"*American Idolatry* is the book I would hand to anyone who is just beginning their journey of understanding white Christian nationalism or who is suspicious that it is even a problem. Andrew Whitehead combines his incisive perspective as a sociologist with his personal journey as one whose early faith was shaped by this ideology. *American Idolatry* moves beyond an academic analysis and reveals the deep and harmful human impact of white Christian nationalism."

—**Jemar Tisby**, *New York Times* bestselling author of *The Color of Compromise* and *How to Fight Racism*; professor, Simmons College of Kentucky

"This is a book whose time has come. With the precision of a scholar and the passion of a faithful Christian, Andrew Whitehead clarifies the difference between Christianity and Christian nationalism. He calls out Christian nationalism for what it is: 'a cultural framework . . . draped in religious rhetoric . . . irrevocably linked' to white racist and xenophobic attitudes. He also makes clear that it is not enough simply to declare that one is not a Christian nationalist; rather, one must embody what it means to be Christian—beginning with recognizing Christianity's complicity in creating and sustaining racism and actively working for racial justice. By the end of this book, one discovers that it's not only Christian nationalists who betray the gospel but also those Christians who remain quiet in the face of it. *American Idolatry* is required reading for anyone who claims to be Christian in this time of Christian nationalist fervor."

—**Kelly Brown Douglas**, former dean of Episcopal Divinity School, professor, Union Theological Seminary

"We need this book. Now. Whitehead uses his academic expertise and personal experience to explain how we can be both faithful Christians and faithful citizens without being seduced by Christian nationalism. With skill and grace, he explains the dangerous ideologies undergirding Christian nationalism, traces how it has infected the church, and provides practical guidance for those of us fighting it in our own communities. This is a book you should give to your friends, your family, and your pastor."

—**Beth Allison Barr**, professor, Baylor University; author of *The Making of Biblical Womanhood: How the Subjugation of Women Became Gospel Truth*

"In *American Idolatry*, Whitehead enters the belly of the beast, where he ventures forth not with a sword or with a dagger but with a light—shining beautifully and brightly in the form of his own journey, his own imagination, his own witness. It is said that salvation is not only about life in the future but also about life right now. Whitehead reveals that life, that love, and the truths that remake us. At a moment in time when people are not taking Christianity seriously, or have been hurt by the faith, Whitehead invites us into repair. *American Idolatry* is a reckoning with a faith that desires power more than love. But it is also a redemption. A resurrection. And quite possibly for those who need it—a revolution. Stories indeed can save us and heal us. Whitehead has an important story to tell."

—**Danté Stewart**, award-winning author of *Shoutin' in the Fire: An American Epistle*

"Sociologist Andrew Whitehead's scholarship has greatly deepened America's understanding of white Christian nationalism. In *American Idolatry* he powerfully engages the subject on intimate terrain, that of a Christian believer deeply grieved by the ways white Christian nationalism has weaponized the faith he loves. With both passion and acuity, he cites the dangers it portends for both American society and the Christian faith: its grotesque distortion of the gospel message of peace and love for neighbors, its poorly veiled inherent racism, its antidemocratic obsession with authoritarian power, its fearmongering and 'us' versus 'them' view of the world, and its willingness to use violence to fulfill what it believes to be its ultimate duty of dominating every aspect of American society. But just as importantly, he also looks at the ways that it is being confronted on the terrain of faith. A lively and lucid read, *American Idolatry* is a significant contribution to our understanding of white Christian nationalism and the social and psychological forces that underlie it."

—**Obery M. Hendricks Jr.**, author of *Christians against Christianity: How Right-Wing Evangelicals Are Destroying Our Nation and Our Faith*

AMERICAN IDOLATRY

AMERICAN IDOLATRY

HOW CHRISTIAN NATIONALISM BETRAYS
THE GOSPEL AND THREATENS THE CHURCH

ANDREW L. WHITEHEAD

Brazos Press

a division of Baker Publishing Group
Grand Rapids, Michigan

Published by Brazos Press
a division of Baker Publishing Group
Grand Rapids, Michigan
www.brazospress.com

Printed in the United States of America

Library of Congress Cataloging-in-Publication Data
Names: Whitehead, Andrew L., author.
Title: American idolatry : how Christian nationalism betrays the gospel and threatens the church / Andrew L. Whitehead.
Description: Grand Rapids, Michigan : Brazos Press, a division of Baker Publishing Group, [2023] | Includes bibliographical references.
Identifiers: LCCN 2022056548 | ISBN 9781587435768 (cloth) | ISBN 9781493441976 (ebook) | ISBN 9781493441983 (pdf)
Subjects: LCSH: Christianity and politics—United States—History—21st century. | Christianity and culture—United States—History—21st century. | Nationalism—Religious aspects—Christianity. | Nationalism—United States—History—21st century.
Classification: LCC BR526 .W52 2023 | DDC 277.308/3—dc23/eng/20230320
LC record available at https://lccn.loc.gov/2022056548

Scripture quotations are from THE HOLY BIBLE, NEW INTERNATIONAL VERSION®, NIV® Copyright © 1973, 1978, 1984, 2011 by Biblica, Inc.® Used by permission. All rights reserved worldwide. Italics in quotations are the author's addition.

The author is represented by The Anderson Literary Agency, Inc.

Baker Publishing Group publications use paper produced from sustainable forestry practices and post-consumer waste whenever possible.

23   24   25   26   27   28   29   7 6 5 4 3 2 1

For Kelly,
always and forever

CONTENTS

Preface *xi*

Acknowledgments *xvii*

1. A Hollow and Deceptive Philosophy   1

2. What Is Christian Nationalism?   23

3. Turn the Other Cheek?   51

4. Do Not Be Afraid?   81

5. Lay Down Your Sword?   105

6. May Your Kingdom Come, on Earth as It Is in Heaven?   129

7. And Who Is My Neighbor?   159

8. Remaking American Christianity   179

Notes   *193*

PREFACE

I F YOUR FAITH JOURNEY has been anything like mine, you've likely wrestled with some big and important questions. Over the last twenty years or so, here are some that have unsettled me personally:

- If our nation was built on Christian principles, why did our forebears treat Native Americans so viciously? Why are some committed to ignoring this history today?
- If Christian theology so profoundly shaped our national values of liberty, human rights, and full equality, why did even the most devout Christian citizens enslave Africans, ripping them from their land and destroying their lives and families? Why did our political leaders and the people who supported those leaders bar Black Americans from the full rights of citizenship for so long? Why do Black Americans continue to face hurdles today?
- If the United States is a Christian nation, a beacon of hope and democracy to the world, why do we often treat immigrants and refugees with such disdain and sometimes outright violence? Why don't we do more to help them?[1]

- Can we be faithful Christians and critique the United States?
- Can we be faithful Christians and patriotic?
- Can we be faithful Christians and celebrate this country and our citizenship?
- Can we be grateful for this country without baptizing and rationalizing away all the evil perpetrated in its name?

These are difficult questions. Perhaps some of them look familiar. Perhaps some of them do not. If you've wrestled with at least one of these, then we're likely on the same journey. We're trying our best to understand how our faith tradition and our place in this world should interact.

These questions are difficult because they highlight how closely intertwined the Christian faith is with American national identity for many Christians in the United States. And when the dictates of the Christian faith seem to so clearly oppose the actions of the nation, profound dissonance starts to reverberate.

In my own journey—much of which is reflected in this book—I've come to believe that in order to faithfully follow the teachings and example of Jesus of Nazareth, I must work to disentangle Christianity from Christian nationalism. The two cannot coexist. I must serve one or the other.

Therefore, the first goal of this book is to make clear that Christian nationalism—a cultural framework asserting that all civic life in the United States should be organized according to a particular form of conservative Christianity—betrays the example set by Jesus in the Gospels. Christian nationalism leads us to practice various forms of idolatry, revering a god or gods other than Jesus, trusting in them for protection and provision.[2] I hope this book will encourage continued discussions within American Christian circles about what Christian nationalism threatens and why it's so important for us to confront this idolatrous ideology. It can be a difficult conversation but is worth having.

What I've also found on this journey is that I am not alone. I've interacted with hundreds of Christians like me who are confronting Christian nationalism in their daily lives, congregations, and communities. I'm confident many more exist. Highlighting some of these people and organizations is the second goal of this book. We need to see how we can do the work of disentangling Christianity from Christian nationalism by following those already on this path. I draw on the wonderful work and writing of fellow pilgrims, and I encourage you to seek out their work, support their efforts, and follow their lead, as I am. So this book is a continuing word, not the first and not the last.

I also want to clearly identify what this book is *not*. This book is not a scholarly treatment of Christian nationalism. My colleague and friend Samuel Perry and I have already addressed this in *Taking America Back for God: Christian Nationalism in the United States*. A related work is *The Flag and the Cross* by Philip Gorski and Samuel Perry. I continue to publish academic journal articles on this topic, and interested readers can see those studies for more in-depth details about our research.

Likewise, this book does not directly examine the threat that Christian nationalism poses to democracy in the United States—although that threat is very real. Fellow scholars document how Christian nationalism is closely associated with desires to restrict access to the voting process, a rejection that voter suppression exists, and a comfort with engaging in violence to overturn an election outcome deemed disagreeable.[3] Christians can and should care about the health of our democracy. I aim to help fellow Christians confront and oppose Christian nationalism, and I hope it will spill over into their views toward democracy and the right of *everyone* to have an equal say in how we organize our society.

This book does not argue that Christians should abstain from politics. Exiting the public square is not the avenue through which we confront Christian nationalism.[4] Standing against Christian nationalism is not the same as saying that Christians (from anywhere on the theological or political spectrum) should stay out of politics. Christians can and should participate in the political process in their communities, states, and nations. The question concerns *how* we are active and to what ends. Christian nationalism points us in one direction. I'm convinced Christians should seek another path.

This book does not argue that Christians should reject patriotism. Christian nationalism and Christian patriotism are different things. Christians can love their home country, can steward its vast resources with care, and can sacrifice to make the lives of their neighbors better. Christians can and should celebrate the good elements of their country's history and makeup while striving to make things better. Again, the question concerns *how* we define and express patriotism and to what ends.

I wrote this book with a particular audience in mind: fellow Christians. Throughout, I will make normative and moral claims flowing from my identification as a Christian. While I ground my beliefs about the harmful nature of Christian nationalism in empirical, scholarly research, this book is also deeply informed by my faith and by historical Christian teachings, the life of Jesus, and the Bible.

This book does not delve into some topics as deeply (or even at all) as some might expect. While I offer my expertise and thoughts as a social scientist as to how we can and should confront Christian nationalism, I look forward to hearing and continuing to learn from experts in fields other than social science. The only way we make headway is by doing it together, in community.

I must also note that I'm a white, able-bodied, Protestant Christian man born in the United States. My voice and the voices of people who look like me have always been central in these conversations. While I am one of a handful of academic experts on Christian nationalism in the United States, I advocate for raising up and listening to people who live and lead on the margins, those historically silenced and minimized. I firmly believe this is where

Jesus most often located himself. Therefore, throughout this book I cite the thinkers and writers who are usually on the margins in the religious tradition of my youth. I've come to find these voices later in my journey. I hope you find, buy, and read their books and learn as much as I continue to.

I was raised in an evangelical Christian community and attended largely white evangelical congregations the majority of my life. I made a personal decision to follow Jesus as a young child and then again as a freshman in high school while on a spring-break service trip with my youth group. I was baptized at a Sunday-evening service out in a fellow congregant's pond. I was in church Sunday mornings and Sunday and Wednesday evenings. The church was a shelter for me during some trying times as an adolescent. I knew I was accepted, loved, and welcome.

I've memorized scores of Bible verses, even a whole book. In college I attended and led Bible studies and participated in the Navigators (a parachurch organization like Cru) in addition to participating in a church home on Sundays. This world made me, and I can speak with an insider's perspective on its strengths and weaknesses. I have experienced both firsthand. My faith, albeit different today than twenty years ago, is still a fundamental aspect of who I am. I continue to try my best to follow Jesus, who at the beginning of his ministry told us he came "to proclaim good news to the poor" and "to proclaim freedom for the prisoners, and recovery of sight for the blind, to set the oppressed free, to proclaim the year of the Lord's favor" (Luke 4:18–19). I'm compelled by the great mystery of God, as we read in Colossians 2:2, which is Christ in us, the hope of glory. I will share more of this journey in the coming pages.

I write this book as a sociologist and a Christian. I approach this subject with both identities in hand, writing to fellow Christians to show that Christian nationalism is opposed to the way of Christ. I entertain no fantasies of convincing everyone to see things exactly the way I do. But I hope you will genuinely grapple with whether and how the particular Christian expression and community of believers you most identify with embrace aspects of Christian nationalism. We are all on a journey, and I continue on mine. I have not arrived. I have more to learn.

Finally, in the chapters that follow, I share how American Christians are faithfully confronting Christian nationalism. It is not just a "progressive" or "liberal" Christian activity. Pastors, teachers, and lay Christians like me across a wide spectrum of theological views recognize how aspects of Christian nationalism are contrary to the life and teachings of Jesus Christ. May their stories inspire us to confront and oppose the idols of Christian nationalism.

This book aims to be a resource that you can quickly turn to as we together do the work of disentangling Christianity from Christian nationalism.

ACKNOWLEDGMENTS

I LOVE WRITING ACKNOWLEDGMENTS. It reminds me I am not alone when so often this work can feel that way. While I am responsible for any mistakes or errors in this text, and what I wrote does not necessarily reflect the views of anyone mentioned here, so many people have shaped and formed my thinking and supported me through this process.

First, thank you to the entire Brazos team, including Paula Gibson, Erin Smith, Kara Day, Katie Pfotzer, Julie Zahm, and especially to Katelyn Beaty, for reaching out to me with an idea and being there from the beginning to the end.

Thank you to Giles Anderson for representing me and helping round out the project proposal. I am grateful to Brian Steensland, Phil Goff, Nate Wynne, Lauren Schmidt, IUPUI, and the Center for the Study of Religion and American Culture. Thank you to Robby Jones, Kelsy Burke, Dan Winchester, Jeff Guhin, Ruth Braunstein, Gerardo Martí, Phil Gorski, and the RRJN for the camaraderie. Michael Trexler and Jeff Ballard were also there offering support and encouragement from start to finish, through ups and downs.

I am grateful to my lifelong pals: Keith Fishburn, Chunny Lech-litner, Ben Myers, and David Cramer. You guys lift me up. I give credit to Reese Roper for the closing line of this book.

Many thanks to those who offered feedback at the proposal stage or on portions of the book: Sam Perry, Kristin Kobes Du Mez, Beth Allison Barr, David Cramer, Danté Stewart, Jeff Ballard, Drew Strait, Amy Edmonds, Jonathan Wilson-Hartgrove, and Andrea Cramer. Rob Saler was there from beginning to end and never hesitated to read and reread chapters. I'm grateful to Joseph Baker, who at one of my lowest points demanded (perhaps even lightly threatened) I send him what I had, and he read every single word.

Many thanks to those who allowed me to interview them and whose stories and perspectives I share: Scott Coley, Amanda Tyler, Andrea Cramer, Amar Peterman, Trevor Bechtel, and Asma Uddin.

I also want to acknowledge that the institution where I work in Indianapolis sits on land that once belonged to scores of African American families who were forced from their homes. The community where I live sits on the land of the Kiikaapoi, Kaskaskia, and Myaamia nations. The histories of where we find ourselves matter.

Thank you to my parents, who set me on the path to where you find me today, playing a role in helping me pierce through the veil at various times. I am also grateful to my in-laws for their unwavering support of our family—with all the challenges that entails—and for their unconditional love no matter where my work leads me.

To my kiddos: Thank you, Joel and Theo, for your giggles, smiles, cuddles, hugs, and hidden treasures. Thank you, Natalie, for your irresistible spirit and bringing so much light to our lives.

Finally, to Kelly: You are my best friend. You are my greatest strength. You are everything I ever hoped for and so much more than I ever deserve. Thank you for choosing me every single day.

A HOLLOW AND DECEPTIVE
PHILOSOPHY

See to it that no one takes you captive through hollow and deceptive philosophy, which depends on human tradition and the
elemental spiritual forces of this world rather than on Christ.

—Colossians 2:8

GROWING UP IN CHRISTIAN SPACES, I routinely
heard that one of the greatest threats to Christianity in
the United States was secularism. If you weren't careful,
it would draw you away from God. Secularism—defined for us as
a philosophical system that rejects religion, or at least rejects its
place in the public square—wanted to take prayer and the Bible
out of public schools. The Supreme Court and "activist justices"
(which always meant the liberal ones) were committed to moving
our country away from its Christian roots.

Democrats threatened our faith too. They advocated for abortion, accepted homosexuality, and wanted to take what we rightfully earned and redistribute it. I was told to detest both communism and socialism, as those economic and political systems were godless, while capitalism was the route to ensuring a fair, free, and prosperous nation blessed by God.

I heard that some of the greatest threats to Christianity in the United States were divorce, feminism, and the absence of strong fathers. Families needed a mom at home and a dad at work in order to flourish. Moreover, our nation needed strong families or else it would go the way of ancient Rome. Gay marriage and homosexuality were a clear threat to the family, one that we were expected to oppose.

We generally ignored immigrants and refugees. They likely brought false religions like Islam, Hinduism, or Buddhism to our shores. We should go to other countries to evangelize, and we should be kind to the few foreign families who might live among us. But we rarely had to think about it as few lived in our communities.

But what if the greatest threat to Christianity in the United States was never from these or any other outside sources? What if the greatest threat to Christianity in the United States came from within, a wolf in sheep's clothing, something familiar enough to evade detection so most would not even realize the threat? What if, for many American Christians, confronting this threat felt akin to opposing Christianity itself?

What if all along the greatest threat to Christianity in the United States was white Christian nationalism? (I explain the racial component of Christian nationalism in detail in chap. 2.)

My Story

I was born and raised in a small, rural, close-knit community in the Midwest. We had one stoplight, two if you counted the blinking red light on the way out of town. Farming and manufacturing were the primary drivers of the local economy. It was blue collar through and through.

Over the past forty years, the population has hovered around sixteen hundred people, served by no less than fourteen Christian congregations in a five-mile radius. Families, faith, and American pride were paramount. If it was Sunday morning, or Wednesday or Sunday evening, you were in church, worshiping beside neighbors who might also be your teacher, florist, electrician, or insurance agent.

For most residents, this resulted in a strong sense of community. You knew everyone and they all knew you. If a family was in need, you took them a meal. If someone was laid off, you poked around to see where work might be available. It was here that I first learned how to love and sacrifice for my neighbor. I am confident that even now if I was in need, those who knew me when I was growing up would do all they could to help.

The congregations in this community instilled in me a love for Jesus, the Bible, and the Christian church. It was in this context that I learned what it meant to be a Christian: accept the correct beliefs, care for those around you, stand up for what is right, and ensure that our Christian convictions prevail in the public square. Doing these things made you a good Christian and a good American. The American flag and the Christian flag at the front of the sanctuary symbolized this relationship. To be one was to be the other.

Our community maintained a number of beliefs to be obviously true:

- Families are the cornerstone of society, and when the family breaks down, society breaks down. Families are made up of a dad, a mom, and kids. Children obey parents, and fathers are the head of the household.
- Christianity always works for the good throughout society. The United States is great, and that is due to its Christian heritage.

- Christians should categorically oppose abortion, homosexuality, and divorce because the Bible clearly teaches each is wrong. The extent to which we allow each to exist in our society will erode the greatness of our nation, ensuring its collapse.
- War might be terrible, but the United States has always fought for good, helping achieve God's will for the world. Therefore, war is sometimes necessary, even godly.
- Secular society will destroy your faith, so you must be careful what you read, listen to, or interact with outside church.

These and other beliefs suffused my worldview. However, despite the taken-for-granted nature of these beliefs, there were moments when cracks and inconsistencies became visible.

One such instance was when I was discussing war with a youth pastor of the evangelical megachurch I attended in high school. In my mind, there was little to no dissonance between the dictates of the Christian faith and the righteousness of fighting to defend our country, which would include killing those on the other side. He asked me, "But what if the person we kill on the other side is a fellow Christian? What then? Did we just send that person to heaven? Is that what God would want for us?"

I was taken aback. I could not stop thinking about the implications of his questions. It was uncomfortable to think about the tension between my identities as an American and as a Christian. I began to see how my categories of "us" and "them" were influenced by much more than my faith. It was awkward to contemplate how being faithful to one identity might lead to being unfaithful to the other. Up until then, they had perfectly complemented each other.

Another instance was brought on by the music I listened to while in high school youth group. One of the bands my friends and I loved had several songs that questioned the narratives about the righteousness of the United States. For instance, in one song they sang about how the budding nation had slaughtered Native Americans in order to manifest its "destiny."[1] This was quite different from the mainstream contemporary Christian artists I listened to back in the 1990s and early 2000s.

These and other experiences began to raise questions in my mind. Can Christians, in good conscience, fight and kill other Christians if the nations we were born into by historical accident demand we do so? How could Christians send missionaries and soldiers to the same country? How could a loving God make room for Christians in a new land through genocide? I would try to imagine Jesus—who I was taught was the perfect representation of God—acting in these ways. I just couldn't see it.

These questions found additional purchase during my first semester of undergraduate education at Purdue University. I was in a survey course of American history from the colonies up until Reconstruction. Frank Lambert, a leading historian on religion and the founding period, taught the course.[2]

I distinctly remember the day, when discussing various founding fathers, Dr. Lambert said that while some were religious in their own right—many were deists, believing in a Creator God, who could be understood via reason—the founding fathers were certainly not "evangelical Christians."

In this moment, a key in my mind slid into place, cleanly releasing a previously locked door. In one instant, an expert in early US religious history justified the questions I had about the relationship between Christianity and the founding period. The present and past had a much more complicated and circuitous relationship. Things were not so cut and dried.

Nevertheless, this moment was also disorienting. The history I grew up hearing was not entirely accurate. The implications of this revelation began to slowly bubble to the surface. Because so much of the public role of Christianity in the United States relied on a narrative about the nation and its founders being essentially evangelical, I had to entirely rethink how my faith should work itself out in public life.

It was at this point that I began to recognize my enduring interest in the relationship between religion and culture, particularly in the United States. One year after I graduated from Purdue, I realized that I wanted to be a student forever. Off to graduate school I went with the desire to study the only thing that ever consistently captivated my attention: how religion both influences and is influenced by culture.

In my first year of graduate school, I read Greg Boyd's book *The Myth of a Christian Nation*. This work crystallized so much of what I had been considering for years. It delineated the differences between the kingdom of God and the kingdoms of this world. It pointed out how the temptation to exercise power *over* others has consistently led Christians to commit all sorts of atrocities. Rather than seek power over others, Boyd argues, Christians should imitate Christ and his "upside-down" kingdom, where power *under* others is the way.[3] It felt like I could finally put my finger on why culture-war Christianity felt so hollow and devoid of the fruit of the Spirit. Christianity was not about culture-warring or dominating the public square. Thanks to Boyd and a new understanding of historically marginalized communities, I began to see how Christians are called to serve, give of themselves, and leverage their power and privilege for the common good.

I found this to be a much more beautiful vision of the gospel. This vision of the kingdom captivated me. My faith would never be the same. Instead of fear and control, this gospel was about freedom and liberation.

While the faith of my youth was being refined and reformed to align with a Jesus who came not to be served but to serve (Matt. 20:28), I was learning the methodological and theoretical tools of my craft, sociology. As luck (or providence?) would have it, the graduate program I attended consistently collected high-quality quantitative data on the American public.

In two early surveys, they asked a series of questions about how Americans view the relationship between Christianity, religion, the federal government, and civic life in the United States. Following the work of others, I used these questions to create a scale that measured Christian nationalism. I sent an email to a new colleague with whom I had just written another paper: Sam Perry.

We began working on several studies making the case that above and beyond the usual measures of religious belief, belonging, and behavior, as well as political party and ideology, Christian nationalism tells us something unique about how Americans see the world. We soon found that Christian nationalism—which I define briefly below and more fully in the next chapter—was indeed one of the strongest predictors of Americans' attitudes toward several social issues. One paper explored attitudes toward same-sex unions (this was back before *Obergefell v. Hodges* legalized same-sex marriage across the United States). Perhaps more transformative for us was our paper showing that greater acceptance of Christian nationalism predicted much more negative views of interracial marriage. Again, Christian nationalism was consistently one of the most powerful predictors.

It made us wonder: Why are the questions we use to measure Christian nationalism, which make no mention of race, so powerfully related to white Americans' attitudes toward interracial marriage? What is it about holding "Christian nation" views that makes white Americans more likely to believe marrying Black Americans is wrong? We started to realize that we were onto something much bigger than anticipated.

Not long after these papers appeared in peer-reviewed journals, I applied for funding to place these questions about Christian nationalism on another national survey. I decided then that I would use this data to write a book on Christian nationalism. Scores of historians had examined the Christian nation narrative and mythology. Several journalists had written books on Christian nationalists in the United States. However, there was no book examining Christian nationalism with high-quality empirical data of the American public.

Sam agreed to collaborate with me, and our work culminated in *Taking America Back for God,* published in 2020. While writing the book, along with the many peer-reviewed articles on Christian nationalism we wrote together and with several close colleagues, I became more and more convinced of the detrimental influence Christian nationalism has on multiple aspects of American life. I became even more convinced that Christian nationalism was detrimental to the church. Christian nationalism makes American Christians less Christlike. As we write near the end of our book, "The desperate quest for power inherent in Christian nationalist ideology is antithetical to Jesus' message. At its core, Christian nationalism is a hollow and deceptive philosophy that depends on human tradition and the basic principles of this world, rather than on Christ."[4]

I share this to show how my desire to confront Christian nationalism flows from two parts of my history and identity. First, I am a follower of Christ. Born and raised in Christianity, I was taught to take seriously the commands of Jesus and the gospel message. Second, I am a social scientist. I am trained in how to gather and analyze high-quality data to make sense of our social world. Both parts of my identity compel me to seek after and to stand for truth, no matter what. Both parts of my identity have led me to the same conclusion: Christian nationalism betrays the gospel and is a threat to the Christian church in the United States.

It is from this perspective that I write this book. I want to make clear to my fellow white American Christians how much Christian nationalism threatens our faith—not only our individual expressions of it but also our organizations and institutions. It threatens our capacity to love our brothers and sisters in Christ who are minorities. It threatens our capacity to love and serve our brothers and sisters in Christ from countries around the world. It threatens our capacity to love and serve fellow bearers of God's image at home and abroad who don't share our faith at all. And it threatens how our organizations function, causing them to reproduce inequality and further harm the marginalized.

I am convinced that Christian nationalism makes us bad Christians.

What Is the Gospel?

In recent years, some of us have seen the fruit of Christian nationalism in our churches and among our friends. We are rightly troubled and wonder, *Has it always been this way?* We no longer recognize our faith tradition. Some of us leave. Others of us stay but grieve the current state of affairs. We try to imagine a different future in which our collective example to those outside the faith is one that attracts rather than repels.

Based on both my personal and my professional experiences grappling with Christian nationalism, this book seeks first to demonstrate how several central aspects of white Christian nationalism are antithetical to the gospel. Each chapter represents a distinctive lens through which we can see how white Christian nationalism betrays the life and teachings of Jesus—the gospel—as found in the Bible.

What is the gospel? Growing up, I would have defined it as recognizing that (1) I was born a sinner separated from God, (2) the wages of sin were death and eternal punishment, (3) I was in need of Jesus's sacrifice on the cross to pay my debt, (4) accepting by faith Jesus's sacrifice would save me from the punishment I deserved and promise me eternal life, and (5) I was now at peace with God in a personal relationship with Jesus. This may look familiar to you or reflect your current definition of the gospel.

Today, I believe this picture of the gospel is an important foundation yet incomplete.[5] It reflects only one aspect of the gospel, what my philosopher friend Scott Coley suggests we might label the *doxastic gospel*. Think of the doxastic gospel as a set of theological claims that we either believe or do not believe, such as the death and resurrection of Jesus, the nature of atonement, and the work of the church.[6] The doxastic gospel focuses mainly on me and my relationship with God and whether I believe the right things. However, as theologian Kat Armas says, "Spirituality includes all the dimensions of human, personal, and societal living that combine to make human life human—the measure of the fullness of God's gift."[7] When we apply the gospel only to our personal lives and cherry-pick Bible verses in support, we miss the clear theme of justice throughout the Bible and ignore the broader work of God in the world.

We must embrace the second aspect of the gospel, what we can label the *practical gospel*—practices that flow from the doxastic gospel, such as loving one's neighbor, seeking justice for the oppressed, and caring for orphans and widows.[8] Scott pointed out to me how throughout the Bible the doxastic gospel is inextricable from the practical gospel. The book of James and the Beatitudes are two clear examples of this. We can also see it in Jesus's first public message.

Consider his claim in Luke 4:16–21. In a synagogue on the Sabbath, he stands up and reads a passage from Isaiah:

> The Spirit of the Lord is on me,
>   because he has anointed me
>   to proclaim good news to the poor.
> He has sent me to proclaim freedom for the prisoners
>   and recovery of sight for the blind,
> to set the oppressed free,
>   to proclaim the year of the Lord's favor. (4:18–19)

In his first public sermon, Jesus does not emphasize the forgiveness of *my* individual sins. Instead, he points to how his project is liberating all of humanity from *our* enslavement to sin, including the ways sin is baked into the structures of our common life and harms our neighbors. We, like Jesus, cannot read the words of Isaiah and other prophets honestly and come away thinking God cares more about our personal salvation than how we treat other people, including through the social structures that oppress them.[9] "The good news was both about the *coming* of the Kingdom of God and the *character* of that Kingdom," writes Lisa Sharon Harper.[10]

The definition of the gospel from my youth reduced Christianity to the doxastic gospel, ignoring the practical aspect of it. This sheds light on why so often the gospel amounted only to person-to-person evangelism, getting people "saved." This gospel limited the work of Jesus to each person's spiritual condition. It had little to say about the political and social realities of our fellow humans. I began to ask myself, "What if I preached this gospel to someone enslaved in 1845 or someone being forcibly removed from their land in 1832? Would they receive this promise of future salvation that says nothing about their current suffering as 'good news'?"

We all are to join God in the work of renewal that entails the flourishing of all, likewise proclaiming the Year of Jubilee that Jesus inaugurated that day in Nazareth. Jesus came "that they may have life, and have it to the full" (John 10:10)—not just spiritually but in our bodies, our relationships, and the social systems that organize our collective lives. "God's redemptive plan throughout history has consistently concerned all of creation, and he repeatedly admonishes his people to seek the flourishing of the whole world."[11]

Severing these two important aspects of the gospel obscures how Jesus proclaimed a fundamental realignment of the power structures of society *in addition* to personal spiritual salvation. It also ignores how Jesus understood his ministry and rescue mission to all of humanity as beginning here and now. Jesus was inaugurating God's kingdom on earth, and this held political and social implications, for systems of power *and* individuals. Those listening to Jesus in the shadow of oppressive empire understood this. Those marginalized in our society hear Jesus in this same way.

Indeed, much of the Christian tradition, from the time of the early church forward, has stressed that salvation itself is a communal reality that encompasses all of creation. Thus, if salvation is understood as a personal possession with no implications for how I fight the evil that hurts my neighbor, then not only is that a misunderstanding of the teaching of Jesus but it is also a misunderstanding of the nature and scope of salvation itself.[12]

And it is the broad acceptance of an incomplete view of the gospel—the doxastic aspect that focuses on individual salvation alone—that hinders many American Christians from seeing how Christian nationalism betrays the life and teachings of Jesus in two important areas: racial inequality and xenophobia.[13] In these two areas, white American Christians tend to ignore the practical aspect of the gospel, including justice for the oppressed, thinking that as long as we believe the correct theological claims and encourage others to embrace those theological claims as well that we are doing all we need to do. Likely, this is because we are *already* free. We *already* enjoy so much in the here and now. What use do those of us who are white American Christians have for overturning systems of oppression when we have long benefited from those very systems?

Jesus realigned how we are to view power and called for a people whom the world would know by their sacrificial love—a love that leads to the disruption of oppression in the world. Part of our loving the poor, the widow, the orphan, and the immigrant is recognizing our own complicity in the systems of injustice that create and perpetuate their marginalization and suffering.[14] This sacrificial love participates in God's ongoing mission of disrupting sin and its destructive effects on human relationships. Christians are to leverage their power, position, and privilege to the benefit of all rather than for their own self-interest.[15] In the dozens of studies others and I have conducted in recent years, we find repeatedly that the practical fruit of Christian nationalism is certainly not love. It is power, control, domination, fear, and violence.

Once we see the gospel as good news for the present, good news for the marginalized, good news for the prisoner, good news for the poor, good news for the blind, and good news for the oppressed, we can begin to take the evidence that social science hands us about Christian nationalism and recognize this ideology as limiting—and in many cases outright opposing—the work Jesus claimed he came to do and commanded us to do likewise (Matt. 22:37–40).

Comparing this gospel with the evidence I will share is an important step in faithfully diagnosing and understanding the problems the American Christian church faces. It will show how Christian nationalism betrays the gospel. We have to look straight into the mirror and not try to hide or diminish the imperfections we see. Only then can we begin to imagine something new. Part of this work is recognizing that the God we worship has no particular interest in the greatness of the United States. The survival of any one nation over another is not paramount. The kingdom of God needs no global superpower in order to flourish. Rather, as Jesus's parable teaches, it spreads and grows from the smallest of seeds, soon providing shade to the whole garden (Mark 4:30–32).

Again, recognizing that human flourishing in the kingdom of God and in the United States (or any other nation) are not synonymous does not mean that Christians should not invest in the flourishing of a nation and its people. We can work toward peace, justice, and care for all who live and work within the boundaries of our home country. We can collaborate with God and those around us to create a more loving and liberating country for all our neighbors. We can seek shalom—"a vision of a Kingdom that provides for all," in Harper's words.[16]

Therefore, it is not a question of *if* we should engage in work to benefit those around us. It is a question of how broadly we define the "us" who benefits. The gospel can and does *empower* us to enter more deeply into our neighbors' needs, serving them out of gratitude to God. We can advocate for "coercive" policies— like the Voting Rights Act—that benefit all our neighbors. To do so faithfully in a pluralistic society, however, requires us to build coalitions for the public good, collaborating and cooperating with our neighbors no matter how different we perceive them to be. We will need to practice humility, vulnerability, and empathy in a way that befits the gospel.

Where Are We Going?

To help us imagine a future full of possibility, in later chapters I share stories and examples of American Christians who are currently confronting white Christian nationalism as it relates to their congregations and communities. These Christians are seeking shalom among all their fellow citizens, not just those fellow citizens who they might feel are most "deserving." As Dr. Martin Luther King Jr. showed us, "We are caught in an inescapable network of mutuality, tied in a single garment of destiny."[17] Injustice experienced by one community is injustice experienced by all. The stories and examples will model how Christians can be committed to all. We can expand the "us" to all of humanity, so that if particular policies that harm minority communities are "being implemented in the name of Jesus, we have a particular obligation to show up, resist, and demonstrate a better way."[18]

We will learn about a group of Christians who collaborate with secular Americans to advocate for the right of all people to practice or not practice religion without governmental interference. We will discuss Christians who practice empathy to confront fear that so easily turns us against one another. We will hear from a congregation who took a step of faith with their own reparative act, collecting and donating funds to give away to their Black sisters and brothers. I will share the story of a friend from my own youth group who recognized that "no friendship is apolitical" and decided to enter into the challenges facing immigrants and refugees to ensure that they are truly welcomed to her community. These examples help us see what is possible. Life is springing from the cracks in the concrete.

But first, we will begin the journey defining Christian nationalism and describing its depth and breadth across American society (chap. 2). In short, white Christian nationalism is a cultural framework asserting that civic life in the United States should be organized according to a particular form of conservative Christianity. Beyond any theological or religious beliefs associated with Christianity, white Christian nationalism brings with it a host of cultural assumptions, particularly a moral traditionalism predicated on maintaining social hierarchies, a comfort with (the "right kind" of) authoritarian social control that includes the threat and use of violence, and a desire for strict ethno-racial boundaries designating who can fully participate in American civic life. As we'll explore later, it centers and privileges the white Christian experience because it essentially teaches that this country was founded by white, conservative Christian men for the benefit of white, conservative Christian citizens.[19]

After defining Christian nationalism, we will work through examples of where and how it exists in our congregations, personal lives, and communities. We will touch on whether we can oppose Christian nationalism and still be patriotic Christians and how Christians can commit to a common good that does not favor one group over another.

Then we'll turn to three distinctive idols of white Christian nationalism (chaps. 3–5). I like how Kaitlyn Schiess defines idolatry in *The Liturgy of Politics* as "capitulation to a different story and set of values. Idols make promises of protection and provision, and they require allegiance."[20] Bible scholar Drew Strait tells us that idols "co-opt our theological imaginations" and "distort our knowledge of God and neighbor," leading us to betray our loyalty to Jesus and the gospel.[21] Power, fear, and violence are not the only idols of Christian nationalism, but they are the three most powerful. We'll see how they promise protection and provision but only deliver on those promises by forcing us to exploit our neighbors.

First, Christian nationalism is wholly obsessed with power used to benefit "us." It seeks to create hierarchies in which some deserve (on the basis of "the will of God") to be at the top with unfettered access to power and privilege, while others exist in lower sections of the social hierarchy. We will explore how Jesus related to power throughout the Gospels. We will examine fellow Christians who are thinking deeply about power and how to wield it faithfully. And we will look at how Christians can confront Christian nationalism through defending true religious liberty and siding with those marginalized across American society.

Second, Christian nationalism is intimately intertwined with fear and a sense of threat. It constantly pushes us to see the world in terms of "us" versus "them," with "them" always threatening "our" power and privilege. It operates from a scarcity mindset, that there is not enough for all of us to experience abundance. Those wielding power to selfishly benefit white Christians have for decades traded in fear alongside Christian nationalism to great effect. They mobilized countless Americans to particular ends, even when those ends ultimately cost the lives and livelihoods of our fellow Americans from minority populations. However, should Christians live in fear? What if Christians did not buy into fear, especially the fear of losing what they see as rightfully theirs? What if Christians could reject us-versus-them thinking, which encourages us to see other humans as enemies to subdue and hold in contempt? What if we instead embraced the gospel highlighting the good news of abundant life for all, in the here and now, where we can empathize with our neighbors instead of demonizing them? The message of this gospel dispels the group-level fears of white Christian nationalism centered on loss of power, privilege, and prosperity.

Third, Christian nationalism is completely comfortable with, and at times demands, the use of violence. Because the protection of "our" power and privilege from "them" is paramount, all means of achieving such ends are acceptable. History demonstrates how violence is the result of quests for power that are based on fear, especially when power and fear revolve around hierarchical relationships predicated on "us" versus "them." Ultimately, the use of violence signals a distrust of the work of God in the world and seeing the image of God in all people.

Throughout our nation's history, these three idols have resulted in horrific violence, expressing themselves through creating and maintaining "proper" hierarchies between various groups and the mistreatment of those groups. There are many examples of this dynamic at work, including the subjugation of women. For centuries, women have been victims of the idols of power, fear, and violence intertwined with white Christian nationalism. Because the "Christian" content of Christian nationalism tends to revere cultural traditionalism in all its forms, social science consistently demonstrates that calls for a "more Christian nation" are essentially calls for a more patriarchal social and political system within our families, congregations, and political institutions. Unchecked sexual and psychological abuse, limitations on women's autonomy, and the silencing of women's voices and gifts are just a few of the ways white Christian nationalism and its idols have harmed women. I have learned so much from books like *Jesus and John Wayne* by Kristin Kobes Du Mez and *The Making of Biblical Womanhood* by Beth Allison Barr and encourage you to wrestle with these histories and their implications.

In this book, however, I will focus on how the three idols of Christian nationalism perpetuate racism and xenophobia. One avenue through which we have identified the "other" for centuries is the construction of racial categories. White Christian nationalism is closely intertwined with systemic racism. Rather than minimizing this connection, white American Christians can acknowledge our complicity in upholding the systems that maintain racial inequality. While we personally may not have played a role in setting up these systems, we do participate in and benefit from them. Listening to our brothers and sisters from minority racial and ethnic groups will help us find a new path toward more faithful Christian love.

Alongside fear of racial and ethnic minorities, fear and antipathy toward immigrants, refugees, and pretty much anyone not a natural-born citizen is another harmful result of the three idols of white Christian nationalism. The "other" includes anyone not "born here." Why do we discriminate against other children of God just because they were not born here by historical accident? Even if we assented to the idea that God chooses the nationality of every human being, how does that excuse us for selfishly holding on to the blessings and comforts of being an American citizen?

If God truly chose some of us to be Americans and enjoy living in arguably the wealthiest country in the history of the world, shouldn't we be trembling with fear that we might cruelly withhold sharing our undeserved blessing and grace with others? Consider the parable of the unmerciful servant (Matt. 18:21–35). Blessed with a gift of mercy he could never repay, he fails to extend even a shred of such blessing to those in need. What if American Christians applied this lesson to ensure that we do not likewise hoard blessings at the expense of others?

But instead of welcoming and serving the alien and stranger, Christian nationalism encourages an outright rejection of these people. Throughout the Christian scriptures and especially in the teachings of Jesus, Christians are commanded to do the exact opposite.

As we will see throughout each chapter, American Christians are confronting the idols of Christian nationalism in various ways. We can join in this work both individually and in our communities. While we can seek to renew our individual hearts and minds, we cannot stop there. Indeed, a key insight from my field of sociology is that focusing solely on changing individual hearts and minds will only perpetuate the current situation. We will need to commit to changing how our congregations, denominations, other faith organizations, and the political systems in our states and nation—the social groups and systems of which we are all a part—operate. Only then can we hope to remake American Christianity.

We can acknowledge and grieve the harm that we and our organizations have done as we have chased unfettered power to enact a particular vision of the world on those around us. We can begin to recognize that Christians were *never* called to "win" their culture for Christ (whatever that might mean) or vote only for Christians like them to hold political office. Jesus did not call us to advance any particular kingdom of this world by selfishly wielding power. Jesus did not call us to win the culture and lord our privilege and influence over others. Our commitment to these pursuits has made us unloving neighbors.

Those outside Christianity, as well as those who have left, clearly recognize we sometimes treat Jesus as a mascot, useful only for baptizing our efforts to (re)make American society as we see fit by protecting and increasing our power and privilege. We claim that by increasing our privilege and selfishly employing our power, we will win more to the faith.

The project to win the culture for Jesus has backfired. Consider how the latest iteration of white Christian nationalism born out of the culture wars—from the rise of the Christian Right in the late 1970s until today[22]—has been completely ineffective in countering the numerical decline of American Christianity in the face of broader trends of secularization happening in the West. Consider the following:

- More Americans today affiliate with no religion at all than with any Christian religious tradition.

- The rates of disaffiliation show no signs of slowing; over 10 percent more Americans have disaffiliated from religion in the last decade alone.
- Young people are disaffiliating or never affiliating at higher rates than previous generations.
- From 2017 to 2021, 12 percent more Americans reported believing that "conservative Christians" want to do them physical harm.[23]

Gaining and selfishly employing political power has *not* served to bring more Americans into the Christian fold. Study after study demonstrates that one effect of the culture-warring of the Christian Right was to actively push people out of the Christian tradition. The following chapters highlight various aspects of the history of the Christian Right in relation to white Christian nationalism and the idols of power, fear, and violence.

The result of the Christian Right's commitment to culture-warring was that while we were trying to convince those outside the church that we loved them, our commitment to white Christian nationalism ensured that they perceived that narrative as a lie. The same trends continue today. More and more Americans are leaving the Christian faith, and fewer and fewer have any desire to return or come for the first time at all.

In our effort to retain what we thought was a Christian nation, we have succeeded in pushing more Americans away from the faith. In our effort to ensure that our society is structured according to "God's laws," we have only convinced many Americans that we care more about achieving our vision for the country—which looks a lot like taking care of ourselves and our comfort—than loving and sacrificing for "the least of these" (Matt 25:40).

Following Jesus necessarily means we confront the various idols of Christian nationalism. White American Christians have too easily idolized power, fear, and violence. Each stands in contrast to the example set by Jesus. The longer American Christians actively embrace or tolerate white Christian nationalism, the greater the likelihood that our witness will continue to suffer and become effectively naught, if it isn't so already.

When Do We Begin?

Historian Jemar Tisby, in his book *The Color of Compromise*, notes that history is contingent.[24] By this he means that people and organizations in our collective past made particular decisions at particular moments that resulted in where we find ourselves at present. By extension, had they made *different* decisions, Tisby notes—with no small measure of hope—we could well have inherited a very different world. He encourages us to arm ourselves with this knowledge to build a different world for tomorrow. Our decisions today matter and can have a broad impact, for good or ill.

The same is true as we seek to confront Christian nationalism. We can help make a new world through our decisions to confront this ideology in its various forms today, tomorrow, and into the future. It will not be easy. It will take time and effort. But we can forge a new path for American Christianity, one freed from the temptation to protect our own and exert power over others toward selfish ends.

In virtually every movie about time travel, someone warns the protagonist not to influence the lives or choices of those in the past too much. The repercussions could be so far-reaching as to completely remake the present. One little choice could radiate outward in unimaginable ways, altering the very fabric of reality in the present day. When watching *Back to the Future* or *Avengers: Endgame*, we naturally accept this idea. However, we rarely apply the same logic to our own lives. We fail to see how a seemingly insignificant decision we make today could dramatically alter the future.

What if we began to live our lives believing that even small actions we consistently take now—a practice of faithful resistance—can reverberate through our communities, congregations, denominations, nation, and world? Changes we make to our organizations and institutions now can dramatically alter their functioning in decades to come. Even simple questions we pose to fellow Christians and our organizations that break through the taken-for-grantedness of Christian nationalism can have an impact. Questions like those that I faced at various moments of my journey might alter individual and organizational trajectories.[25]

While we cannot go back and change the past to reduce the negative influence of Christian nationalism on our civic life today, we *can* act today in order to change tomorrow. I am convinced we must at the very least try.

What you choose to do today to confront white Christian nationalism—in your own life, the lives of those around you, or the systems of which we are all a part—matters. We can commit now to consistently making these choices, hoping that the seeds planted, however small, will someday grow and provide shade to the entire garden—where we *all* can flourish.

WHAT IS CHRISTIAN NATIONALISM?

To me, God and country are tied—to me they're one and the same. We were founded as a Christian country. And we see how far we have come from that.

—Jenny Cudd[1]

LIKE MANY AMERICANS, I was working from home on January 6, 2021, as we were all living through the winter COVID-19 surge. The 2020 election was two months past, and Congress was set to certify the Electoral College results. Finally, the election would be over. We could move on with life. In almost every other presidential election—especially those with such a clear victor, as in 2020—this largely bureaucratic procedure came and went quickly and quietly.

However, since November 4, then president Donald Trump and his followers had been intent on sowing seeds of distrust, claiming the election was stolen or rigged against him. Trump and his supporters were keen to fan the flames of suspicion, calling on his followers to "Fight," "Don't be weak," and "Don't let them take it [the presidency] away!" Trump foreshadowed the January 6 protest on December 19, claiming (without evidence), "Statistically impossible to have lost the 2020 Election. Big protest in DC on January 6th. Be there, will be wild!"[2] Across social media and especially within the news outlets that had long supported Trump, truth mattered little.

Prominent religious leaders joined in on casting doubt. Franklin Graham, son of famed evangelist Billy Graham and leader of two large evangelical ministries, said, "The votes are in, but is the election over? I have no clue. I guess we just have to wait and see."[3] Paula White-Cain, a prominent televangelist and one of Trump's spiritual advisers, claimed that "demonic confederacies . . . are attempting to steal the election from Trump."[4] Eric Metaxas said, "This is God's battle even more than our battle."[5]

In the weeks following Election Day, however, no one ever produced evidence of electoral improprieties. Trump's lawyers, once under oath in a court of law, repeatedly confessed that they could not claim the election was stolen or fraudulent.[6] They have since faced legal repercussions for embracing such falsehoods.

Despite this, the Big Lie had already taken hold. A number of rallies protesting the election outcome were held in Washington, DC, from January 3 through 5. The next day, the mounting pressure found release. Trump spoke at noon and encouraged the protestors to march to the Capitol. Over the next two hours, rioters overwhelmed various perimeter barricades and then within minutes broke through windows and doors, unlawfully entering the Capitol building. Five people died as a result of the violent insurrection. In the summer of 2022, the Select Committee investigating the January 6 attack began presenting evidence of Trump's involvement with the attack and his desire to see the rioters violently impede the democratic process for his benefit.

The images from that day were certainly shocking, but they were not surprising. The fear, sense of displacement, quest for superiority, militarism, violence, conspiratorial thinking, and unquestioned allegiance to Trump had been building for years. It was only a matter of time until they broke free. While there is no single explanation for the attack on the Capitol that day, it is impossible to ignore the influence of Christian nationalism.[7]

As I sat glued to the news and Twitter as the events unfolded, the presence of various Christian symbols among the rioters was apparent. "Jesus Saves" and "God Is with You" signs, crosses, and the Christian flag were all visible. Videos posted from those storming the Capitol revealed prayer circles and screams of love for Jesus. Pastors, politicians, and other religious leaders from around the United States reveled in their participation.[8] In their own words, the insurrectionists explained that this was *their* country, the Christian God had ordained it, and Trump was chosen by God to lead it. And so, if God had ordained Trump the winner of the 2020 election, who were they to allow anything—even democracy—to stand in the way?

Leaders from across Christianity condemned the violence and lawlessness on full display on January 6, even some leading within more conservative traditions. Russell Moore, who at that time still led the Ethics & Religious Liberty Commission of the Southern Baptist Convention, stated, "The sight of 'Jesus Saves' and 'God Bless America' signs by those violently storming the Capitol is about more than just inconsistency. It is about a picture of Jesus Christ and of his gospel that is satanic."[9]

One year later, Moore was no less vehement in his appraisal of the insurrection and the dangers of a blithe acceptance of the violence across American Christianity: "It would be one thing if this were just a matter of the crowd attacking the Capitol that day. It's quite another when people—including people with highlights in their Bibles and prayer requests on their refrigerators—wave the attack away as a mere protest from which we should 'move on.' This represents more than a threat to American democracy—though that would be bad enough—but a threat to the witness of the church."[10]

In January 2021, Albert Mohler, president of the Southern Baptist Theological Seminary, called the "fusion" of Christian symbolism with "symbols of other things with which Christians ought to have nothing to do" horrifying. He identified Christian nationalism as idolatrous. Mohler wrote that Christians' ultimate allegiance and identity reside in Christ and his church. He pointed out that no earthly nation should be mistaken for the kingdom of God: "It is about the church, not any nation that Jesus said, 'Upon this rock, I will build my church, and the gates of hell shall not prevail against it.' There is no such promise to any nation, and as a matter of fact, the Christian biblical worldview makes very clear that every earthly nation is eventually going to disappear. Every single empire will fall."[11]

Mohler's willingness to decry the insurrection and the role of Christian nationalism and to distinguish between the kingdom of God and a kingdom of the world like the United States is notable, especially considering Mohler encouraged Christians to vote for Trump in 2020 after opposing Trump in 2016. However, in the same article, Mohler questioned the prevalence of Christian nationalism, saying, "It is not fair to say that mainstream evangelical Christianity in America is characterized by the kind of fusion and Christian nationalism of an idolatrous sort that's been identified here."

Mohler continued to decry the "events" on January 6, 2021—he refused to call it a "coup" or "insurrection"—but in an article written a year later he notably made no mention of the influence of Christian nationalism on that day. Rather, in his recollection of January 6, the only mention of the role of Christianity was that some in the mob "even dared to carry Christian symbols."[12]

Comparing Mohler's responses one year apart highlights his desire to obscure the role of Christianity and especially of Christian nationalism in the insurrection. Back in 2021, it was clear Mohler worried that paying too much attention to Christian nationalism would ultimately serve to marginalize American Christianity. In his column in early 2022, he followed his own advice, largely keeping Christianity absent from the discussion. In other words, Mohler concedes that, yes, Christian nationalism is bad and American Christians must be vigilant concerning the influence of Christian nationalism; however, he claims, it is also relatively rare and found only in the extreme corners of evangelicalism and consequently should not be equated with American evangelical theology.

Yet Mohler is mistaken about the prevalence of Christian nationalism within white Christianity, especially evangelicalism, in the United States. It does not exist only on the fringes. High-quality surveys of the American public routinely demonstrate that Christian nationalism permeates all corners of white American Christianity. Close to two-thirds of white American Christians are at least favorable toward Christian nationalism, and that number increases to over 75 percent if we look solely at white evangelicals.[13] Christian nationalism is at the very heart of contemporary evangelicalism, not on the fringe.

But more important to Mohler than saying Christian nationalism is dangerous and fringe is his insistence that Christians must guard against any attempt to exclude Christianity from public life. And in his estimation, focusing on white Christian nationalism and its prevalence within white American Christianity, especially white evangelicalism, leads us down the slippery slope to just such marginalization.

Mohler's journey doesn't end here. Just seven months after calling Christian nationalism idolatrous and obscuring the role it played in the insurrection, Mohler *embraced* the label "Christian nationalist" during a July 2022 interview with a conservative philosopher. He declared, "We have the Left routinely speaking of me and of others as 'Christian nationalists' as if we're supposed to be running from that. And, you know, I'm not about to run from that. I'm not about to join their one world order."[14] Mohler now seems to think that if "the Left"—which he never clearly identifies—dislikes Christian nationalism, then it's an identity worth embracing. Other national religious and political leaders have joined Mohler in explicitly adopting the label.[15] This is a regrettable and serious development.

Mohler misses the mark by claiming that attempts to define and measure white Christian nationalism and its popularity within American Christianity will lead to a silencing of American Christians. It is simply untrue that most scholars, religious leaders, or politicians decrying Christian nationalism ultimately desire to suppress the presence of *Christianity* in the public sphere. Mohler and I agree that we must identify exactly how white Christian nationalism is distinct from the kingdom of God. We also agree that confronting Christian nationalism should not mean American Christians abdicate (or be forced to abdicate) any influence or presence in the public sphere. Rather, we should seek to encourage expressions of Christian faithfulness that offer a kingdom-centered rebuttal to white Christian nationalism.

To do so, we must first clearly define white Christian nationalism and understand where it exists across American society. And once we do that, we can explore in subsequent chapters where and how Christian nationalism betrays the gospel. At that point, it will be clear that Mohler's and other Christian leaders' recent embrace of the label "Christian nationalist" only further endangers the witness of the church.

Defining White Christian Nationalism

White Christian nationalism is a cultural framework that idealizes and advocates for a fusion of a particular expression of Christianity with American civic life. It holds that this version of Christianity should be the principal and undisputed cultural framework in the United States and that the government should vigorously preserve that cultural framework.

White Christian nationalism combines a number of elements. The first element is a strong moral traditionalism based on creating and sustaining social hierarchies. Oftentimes these revolve around gender and sexuality. The second element is a comfort with authoritarian social control. The world is a chaotic place, and at times society needs strong rules and rulers to make use of violence, or at least the threat of violence, to maintain order. The final element is a desire for strict boundaries around national identity, civic participation, and social belonging that fall along ethno-racial lines. A "Christian nation" is generally understood to be one where white, natural-born citizens are held up as the ideal, with everyone else coming after.[16]

Cultural frameworks are the scaffolding on which human interaction and societies form. They consist of the stories we tell ourselves about who we are, how we came to be, and where we are going. Christian nationalism is a deep story.[17] Cultural frameworks and deep stories contain the symbols, narratives, and traditions that unite us and dramatize the values we hold dear. Oftentimes we don't even notice them. They just *are*. And to the extent that deep stories are taken for granted, they are most powerful.[18]

Now, you probably noticed the phrase "a particular expression of Christianity" in the definition above. The wording signals a critical point of this book: the Christianity of Christian nationalism is of a particular type. It is not just about acknowledging Jesus Christ as the Son of God and Lord over all. It is not just about agreeing with the Apostles', Nicene, or Athanasian Creed. It is not just about religious or theological beliefs. Rather, the Christianity of American Christian nationalism conveys particular forms of cultural baggage.[19] Chief among these is how it privileges and centers the white experience. Christian nationalism in the United States is inextricably tied to race. Over the centuries, the deep story of white Christian nationalism in the Americas formed around identifying who was in and who was out primarily along racial and ethnic lines.[20] This is why I already have and will continue to modify "Christian nationalism" with "white." Here are three brief explanations as to why.

First, Anthea Butler and Jemar Tisby—both historians of race and Christianity—show that white Christians and white Christian communities were intimately involved in the creation of racial categories from the earliest moments of American history, contending that "white = good and Christian," while "nonwhite or Black = bad and heathen."[21] Such theological work was necessary to assuage guilt or doubts that white colonists (and later Americans) might have for enslaving Africans or committing genocide against Native Americans. Rather, the Christian God was seen to have smiled on their efforts to create a new world. The consequences of this history still reverberate within American Christianity today as well as throughout the broader culture.

Second, the mainstreaming of the modern narrative of the United States as a Christian nation was located primarily within white Christian traditions. Some of the most ardent supporters and purveyors of Christian nationalism in the early to mid-twentieth century were white Christian men preaching to predominantly white audiences. The intersection of race and Christian nationalism can actually be traced even further back to before the formation of the United States.[22]

The intersection of Christian nationalism and race was more recently exposed with the rise of the Christian Right in the 1970s, which began as a result of fears of racial integration being "forced" on them, alongside other culture-war issues like abortion and homosexuality.[23] In a truly Christian nation, they argued, the federal government would not impose such practices but would allow local communities, and Christian schools in particular, to follow the dictates of their own consciences.[24] While the racial concerns motivating this movement were and continue to be obscured, the effect of mobilizing primarily *white* Christians and organizations to the cause of Christian nationalism persists.

Third, social science research consistently finds that Christian nationalism operates quite differently for white Americans than for Black Americans across a host of issues. Christian nationalism among whites primarily serves to draw sharp boundaries around who is truly "American," ensuring that the various rights and privileges of citizenship are for them alone. "Christian nation" rhetoric is racially coded for whites. It functions in such a way that allows white Americans to remain ignorant to historical and current injustices.[25] For Black Americans, embracing Christian nationalism tends to make them *more* accepting and open to the civic participation of potential out-groups.[26]

For these and other reasons, the Christian nationalism discussed throughout this book focuses primarily on privileging *white* Americans, organizations, and cultural values. However, the cultural baggage attached to Christian nationalism does not end with race and ethnicity.

Christian nationalism also privileges conservative political ideology. It asserts libertarian conceptions of self-governance and free-market capitalism. It also assumes the importance of being a natural-born citizen. It insists that men are best suited to lead. It encourages the use of power to subdue all dissent. It elevates the production and protection of wealth as an unquestioned good. It idealizes the use of violence in order to conquer all enemies.

So, when we talk about the *Christian* in Christian nationalism, remember that in this sense it carries with it all this extra cultural baggage. Recognizing this is important for two reasons. First, acknowledging this baggage shows how it serves as a signal to those with ears to hear. The scaffolding of this cultural framework helps them imagine a very particular type of nation, with a particular set of people in power. Second, it helps us distinguish the Christianity of Christian nationalism from other expressions of Christianity. This is not to say that Americans who embrace Christian nationalism are not Christian. Many are devout Christians and hold various theological beliefs in common with many Christians of color, those arguably most dispossessed by the ideology of Christian nationalism.

This also isn't to say that other expressions of Christianity do not contain and convey particular sets of cultural baggage. All religious expressions shape and are shaped by their surrounding culture. My argument is that we can and should work to combat the particular cultural baggage of white Christian nationalism. We should seek out expressions of Christianity that do not groan under the weight of these particularly harmful and unnecessary additions that betray the gospel.

Imagine Christian nationalism as a pair of glasses through which Americans see and experience their social worlds. At one end of the spectrum, these glasses are relatively clear. These could be folks who reject white Christian nationalism. Moving from one end to the other, an orange tint becomes more noticeable, intensifying the further along you go. Those who wholeheartedly embrace Christian nationalism see a world awash in a deep orange hue.

For some Americans, the world they see has very little orange tint. They believe, behave, and live accordingly. For other Americans, all they see is a deep orange, which obviously signals something quite different to them, altering their behaviors and attitudes.

Consider how communication between people on opposite ends of the spectrum can be so difficult. They each see very different worlds. To some extent, they experience *completely* different realities. Is it any wonder we struggle to find common ground? Christian nationalism is indeed corrosive to a culture of democracy in which, working from a similar set of facts, we collaborate and at times argue in order to find compromise.[27]

The question remains: How many Americans are wearing these glasses and see the world awash in various shades of orange? Is

Al Mohler correct? Is Christian nationalism just a fringe cultural framework within white evangelicalism? Or is it much more widespread? Thankfully, social science provides a clear answer.

White Christian Nationalism across the United States

The short answer to whether Christian nationalism is only a small-scale phenomenon is a resounding *no*. Christian nationalism is not relegated to the fringes of white evangelicalism. Survey after survey of the American public from the late 1990s until today repeatedly underscore one basic fact: a substantial portion of Americans—especially within but also outside white evangelicalism—embrace Christian nationalism. Any pastor, religious leader, or politician who downplays or minimizes the degree to which Christian nationalism endures throughout the broader population and especially within white evangelicalism is either lying or misinformed.

A longer answer builds on this basic fact and contains a few surprises that are vitally important to understanding and then confronting Christian nationalism. If we have any hope of opposing white Christian nationalism, we must be clear about its extent and severity. Here are five basic facts about Christian nationalism across the US population that everyone should know.[28]

First, close to half of Americans embrace Christian nationalism to some extent. In our book *Taking America Back for God*, Sam Perry and I label these folks "Accommodators" and "Ambassadors." Accommodators, who make up a third of the population, are those Americans who believe Christianity should be a visible part of our public sphere but stop short of saying it should completely dominate all other expressions of religion or secularity. As we write, "Their support [of Christianity] is undeniable, but it is not unequivocal."[29] Ambassadors, however, completely embrace privileging Christianity throughout American society. They believe the United States was founded on Christian principles and must maintain this identity to prosper. Ambassadors represent about 16 percent of the population. Together, these two groups represent just under half of Americans who support Christian nationalism to varying degrees. A recent Pew survey underscores the reach of Christian nationalism as well as the variation within. Researchers found 45 percent of Americans believe the United States "should be" a Christian nation, but there was no clear concensus as to what exactly that means.[30]

Second, white Christians, and especially white evangelicals, are most likely to embrace Christian nationalism. As I mentioned, Christian nationalism as we define it and as it manifests throughout the United States is primarily a phenomenon anchored in white cultural institutions and organizations, particularly the white Christian church. It is therefore unsurprising that white Christians are most likely to embrace white Christian nationalism.

Looking at all white Christians (Catholics, mainline Protestants, and evangelical Protestants) in the United States, we found that around 24 percent are Ambassadors and just over 41 percent are Accommodators. Together, just under seven in ten white Christians are at least favorable toward Christian nationalism. For white evangelicals the numbers are even higher. Just under eight in ten are either Accommodators (36 percent) or Ambassadors (39 percent).[31]

These first two facts demonstrate that white Christian nationalism is not fringe in American evangelicalism or even the broader US population. Even if we look at only Ambassadors—Americans who score in the highest quartile of our Christian nationalism scale—they represent a third of all white Christians and 40 percent of all white evangelicals.

Third, Christian nationalism is not located solely within white Christianity or white evangelicalism. While white Christian nationalism is largely a product of white Christianity in the United States, it is not limited to the congregations or the people who make up these groups. Rather, the cultural influence of white Christianity helped diffuse the tenets of Christian nationalism across the population. This means that Americans in other religious traditions, and even those who do not affiliate with a religious tradition, can and sometimes do embrace Christian nationalism to varying degrees.

Therefore, Americans both in and out of organized religion use Christian nationalism as motivation and justification for their actions. While we have no data on those physically present at the Capitol insurrection, videos show rioters claiming a desire to take this country back for God and claiming that the United States is a Christian nation.[32] Some supporters of Christian nationalism may attend religious services regularly; others may not. But the utility of Christian nationalism remains the same for all. It justifies their actions in the will of the Divine, defending what they see as their rightful place atop the social order.

The diffusion of Christian nationalism across the population underscores the power and resilience of white Christian nationalism in the United States. While white Christians must take the lead in responding to Christian nationalism within their congregations and communities, we need to acknowledge that Christian nationalism exists beyond these groups. It will take a concerted effort from all of us to confront white Christian nationalism consistently.

The diffusion of Christian nationalism also underscores the fact that white Christian nationalism is not reducible to white evangelicalism alone. A significant minority of white evangelicals are taking real steps to confront Christian nationalism. About 25 percent of white evangelicals are "Rejecters" or "Resisters" of Christian nationalism.[33] Readers and leaders outside white evangelicalism confronting Christian nationalism ignore those allies at their own peril. Successfully opposing Christian nationalism will require all of us—Rejecters, Resisters, and hopefully increasing numbers of Accommodators—to work together. To achieve a better version of a democratic society, those who identify as religious and those who do not must at least agree on the threat Christian nationalism poses to all and confront it simultaneously, despite our differences across other important issues.[34]

Fourth, Christian nationalism exists across all sectors of society. Similar to the previous assertion, Christian nationalism is not confined to people living in a particular region—such as the South. Americans with varying levels of education embrace Christian nationalism. It isn't found only among the rich or the poor. Christian nationalism exists in rural, suburban, and urban communities. Racial and ethnic minorities embrace white Christian nationalism. It is not limited to white Americans alone.

It is important to mention here how the "white" of white Christian nationalism does not necessarily refer to the skin color or racial identity of an individual American who might embrace it. Rather, it refers to "whiteness," the values, habits, beliefs, behaviors, and attitudes that result in the organization of society in such a way that white Americans, as a group, tend to have greater access to power, privilege, wealth, and other benefits bestowed by various social institutions. Therefore, nonwhite Americans can still participate in and perpetuate systems or cultural frameworks, such as white Christian nationalism, that serve to uphold a racialized society in which one group tends to benefit at the expense of other groups.

Remember how Christian nationalism has diffused across American society. While the meaning and benefits of Christian nationalism might differ for various social groups, as a cultural framework it is flexible enough to be useful across dramatically different social locations. It can fit the needs of the down-and-out, the CEO, the big-city office worker, or the rural farmer.

Fifth, Christian nationalism is not becoming more prevalent. Perhaps the most frequently asked question I receive about Christian nationalism is whether it is growing. Many assume that because they hear about Christian nationalism more often now than in the past that it must be spreading like wildfire across the United States. Many a headline writer wishes they could truthfully write that Christian nationalism is "sweeping the nation!"

Christian nationalism is not some new phenomenon bringing more Americans into the fold every day. If anything, evidence from the past ten to fifteen years suggests that the number of Ambassadors—those who most strongly embrace Christian nationalism—are shrinking, bit by bit. From 2007 to 2017, the number of Ambassadors shrank from 24 percent to 20 percent of the population. In a national survey gathered in 2021, they made up 16 percent of the population. Other surveys show the number of Ambassadors holding steady from 2020 to 2021 at about 24 percent.[35] Although there is some fluctuation due to sampling differences across surveys, the evidence is clear that Christian nationalism is not growing but rather contracting some in terms of the overall population.

Why does it seem like Christian nationalism is growing even though the data do not support this claim? Part of this perception likely stems from how consistently and skillfully former president Trump and those within his administration employed Christian nationalist rhetoric. For years, the man occupying one of the most powerful positions in the world privileged the claims and desires of a particular strain of Christianity within American civic life. That clearly shaped the discourse in American civic life and the church and effectively normalized such claims. Americans who might have always desired and personally believed Christianity should be privileged perhaps now felt legitimized. This trend is especially true as folks like Al Mohler, Robert Jeffress, and Marjorie Taylor Greene actively embrace the label "Christian nationalist."

We must realize, however, that even if a group shrinks in size, this does not mean their shared identity fades away. The opposite usually occurs. As Ambassadors shrink in number, their shared embrace of white Christian nationalism becomes more salient compared to those around them. Twenty years ago, we may have had more Ambassadors in our midst, but they were likely quieter about it. Today there may be fewer, but they are much more vocal.

While this trend may seem counterintuitive, especially considering events on the national stage over the past several years, it is important to be realistic. There is no evidence to suggest that Christian nationalism is growing more prevalent. This does not mean, however, that it is any less of a threat. The claims and desires of Christian nationalism are likely more salient to the Americans who embrace it. This group tends to be the most religiously and politically active, and so the risk to American Christianity and our democracy remains very real.

A Field Guide to Christian Nationalism

For many, recognizing Christian nationalism is a "You know it when you see it" situation. Sometimes it is as blatant as someone arguing that the United States is God's chosen nation and that to be a good citizen you must be a Christian. Some pastors and laypeople adhere to a form of dominionism or Seven Mountains theology. They believe that Christians must aspire to total control across seven spheres of influence over American culture: media, education, family, religion, arts and entertainment, economy, and, of course, government. Such folks would certainly score as Ambassadors on our Christian nationalism scale.

Most often, however, Christian nationalism is not so explicit. Embracing Christian nationalism is not a binary, either-or situation. Instead, many Americans are somewhere in the middle. Therefore, I prefer speaking about Christian national*ism* rather than labeling people Christian national*ists*. Many Americans may be comfortable with privileging Christianity in some ways but less comfortable with others. The key is for us to be able to consistently identify areas where we, as Christians, may be straying into a form of belief and practice that sets aside the gospel for a form of power over others that aspires to protect our own interests.

Field guides provide lists of characteristics that help readers more accurately identify the world around them. What follows are some possible identifying markers of Christian nationalism you may encounter in interactions with fellow Americans or in Christian congregations. While identifying Christian nationalism may be less straightforward than identifying a particular bird, my goal is that this list will sketch out in a bit more detail where and how Christian nationalism permeates our daily lives. If we can train ourselves to notice some of its features, even those that seem rather innocuous, we can then address it quickly, directly, and faithfully.

In Congregations

▓ The United States Flag Displayed in the Main Sanctuary

A majority of congregations in the United States, just over 60 percent, reportedly display an American flag in their main worship space.[36] Prominently displaying the American flag during worship appears to be a rather innocuous feature of American Christianity. Perhaps you are wondering, How could this make it on his list? Displaying the American flag in our worship space is not an unhealthy practice for those in my congregation. I counter with my own question: What do you think would happen if your congregation removed the flag before next week's service?

I remember reading one pastor's remark that if he ever wanted to anger half his congregation, he only needed to remove the Stars and Stripes from the sanctuary. I am confident his congregation's feelings are not unique.[37] The anger we can imagine from some fellow Christians over the removal of the flag from our sanctuaries is instructive. It tells us a lot about what the flag means to Americans who desire it in their worship spaces.

As we see throughout the Scriptures and church history, identifying idols tends to make people angry. Is a national flag necessary to worship God? And if not, then what purpose does it serve, if not to signal the Christian church's relationship to the nation-state?

▨ Yearly "Celebrate America" Services around the Fourth of July

Every year around July 4, thousands of congregations schedule "Celebrate America" services during their normal worship times or during a special service. These celebrations usually entail various patriotic tunes like "God Bless America," "America the Beautiful," "God Bless the U.S.A.," and various anthems of the United States military. Red, white, and blue are featured everywhere, and a theme of triumphant gratitude pervades the proceedings. A sermon or homily usually directly links the greatness of the United States to the blessing of the Christian God.[38]

Appreciation for the nation and people we were born into is not Christian nationalism by default. That said, these services sometimes veer into exalting the United States over and above every other nation and people. A certainty about God's stake in the ultimate triumph of the United States should give us pause. Of course, some congregations are more careful than others in how they acknowledge the founding of the United States. One service I attended did not shy away from acknowledging the history of racial inequality in the United States. Nevertheless, a big "Celebrate America" service should prompt questions and careful thinking about the assumptions made concerning the relationship between the United States, its history, its military, and Christianity.

▨ Self-Interested or Fearful Messages from the Pulpit

The sermon is the focal point of most Protestant worship services in the United States. Therefore, its content is important for shaping the lives and imaginations of the congregants and for attracting and drawing in new congregants. It is easy enough to identify Christian nationalist rhetoric when a pastor explicitly claims the United States is a Christian nation or chosen by God.[39]

However, more subtle claims that use coded language are equally influential in sustaining white Christian nationalism. One example is limiting the gospel to merely a set of theological claims and ignoring the aspects of the gospel focused on overturning systems of power that oppress our neighbors, which make us more likely to idolize self-interested power, fear, and violence. The following chapters examine additional examples of language and concepts that sustain white Christian nationalism. They can be used to listen for where religious leaders are possibly promoting the cultural framework of white Christian nationalism.

For now, though, it is important to recognize when messages from the pulpit engage with social issues but revolve around particular sets of "moral values" that are taken for granted and treated as the only truly biblical values. In white evangelicalism, these tend to be limited to things like traditional marriage, opposition to abortion, or sexual morality. Usually, such claims are followed by an exhortation that Christians should gain access to more levers of power to ensure that the nation faithfully embodies these moral claims. When the discussion of moral issues is limited to the same few topics, however, the topics omitted are usually absent in service of white Christian nationalism. Racial inequality, poverty, the death penalty, the criminal justice system, and immigration are moral issues as well, with plenty of biblical support for ameliorative actions by Christians. Some work hard to classify such issues as leftist to ignore them, but are not Christians called to take seriously the entirety of historical Christian teachings and scriptures?

In general, those preaching from the pulpit and those of us listening need to determine whether such messages encourage us to love "the world" or to fear and defeat those out in "the world." Do the messages encourage Christians to seek justice, love kindness, and walk humbly, or is justice a dirty word? Are we supposed to focus on only a few issues or broaden our perspectives to engage with the experiences of various marginalized groups? Essentially, do the messages instill fear and a sense of threat, or do they inspire Christians to partner with Jesus in the work of confronting the sin and systems of oppression that harm us all? After hearing a message, consider whether the speaker was encouraging you to embrace love and liberation or power and control.

Among Fellow Christians

A Focus on Defending Access to Power

Christian nationalism is fundamentally concerned with wielding power for the benefit of one's own group. It is focused on defending "our" rights, practices, history, or privileges. Americans who embrace Christian nationalism to varying degrees consistently emphasize how others, those on the outside, are trying to take away their cultural and political power. It doesn't matter whether the threat is real. It is the perception of loss that matters most. Feeling aggrieved is a powerful motivator and for decades motivated many Americans to "defend the faith" and "defend the country."

In one sense, white Christian America is declining demographically and will never again enjoy being the unquestioned center of the culture. Unchallenged access to privilege and power is disappearing. However, this does not mean that white Christians will be given *no* access to avenues through which they might influence civil society. As many of my colleagues in the social sciences might say, when a group is used to privilege, equality feels like discrimination.

A Focus on Fear

Because white Christian nationalism seeks power and privilege, fears of losing unfettered access to cultural and political power engender narratives of persecution. These narratives center on how "they" are taking away what is rightfully "ours." White Christian nationalism imagines a nation that privileges particular cultural values over and above the desires of all other groups. Even considering other views or possibilities is interpreted as persecution and an attack.

The stories that Christian nationalism tells revolve around attacks on their group or how other groups will change the nation for the worse. As with feelings of grievance, fear of persecution is a potent motivator. White Christian nationalism trades in fear because of how powerfully it can delineate the "us," who should be afraid, from the "them," who are intent on persecuting the faithful.

▉ Us-versus-Them Thinking

Relatedly, Christian nationalism draws distinct and robust boundaries designating who is in and who is out. Quests for power motivated by fear require clear statements on who is on "our" side. "We" must know who we should be afraid of and why we must oppose them and their access to power at all costs. As we will discuss soon, these boundary lines are most often drawn using race and ethnicity, nationality, and religion. Christian nationalist rhetoric concerning the lines around "us" also involves aspects of both religious and national identities.

For instance, some Christians question the Americanness of anyone protesting under the banner of Black Lives Matter. In the next breath, they might hint at how these protests call into question how anyone associated with this group could be aligned with God's desires. Additional examples abound, like Al Mohler drawing lines in the sand against "the Left." The key factor is clearly highlighting who "we" are not. This is the quickest and easiest way to define who "we" are without having to make any definitive declarations concerning what "we" are for or what features define "us." Christian nationalist rhetoric consistently resorts to demonizing an "other." The other might be those of a different race, nationality, political ideology, or religion. This rhetoric claims there are people or forces we should all be very afraid of, as these people or forces are intent on diminishing us. Moreover, when Christian nationalism stokes the fires of fear because "they" are out to take our rightful power, violence is a natural result.

▊ A Comfort with Violence

Any quest for power over others that is motivated primarily by fear will likely resort to violence at some point. A key marker of Christian nationalism is a comfort with violence defined as righteous. Such violence may be interpersonal, such as when an American defends his home using a firearm. Or it may be collective, such as going to war to defeat evil, whether evil is made manifest by countries or by transnational groups like terrorist cells. This comfort with violence is intertwined with views toward authority. White Christian nationalism tends to see the enactment of violence by authority figures against out-groups as above reproach and trusts that this is part of God's working in the world. Because Christian nationalism so adeptly ostracizes out-groups, implicitly or even explicitly labeling them evil, using force and violence toward them is understandable and perhaps even celebrated.

▊ Nostalgia for the "Good Old Days"

Another signal of white Christian nationalism is appeals for a bygone era when everyone got along, America's goodness was unquestioned, people's roles in society were clear, and Christian beliefs, practices, and symbols permeated our social and civic lives. The assumption is that it was in this time that the United States was clearly fulfilling God's desires in the world.

Nostalgia for this imagined period—imagined because, of course, life in America wasn't ever quite like this—naturally sets Americans up for a lament of where the country now finds itself. Social strife, criticism of the United States from seemingly all corners, shifting roles, and Christianity no longer being the unquestioned center of culture are clear signs that this country is falling out of God's good graces. This nostalgia for the "good old days" with an accompanying narrative of decline from those days is a powerful motivator as well. It highlights a loss of power and privilege while activating fear over what is yet to come. It primes people for action. It implants a desire to resist and fight back.

Staying attuned to who is nostalgic and what they are nostalgic for will help Christians recognize white Christian nationalism. Nostalgia for the good old days also raises questions: Were the good old days good for everybody? How accurate are our memories of the good old days? As Christians, we must commit to stay grounded in the truth about who we are as a nation and where we have come from. If we do not, how can we claim to be following God's truth?

A View of the Founding Fathers and Foundational Documents as Christian (Just like Us)

Factually incorrect statements about the founding fathers and foundational documents relate to nostalgia for an imagined period in the past. Clearly, Protestant Christianity was influential during the founding period. No reputable historian disputes that. However, claims that the founding fathers and the accompanying foundational documents were explicitly focused on privileging Christianity—and that we as a country need to return to such a time—are a fundamental aspect of the cultural framework of Christian nationalism.[40]

Religious and political leaders push this narrative because it establishes a foundation from which they can argue that their particular values should take precedence. If they can convince Christians that George Washington and Thomas Jefferson embraced the idea of a Christian America, then the modern-day values and policies embraced by those who want to return to a Christian America become central markers of a true American identity. These folks also tend to ignore the dangerous game they are playing. If the founding period was particularly Christian, why did it include the genocide of native peoples and the enslavement of Africans?

There are a number of balanced examinations of the religious faith of the various founding fathers and the role of religion during the founding period.[41] However, when politicians, religious leaders, or those in our communities claim that the founding fathers or the foundational documents set out to establish a Christian nation with laws and policies that just happen to align perfectly with one current political party, we can see Christian nationalism at work.

Can I Oppose Christian Nationalism and Still Be . . .

Now, a common set of questions arises whenever I suggest that Christians must oppose Christian nationalism. Some ask, with good intentions, whether we can no longer be Christians, or allow our faith to influence our political decisions, or be patriots. Others raise these questions to evade reckoning with the negative consequences of Christian nationalism. I offer my assurance that opposing Christian nationalism allows us to be both Christians and patriots.

. . . a Christian?

Yes! Identifying expressions of Christianity that oppose Christian nationalism is one of my key goals. I hope that by sharing a bit about my research, my own journey, and the stories of others you can see several examples of committed Christians who express their faith without resorting to the idols of Christian nationalism.

I'll even go one step further: we can oppose Christian nationalism, be Christians, and still be involved in the public sphere. In fact, I do not know how we could be Christians and faithfully follow the dictates of our faith *without* being involved in the lives of those around us. The key question, though, is how we live out our faith in the public sphere and for whose benefit.

For centuries, and particularly since the 1970s, the prevailing mode of white Christian involvement with politics and civil society has been one of domination and control. Various expressions of Christianity show us a better way. Rather than moving to privilege or protect "us," these Christians work to lift up others, especially those on the margins. They work to protect the rights of all people to participate in civil society and live in peace.

... a Patriot?

Yes! Christians can be grateful to the United States for all the opportunities and privileges it provides. We can celebrate the good that exists in this country. We can honor the people and moments in this country's history that moved us toward a more just and kind world. In the words of Paul Miller, we can oppose Christian nationalism and express "affection and loyalty to a specific part of God's creation" that encourages us to "do the good work of cultivating and improving the part we happen to live in."[42]

Being a patriot, though, does not mean Christians should ignore the difficult and at times heinous aspects of our collective history. We cannot truly love something if we are unwilling to tell the truth about it. I appreciate how Kat Armas says it: "We cannot belong to one another if we're not committed to telling the truth about ourselves and each other. Injustice affects both the oppressor and the oppressed, so we must tell the truth about the past . . . [to] heal our future."[43]

I'm not alone or the first one to say it: being a patriot means we tell the truth about our nation's history and work toward a future in which everyone is able to participate. Doing so "reveals artificial stories for what they are and creates space for truer ones."[44] We can then fulfill the unrealized aspirations of the founding period, creating a space where *all* are able to enjoy life, liberty, and the pursuit of happiness. Christians can and should wholeheartedly endorse this project. Only when we recognize the kingdom of God as superior to the nation can we speak truth to power and maintain a prophetic stance advocating for those on the margins.

When we consider ourselves part of the kingdom of God, we can acknowledge that politics and power in this world can be leveraged for the benefit of all, not just those most like us. We can commit to demanding that the hurting, the sick, and the powerless live without fear of violence, receive healing care for their wounds, and be able to exert influence on our communities and nation as bearers of the image of God. Advocating for the rights of our neighbors is the work of Christians. That sounds like patriotism to me.

However, Christian nationalism, like other forms of exclusive nationalism, lead us a place where we demand and defend our own rights at the expense of others, not alongside them. Where patriotism can move us to care for our neighbor out of a shared love of our country and all its inhabitants, nationalism demands that we draw sharp boundary lines around who is truly a part of our country and that we take control of our country to ensure that "we" benefit most from all it has to offer, the rights and needs of our neighbors be damned.

When those in power are made to see and serve the least in society, a nation can play a role in ensuring the flourishing of its people. That is good. That is holy. That aligns with the gospel of Jesus Christ. That is patriotism. There is nothing anti-Christ about the government ensuring that the wealth of the nation benefits all citizens and not just the already wealthy.

When we love someone or something, we commit to telling the truth. A patriot and Christian should tell the truth about their country. A patriot and Christian should work toward a civil society in which *all* are able to participate and flourish.

Where Do We Go from Here?

Many American Christians from across the theological and political spectrum were troubled by the violent insurrection at our nation's Capitol on January 6, 2021, and the ensuing revelations unearthed in the congressional hearings. They wanted to know why their fellow Americans would attack police officers and storm the Capitol building, why elected leaders stood by and watched the carnage, and why the insurrectionists carried crosses, "Jesus Saves" signs, and the Christian flag.

Christian nationalism is not the sole explanation, but it is a key factor in that story. The idols of power, fear, and violence in service of protecting what God has granted "us" provided the theological motivation and post hoc justification necessary for thousands of rioters to violently demonstrate that this was "their" country. Some commentators, like Albert Mohler, have suggested that Christian nationalism is fringe. Survey data show such a stance is indefensible. But we also shouldn't adopt the label to antagonize "the Left." Others decried the violence and argued that a more faithful expression of Christianity cannot coexist with what we saw on January 6.

Survey data collected just after the insurrection and then again months later tell us a sobering story. White Americans who embrace Christian nationalism were more likely to look favorably on the rioters and the insurrection.[45] These same Americans were also much more likely to endorse violence as a necessary means to "take America back." The undercurrents motivating January 6 are still flowing.

The insurrection is not an outlier event in our nation's history. Nor will it be the last example of violence suffused with Christian symbolism unless and until American Christians consistently confront Christian nationalism.

The first step in confronting Christian nationalism is knowing what it is and how prevalent it is, which has been the aim of this chapter. The second step is to explore the idols of Christian nationalism and examine alternative expressions of Christianity that can help us dismantle those idols. To start, we turn to the central idol of Christian nationalism—power.

TURN THE OTHER CHEEK?

We've turned the other cheek, and I understand, sort of,
the biblical reference—I understand the mentality—but it's
gotten us nothing. Okay? It's gotten us nothing while we've
ceded ground in every major institution in our country.

—Donald Trump Jr.[1]

POWER IS THE ABILITY to do what you want—as well
as get others to do what you want—despite resistance.
Power can be exercised by individuals, organizations, or
even larger social institutions like the economy, government, or
education.

Power may be physical, psychological, emotional, or a combination of these. Most view power as a scarce resource. If one
person or group has more, then others must necessarily have less,
like a seesaw. This suggests that in every interaction—whether
between people, groups, or organizations—the competition for

power necessarily creates an us-versus-them dynamic: if they have more power, then we'll have less, and vice versa.

Therefore, power can be as straightforward as one person forcing another to surrender some coveted good, or as complex as the cultural assumptions that influence how groups of people define and defend the boundaries of belonging.

Christian nationalism is obsessed with power.

Why is it concerned primarily with power? Because the final goal of Christian nationalism rests in safeguarding a space where white, culturally and religiously conservative, natural-born citizens occupy the unquestioned center of the culture and enjoy privileged access to interpersonal, organizational, and institutional control. As author and organizer Jonathan Wilson-Hartgrove says, "White Christian nationalism is the cultural product of people who want to hold on to power."[2]

White Christian nationalism writes a "deep story" in which "we" deserve power and "they" do not.[3] Deep stories are powerful because they give people ready-made narratives rooted in culture that provide organization and structure to the world around them. They are effectively the lenses through which we see and interpret our social worlds. The deep story of white Christian nationalism defines who is a "good" American and a "good" Christian. It clearly identifies the enemies and threats to our country. It provides a specific interpretation of US history, including how the nation should understand itself today. It also imagines the ideal future for the United States and a blueprint for how to achieve those ends.

White Christian nationalism creates a world that works to the advantage of one group while marginalizing others. It legitimizes and even sanctifies the advantages of the in-group, providing them with a divine explanation for their advantage. This is an effective (and sinister) move, as it eliminates accountability for how those advantages create hardships for others and removes any responsibility for repairing what is broken. Those with privilege can merely chalk up their wins to God's favor and their losses to attacks from evil in their midst.

To ensure that their vision of the world comes to fruition, those who embrace the deep story of white Christian nationalism *must* have more political, social, and cultural power than their perceived enemies. They view power in the hands of the "right people"—which most often means white, natural-born, politically and religiously conservative Christians—as inherently righteous. And here is a crucial point: the idol of power in Christian nationalism is a power employed for selfish reasons to benefit the in-group.

To pursue justice, Christians will have to seek and use power; however, this employment of power should benefit all people, especially our neighbors who have been harmed or overlooked. Christian nationalism's vision and use of power is focused solely on extending and protecting a particular subset of largely white Christians' cultural and economic interests. It is important to distinguish between the two uses of power to faithfully confront white Christian nationalism in our society and religious tradition.

In the words of Donald Trump Jr., cited at the beginning of this chapter, biblical ideals like turning the other cheek get us nothing. Instead, we must protect our own with power. Throughout the history of the United States, we see examples of groups and individuals working toward such ends. Most recently, those on the Christian Right have provided a perfect illustration.

White Christian Nationalism's Quest for Power

Growing up in white evangelicalism meant that every presidential election cycle we heard some variation of the following: "It is important that we vote! We need to put a godly person in the White House. Our nation is the greatest on earth because of God's blessing. But right now, our culture is going to hell in a handbasket.

We need to return to God's ways as a nation. Our children's future depends on it!"[4]

The first-order principle for many white evangelical pastors and congregations is that we (as Christians) will be best able to influence our world toward a more Christian future through the power afforded by the office of the presidency, or Congress, or state legislatures, or school boards. For this to happen, Christians must vote in large numbers and for the right people.

Arguments along these lines have a long and storied history. Billy Graham was one of the most well-known evangelists of Christianity throughout the twentieth century. He did not limit himself to altar calls. He was also the leading evangelist of exhorting Christians to be more politically active in order to turn the nation in a particular direction.

In a 1953 rally from the steps of the Capitol, he cast the United States as a Christian nation in need of a revival. Graham firmly believed that to be a good American one must be a Christian: "I want to tell you it is more patriotic, more patriotic, to be a Christian, to live for God, than it is to carry a gun in time of war." He consistently frames the United States as a lone bulwark against the rising tide of communism and atheism. "America," he claimed, "is the great spiritual arsenal of the world."[5] Perhaps it should come as no surprise, then, that he believed from early in his ministry that bending the ear of presidents could pay enormous dividends for inserting Christianity into the public sphere and, in his estimation, making America more Christian.

Of course, Graham was burned several times, such as when he and some friends prayed on the White House lawn for a photo op after meeting with Harry Truman, making Graham persona non grata throughout the remainder of Truman's administration.[6] Graham's most notable political mistake was his long and close relationship with Richard Nixon. It is no coincidence that Graham's ministry focused more on international missions and revivals after Nixon left the presidency in disgrace.

Other white evangelical pastors, religious leaders, and political operatives from the 1960s and 1970s were happy to continue Graham's work. They continued pushing for a public expression of Christianity closely intertwined with conservative politics. In fact, this next generation of leaders took the quest for political power to a new level, creating organizations and institutionalizing processes to help ensure that white Christians understood their role and took seriously their power as a voting bloc.

Jerry Falwell was one of the most recognized leaders of this era. His radio and television ministry reached thousands of religious leaders and millions of American Christians. He recognized the need to get the "right" men in power, as seen in this famous quote aimed at pastors: "We have a three-fold primary responsibility: number one, get people saved; number two, get them baptized; number three, get them registered to vote."[7]

With each election, these leaders warned that the future of the country was at stake. By tying Christianity so closely to the success or failure of the United States, Christians were in effect voting to protect their faith tradition. The message was clear: We need to gain and protect power in order to ensure that our values take precedence in this country.

Consider, for example, what James Dobson, founder of Focus on the Family, had to say concerning almost every presidential election of just the past twenty years:

- 2004: "If you identify with the pro-life and pro-family movement, if you believe there is a right and wrong, if you believe in absolute truth, it's all on the line tomorrow. . . . There is a spiritual battle going on. . . . And we simply must let our voices be heard."[8]
- 2008: "Christians didn't take time to find out who Barack Obama was when they voted for him. Why did they risk our nation's future on him? It was a mistake that changed the course of history."[9]

- 2016: "I believe this great country is hanging by a thread. If we make another tragic mistake after putting Barack Obama in office for eight years, we will never recover from it."[10]
- 2020: "Hordes of angry anarchists are salivating over the next election, hoping to push America over a cliff. If they succeed, . . . Western civilization will never recover."[11]

Repeatedly, Dobson claimed that this country, even Western civilization itself, was hanging by a thread. Only when Christians exert their political prowess can "we" ensure the survival of the land we love. We'll soon explore the use of fear in relation to this quest for power within white Christian nationalism.

Dobson is obviously not alone. Every election cycle, religious and political leaders who espouse Christian nationalism remind white Christians to take seriously this quest for power. On the campaign trail in 2016, Donald Trump Sr. appealed to self-interested power and understood the hold it had on American Christians. While at Dordt University, a small Christian institution, he warned his listeners, "Christians don't use their power. We have to strengthen. Because we are getting—if you look, it's death by a million cuts—we are getting less and less powerful in terms of a religion, and in terms of a force." Trump then promised them, "Christianity will have power. . . . Because if I'm there, you're going to have plenty of power. *You don't need anybody else.* You're going to have somebody representing you very, very well. Remember that."[12]

Before the 2020 election, Pastor Robert Jeffress of First Baptist Dallas highlighted the responsibility of Christians to choose the right leaders in "this Christian nation." In fact, he said that not exercising this right to vote—and ensuring that the right people are in power—"is a sin against God and a sin against this country."[13]

Lauren Boebert, a gun rights activist and congresswoman from Colorado, signaled the centrality of this quest for power as part of

God's plan not only for this country but also for her. She likened her victory to a "sign and wonder" from God and said that she was "called to Congress" as a key part of her "journey with Jesus."[14] In 2022, Boebert said that "the church is supposed to direct the government," that she was "tired of this separation of church and state junk that's not in the Constitution," and that her views represented those of the founding fathers.[15]

Another example of the obsession with self-interested power within Christian nationalism is the collection of political operatives and politicians at various levels of government seeking to enshrine Christianity as supreme in American civic life through legal and legislative strategies. Two are particularly influential: Project Blitz and the National Association of Christian Lawmakers.

Project Blitz is a collection of prepackaged bills accompanied by a systematic process that state lawmakers can use to institutionalize Christian nationalist rhetoric and narratives in local, state, and federal laws. First, Project Blitz encourages representatives to pass seemingly innocent resolutions acknowledging America's Christian heritage. Then representatives are encouraged to push to formalize the centrality of Christianity to American civic life, such as requiring schools to post the national motto "In God we trust."[16] From there they hope representatives will introduce and pass bills that further privilege conservative Christian causes, such as those that will allow religious individuals to refuse service to anyone, perhaps based on gender and sexuality.[17]

Like Project Blitz, the National Association of Christian Lawmakers (NACL) aims to organize Christian lawmakers—both in office and those considering running—and faith-based legislation to fuse a conservative strain of Christianity with American civic life. The founder of the NACL, Jason Rapert, said, "Our ultimate goal and intent is that we restore the Judeo-Christian foundations of our government that were intended from the very beginning" by placing the right Christian people in power to propose and support legislation based on "a biblical worldview."[18] The goal is to gain enough power over others to unilaterally institute laws reflecting their interpretation of Christianity.

NACL leaders also hope to repurpose the concept of religious liberty to fit their political goals. In their view, religious liberty should no longer refer to the right of any citizen to practice or not practice religion without governmental interference. Rather, they seek to redefine religious liberty as the right to bring privately held religious beliefs into the public square. Dennis Baxely, a Florida state senator and chair of the Florida NACL, said, "We think without [religious liberty] there's a tremendous loss in the underpinnings of what America is." Leaders like Baxely believe the United States should be a distinctively Christian nation and consequently that "religious liberty" means the ability to "restore the Judeo-Christian foundations" of the country, as they see them.[19] For those in the NACL and similar groups, this form of religious liberty is just another weapon in the arsenal for ensuring they can privilege their social and political vision over those of others rather than ensuring religious liberty for all.

These illustrations are the tip of the iceberg.[20]

As Tony Perkins, leader of the lobbying group Family Research Council, famously said about Christians supporting Trump despite his non-Christian behavior: "I think they are finally glad that there's somebody on the playground that is willing to punch the bully." White Christian nationalism adores a fighter because fighters embody power. In the same interview, Perkins made his stance clear: "You know, you only have two cheeks. Look, Christianity is not all about being a welcome mat which people can just stomp their feet on."[21]

Within the cultural framework of Christian nationalism, sharing power within a pluralistic democratic society is akin to being a welcome mat being stomped on, or being bullied on a playground. Either their interpretations of the Christian faith are given precedence throughout society, or they are under attack and being silenced and persecuted. The narrative is this stark. There is no middle ground.

It is clear that the quest for power that was paramount for decades and across generations of religious leaders within white Christianity is still pulsing with life today. For these Christian leaders, as well as their followers, sharing control over the levers of power is foolish. As Bible scholar and theologian Obery Hendricks Jr. writes, many "decided that the teachings of Jesus can be ignored when those teachings get in the way of their quest to dominate American society."[22]

In their view, it is only through power over others and the strength to wield such power that Christians can ensure that their vision for this world—which they regard as God's vision—comes to fruition. It is not through service or witness or sacrifice that Christians might influence the world for good. Rather, Christians must force their neighbors to accept the supremacy of their expression of Christianity.

Evidence of Idolizing Power

The quest for achieving and protecting political and cultural power benefiting Christians, led by religious leaders and political operatives who seek to "make America more Christian," clearly resonates with the attitudes and beliefs of Americans who embrace Christian nationalism. My ongoing research, as well as many studies by other researchers, confirms this.

Across various national surveys, analyses show that embracing Christian nationalism is linked to much more authoritarian attitudes and generally a disregard—and at times outright disdain—for sharing power. Consistently, Christian nationalism is suspicious of the opportunity that democracy creates for power-sharing among disparate groups with competing visions for the United States.

There is an internal consistency to this logic. If God has a particular plan for the United States and the *only* way for the United

States to stay in God's good graces is to align itself with God's commands, then those who know (or believe they know) what God commands must do *anything* in their power to ensure that God's desires come to pass. For Americans who embrace white Christian nationalism, setting aside democracy in order to "save" the nation from itself is a worthy sacrifice. If the God of the universe commanded it, who are we to stand in the way? Why would we let democracy and power-sharing undermine our covenant with God?

Consider the following findings among Americans who endorse Christian nationalism. They are

- more likely to deny that voter suppression is a problem;
- more likely to believe the United States makes it "too easy to vote";
- more likely to believe voter fraud is rampant;
- more likely to support requirements to vote, such as passing a civics test; and
- more likely to support laws that would keep those who committed certain crimes from voting.[23]

In sum, those who embrace Christian nationalism desire to limit who gets a say in the democratic process. This relationship is particularly strong among white Americans. Placing boundaries around the democratic process serves to preserve white Christians' disproportionate access to political power. When it comes down to democracy or power, white Christian nationalism will choose power every time. Christian nationalism is interested in a government not for the people, by the people, but rather for a particular people, by a particular people.

It is important for white Christians to recognize the corrupt and immoral history of attempts to restrict access to the vote. White Christian nationalism has been a central factor in efforts to tilt elections in favor of white conservative Christians at the expense of democratic ideals. In 1980, Paul Weyrich, one of the founders of the Moral Majority and the American Legislative Exchange Council, told a group of white evangelical leaders, "Now many of our Christians have what I call the 'goo-goo syndrome.' Good government. They want everybody to vote. I don't want everybody to vote. Elections are not won by a majority of people. They never have been from the beginning of our country, and they are not now. As a matter of fact, our leverage in the elections quite candidly goes up as the voting populace goes down."[24] Weyrich's views have served as central organizing principles on the political and religious Right.

Beyond controlling access to the right to vote to protect privileged access to political power, white Christian nationalism seeks to determine how and when American citizens show deference or respect for this nation and its traditions. Embracing Christian nationalism increases the chances that Americans believe we must force others to show respect for America's traditions.[25]

In a country that supposedly prizes freedom and individualism, is there anything less patriotic than *making* fellow citizens act according to a specific tradition or custom? Of course, it is not really about patriotism or love of country at all. Rather, it is about control. And being in control signals your group has power.

There is a deeper issue at play here. Up for debate are which groups have the right to define American identity and how we should imagine our collective past, present, and future. Consider the professional athletes who have knelt or raised a fist during the national anthem. Most say they are doing so to raise awareness of inequality. This act of raising awareness usually arouses a response aimed at forcing these athletes to "get back in line." We have all read the social media posts telling those kneeling to "just play the game."

It seems many Americans would rather not have to recognize inequality. Doing so would force us to reevaluate our conceptions of this country and how we have benefited from power and policies that overwhelmingly privilege our group. For many white American Christians, highlighting how the United States committed atrocities in the past or how it fails its citizens in the present is akin to an attack on us personally. We then interpret this as an attack on our religion because our personal religious identities are tightly intertwined with our national identity. A threat to one is a threat to the other. We feel lost as to how we should define American identity.

A final example of this quest for power is the ongoing transformation of "religious liberty" or "religious freedom" into a vehicle through which some American Christians argue for the centrality of their own rights in the public sphere. For many white American Christians intent on protecting a Christian America, religious liberty shifted from a protection from interference with freedom of worship to a demand "that individuals should be able to carry religious objections from their private life into their public roles as service providers, business owners, and even elected officials."[26]

Such interpretations depart from historic conceptions of religious liberty and religious freedom that secure the right of all Americans, whether secular or those from any religious group, to believe or act on religious or personal conscience without unnecessary government interference. One recent study shows how in the 2020 election voters who chose "religious freedom" as central to their voting decision preferred conservative Christian supremacy in the public sphere, felt Christians were persecuted in the United States, and believed gender and sexuality minorities were overprotected.[27]

Government neutrality regarding religion is no longer the central goal of the fight over "religious freedom." Rather, "religious liberty" and "religious freedom" are now rhetorical and legal tools in service of gaining power, used to achieve an upper hand in the culture wars and prolong social privileges, even if only for a time. "Religious liberty" and "religious freedom" are now merely "dog-whistle language for conservative Christian supremacy."[28] While there are well-meaning Christians who may have genuine concerns about losing their ability to act according to their conscience in public matters, the goal of the overarching political project is that all Americans abide by the moral values belonging to this expression of Christianity.

Power as Idol

In the Christian tradition, idols are whatever the people of God place their faith in more than God to provide security, provision, and comfort. Throughout the biblical narrative, God consistently calls people to trust in him alone rather than in kings, weapons, or other gods.

Power over others—being able to make them do what we want them to do despite resistance—has tempted much of Western Christendom. In its first three hundred years of existence, Christianity had little in the way of temptation concerning the quest for power. Various emperors of Rome either ignored this small religious sect or, more often, persecuted it. For the early church, the idea of aligning their faith with empire and the power of the sword was a nonstarter. Authors whose main experience of the faith was in a context of marginalization wrote the entire New Testament of the Christian Bible. The age of the martyrs, from around AD 60 until 312, was marked by periodic outbreaks of violence against Christians, prompting Tertullian to write, "The more you mow us down, the more we grow. The blood of the martyrs is the seed of the Church."[29]

The marginalized status of Christians changed in the fourth century, when the Roman emperor Constantine began to favor Christianity and then converted to the faith. Before a battle in which his forces were greatly outnumbered, Constantine reported seeing a vision of light in the sky. It told him, "In this sign thou shalt conquer." The sign—a combination of the Greek letters chi and rho—represented the first two letters of *Christos*.

Constantine and his forces were victorious in the battle. The prevailing explanation for the victory was that the Christian God favored the Roman army. This was likely the first adoption of Christian symbolism in service of military victory and might, of raw power over enemies. The relationship between the Christian faith and empire would never be the same.

I remember first hearing this story of Constantine and his vision from God while an undergraduate student at Purdue University. I was in a history of Christianity course. Growing up evangelical, we were consistently told stories of Romans martyring Christians, and we constantly searched our hearts to discover if we, too, would stay faithful to Christ even if faced with a terrifying death. My sixth-grade public school teacher even screened the music video of Ray Boltz's "I Pledge Allegiance to the Lamb" in class. If you've never seen it, go google it now. The setup to the song shows a father talking with his son about Christian martyrs of the past. It turns out that in the end (spoiler alert!) the father is minutes from being whisked away to his own death as he refuses to reject the name of Christ at the hands of some futuristic unnamed authoritarian regime.

Given Rome's treatment of Christians for a couple hundred years, indeed its slaughter of Christians, Jews, and other religious minorities, it unnerved me to consider why God would give a vision to a Roman emperor promising military victory. Did God do an about-face? What about all those Christians who died at the hands of Roman emperors before Constantine? Was it God's plan all along to win over the most powerful person in the world at that time to now help Christianity flourish? Why didn't Jesus use this same tactic and embrace imperial power? Why would God be interested in helping this emperor leading this particular empire to win this particular battle? Of course, there was and is no way to know what Constantine really saw or what it really meant. One thing, though, is for sure: the track record of Christianity aligning itself with empire in any time and place should unnerve Christians.

From the first moment of comingling the power of the state with the Christian faith, we see repeatedly emperors, kings, prime ministers, and presidents legitimating their power over others, the power of the sword, in the will of the Christian God. They forgive themselves of numerous atrocities by claiming that God has blessed them with the power they wield. They baptize their desire to conquer, capture, and control as divinely ordained. In other words: If God is on your side, who can stand against you?

Just as frequently, we see Christians gladly aligning themselves with those wielding the power of the sword. Surely, we argue, this is the will of God. With the power of the state and sword on our side, Christians will (finally!) be able to broaden our influence over society. We will be able to enact laws, influence customs, and shape culture to align with our interpretations of the Bible. Think of all the lives we will save. We will be able to wield this power over others in a just manner. Just wait and see.

The temptation for self-interested power is seductive. It seems to solve so many problems. Why must we sacrifice our privileged position to ensure that our neighbors flourish as well? However, it is in this failure to empower those marginalized that we begin to treat power like an idol. Our hope and faith are in the possibility that we can defend and extend a world that benefits "us," fashioning a Christendom where we are able to bend the lives and desires of those around us to our vision.

This vision of power is the central idol of white Christian nationalism. This idol tempts us because we believe that only through gaining privileged access to power over others can we ensure our own protection. But is this the way of Christ? What was his relationship to power? I have been asking myself these questions for the past twenty-plus years.

Christ and Power

Through both my personal and my professional journey studying Christian nationalism, I have become more convinced that the life and teachings of Jesus provide us American Christians with a template for how we should regard power. These examples, in addition to other passages throughout Scripture, should encourage white American Christians to be wary of any quest for privileged access to power over others. Striving to establish and defend Christendom is not the same as living as though the kingdom of God that Jesus proclaimed is already among us.

We read in the Gospels of Matthew (4:8–10) and Luke (4:5–8) that Jesus was led into the desert and there faced three temptations. One stands out. In Matthew 4, we read:

> Again, the devil took him to a very high mountain and showed him all the kingdoms of the world and their splendor. "All this I will give you," he said, "if you will bow down and worship me."
>
> Jesus said to him, "Away from me, Satan! For it is written: 'Worship the Lord your God, and serve him only.'"

And in Luke 4, we read:

> The devil led him up to a high place and showed him in an instant all the kingdoms of the world. And he said to him, "I will give you all their authority and splendor; it has been given to me, and I can give it to anyone I want to. If you worship me, it will all be yours."
>
> Jesus answered, "It is written: 'Worship the Lord your God and serve him only.'"

What can we learn from these passages?

First, they suggest that all the kingdoms of this world—their power, splendor, and authority—are under the mandate of Satan. Jesus himself does not dispute this. If nothing has changed since Jesus's time, should we not assume that the kingdoms of this world, including America, are still under the ultimate authority of Satan? A recent national survey showed that 85 percent of self-identified American Christians said that the devil/Satan "definitely" or "probably" exists.[30] Seeking to align Christianity with any kingdom of this world, which includes America, should at least give Christians pause.

Second, we see that Jesus is tempted to bypass the struggle he is bound to engage in, and he *turns down* this opportunity to gain the authority and splendor of the kingdoms of this world.

We can also consider Jesus's interaction with Pilate before he is given over to be crucified (John 18:33–36). Pilate asks Jesus, "Are you the king of the Jews?" Jesus responds by asking if this is Pilate's own idea or if he has heard this from someone else. Pilate then presses, "What is it you have done?" Jesus says, "My kingdom is not of this world. If it were, my servants would fight to prevent my arrest by the Jewish leaders. But now my kingdom is from another place."

This is not the first time Jesus says his kingdom is not of this world. What stands out about his discourse with Pilate is that he's speaking with someone who has the power of empire behind him. Pilate even notes that he can free or condemn Jesus.

Here again Jesus faces a moment when he could aim to leverage the authority of the state for self-interested purposes. But he knows that form of power cannot accomplish the work of his kingdom. The kingdom of God operates by a different principle. It is up to us, as white American Christians, to understand that principle and begin to put it into practice. In these examples, it seems Jesus is showing us that struggling alongside those being crushed by sin and oppressive systems is how we faithfully engage with power in the kingdom of God.

What is the way of Jesus? Mark 10:35–45 provides one poignant example. Two of Jesus's disciples, James and John, ask Jesus to place them in positions of honor and power when he comes into his "glory." At this point in the narrative, the disciples still assume that the culmination of Jesus's work will be Israel's reestablishment as a sovereign nation. They believe Jesus is there to set up an earthly kingdom no longer under the oppressive rule of the Romans.

James and John want to be near the throne of power. We can't blame them for making this rather audacious request. They imagine an Israel that, in the words of former president Trump, "will have power." The seductive nature of power is strong. Jesus takes this moment to instruct them on how they have it all backward. Following him will not lead to positions in which we execute self-interested power. Rather, he tells his disciples, "You know that those who are regarded as rulers of the Gentiles lord it over them, and their high officials exercise authority over them. Not so with you. Instead, whoever wants to become great among you must be your servant, and whoever wants to be first must be slave of all. For even the Son of Man did not come to be served, but to serve, and to give his life as a ransom for many" (Mark 10:42–45).

Here Jesus is encouraging his disciples to reject the opportunity to wield power over others. Rather, we exercise kingdom power when we serve our neighbors and even our enemies. We exercise kingdom power when we stand with the marginalized and demand that those in power use it to benefit the least in society rather than the rich, powerful, or well-connected. We look like Jesus when we leverage whatever earthly privilege, power, or prestige we have in service to others. *For even the Son of Man did not come to be served, but to serve, and to give his life as a ransom for many.* This posture toward power does not fit with white Christian nationalism. We cannot quest for political power to protect our self-interest while living out Jesus's example of turning down access to earthly kingdom power and living a life of service and sacrifice for others. We cannot know the Jesus of the Gospels, "the bicultural, border-crossing, Brown Jesus, the one born in a stable, rejected in his hometown, tortured, broken, and battered," without prioritizing and "centering the voices of" the marginalized.[31]

As James Cone tells us, Christ on the cross "is a paradoxical religious symbol because it *inverts* the world's value system with the news that hope comes by way of defeat. . . . The cross was God's critique of power—white power—with powerless love, snatching victory out of defeat." Recognizing how throughout history power in the hands of humans is generally wielded in self-interest, we come to understand how the revelation of God's goodness and love "must be weak and not strong. . . . Thus, God's revelation *transvalues* human values, turning them upside down."[32]

Recognizing that the way of the cross demands that Christians critique worldly desires for self-interested power and control does not mean that Christians should stay out of politics or not work to leverage systems of power to protect the marginalized. As it was for Jesus, our path is to seek solidarity with the least.

Thus, the *focus* of who benefits from our political actions and systems is what changes. Christian nationalism aims to profit those who have historically benefited from cultural and political dominance. They identify as the in-group, the "true Americans," the "us." In the United States, this has historically meant white, natural-born, culturally and politically conservative citizens. But the life and teachings of Jesus command that Christians serve and work to benefit those marginalized by worldly systems of power. This theme of his life is directly related to God's continual calls to his chosen people to ensure that the entire community took care of and paid attention to "the least of these"—the widows, orphans, strangers, and immigrants.

How can we best do this? What examples are there for how our Christian faith can more faithfully represent Jesus and oppose the idolatry of Christian nationalism in a quest for self-interested power and control?

I believe there are two avenues through which white American Christians can ensure that they are maintaining a faithful and healthy relationship to power. Taking steps to practice these as individuals but especially within our organizations will allow us to reflect Jesus's example of turning power over others on its head in a life of service and love. The first is a commitment to religious liberty for all. The second is a commitment to leveraging our power to benefit primarily those marginalized throughout our society.

Defending Religious Liberty for All

To fulfill the example of self-sacrificial love set by Jesus, American Christians can seek religious liberty for all people. We can reject and resist the temptation to cheapen fights for religious liberty as opportunities merely to make life easier for fellow Christians. Again, religious liberty is the constitutionally ensured right of all Americans, religious or secular, to believe or act on religious or personal conscience without unnecessary government interference. White American Christians can seek to share cultural and political power and privilege so that our neighbors can live, work, and worship in peace.

Therefore, when Christians oppose building permits for other religious groups seeking to build a house of worship, we are abusing our cultural and political power. Consider how this must make our neighbors feel. Do they sense that we see them as fully and deeply loved by God, people whom Christ died for and then called us to love and serve? They become merely objects, those we must control, oppose, or change.

When we demand that symbols of the Christian faith occupy places of honor in the public sphere, we likewise abuse our cultural and political power. Our commitment to faithfully following Christ is not dependent on posting the Ten Commandments at the county courthouse. Our ability to love, serve, and act as salt and light in our communities is not dependent on various symbols of Christianity dominating the civic landscape.

When we demand the right for coaches to lead prayers at the fifty-yard line of a high school football field, we abuse our cultural and political power. We ignore the discomfort of non-Christian or nonreligious student athletes who merely want to participate in team activities but whose sincerely held personal beliefs are trampled on by our desire to center ourselves and our faith. We interfere with the religious freedom of other Christians, too, by ignoring diversity within our religious tradition. Even more, we outright ignore Jesus's distaste toward public, showy prayers (Matt. 6:5–6).

If anything, our continual fight for those symbols and "rights," despite those outside our faith registering their discomfort with what we are doing, merely confirms to them that we are much more committed to our faith standing supreme above any others than to loving or serving them. Jesus calls us to the latter, not the former. And such fights can even serve to empty our sacred symbols of their central meaning, co-opting them in service of other ends.

Our faith can and will flourish in the United States without official governmental support for or opposition to other faith groups or Americans who are not religious. We can vote, rally, give support, and call for a society that reflects the dictates of our faith without seeking Christian dominance.

This is not a call for Christians to exit the public sphere. Far from it. Rather, we Christians should never seek *supremacy* in the public sphere. Participating in a democracy entails exercising some form of political power, whether it be voting, educating others, protesting, or calling our representatives. The problem is not these or other forms of political participation. The problem is when we seek to limit others' access to these forms of political participation and endeavor to dominate others to ensure the supremacy of a particular expression of Christianity. The problem is when we demand that our own self-interested privilege over-shadow the rights or perspectives of our fellow citizens.

I recognize that the intentions of many American Christians are noble and good. They believe in the promise of their faith and that living according to it will help improve the world around them. I hope we begin to recognize, however, that while our intentions might be noble and good, the outcomes of some of our actions toward these ends undermine those good intentions.

For example, efforts like those of Project Blitz or the NACL harm the witness of American Christians to our neighbors— neighbors who have been trying to tell us that actions like these suggest we do not truly care about them, that we care only about whether we can force our particular vision for the nation on them. We can recognize that they, too, have a vision for a flourishing society. If we are interested in living in a pluralistic democratic society where everyone is allowed to participate, then we must agree on shared values that go beyond our particular religious identities and beliefs. Religious liberty is one such fundamental shared value.

How might we begin to stand for religious liberty for all? Those at the Baptist Joint Committee (BJC) are just one example of Christians committed to religious liberty and freedom as an expression of their faith in Jesus. The BJC is a faith-based nonprofit group working to protect religious liberty for all Americans by defending the separation of church and state. They believe all Americans have, and should continue to have, the right to follow their spiritual beliefs without support or encroachment from the government.

Amanda Tyler, the executive director of the BJC, refers to their stance as the "golden rule of religious freedom: Protect your neighbor's religious freedom as you would your own." She and those at the BJC ground this stance in Scripture, specifically in chapter 5 of Paul's Letter to the Galatians.[33] Paul reminds his readers that they are indeed free, but they should not use their freedom in a self-indulgent manner. Rather, their freedom should be used to "serve one another humbly in love. For the entire law is fulfilled in keeping this one command: 'Love your neighbor as yourself'" (Gal. 5:13–14).

In this spirit, the BJC rests firmly in the historic Baptist commitment to religious freedom for all.[34] In the 1630s, Roger Williams left England to escape persecution only to experience more of it in the Massachusetts Bay Colony. He left to establish Rhode Island as a colony committed to religious freedom for all and planted the first Baptist congregation in the colonies.

Martin Luther King Jr., well-known leader of the civil rights movement and also a Baptist preacher, consistently cautioned against Christians grasping for privilege or power through the state: "The church must be reminded that it is not the master or the servant of the state, but rather the conscience of the state. It must be the guide and the critic of the state, and never its tool. If the church does not recapture its prophetic zeal, it will become an irrelevant social club without moral or spiritual authority."[35]

Dr. King and others in the civil rights movement showed us that Christians should certainly be involved with state and political matters. The key is that Christians and Christianity are not used to shore up and protect the powers that be in maintaining an unequal status quo. Rather, Christians and Christianity should focus on advocating for those blocked from enjoying equal rights throughout our nation's history, whether because of religion, race, gender, or other marginalized social identities.

Part of the work of the BJC is confronting and opposing Christian nationalism. In July 2019, they launched the project "Christians Against Christian Nationalism."[36] Their opposition to Christian nationalism flows from their commitment to religious liberty and freedom—that Americans of any faith or none have the right and responsibility to participate equally in our democracy—and their faith in Christ. While their entire statement is an excellent primer for why Christians must confront Christian nationalism, they specifically note how "conflating religious authority with political authority is idolatrous and often leads to oppression of minority and other marginalized groups as well as the spiritual impoverishment of religion." As we will see in later chapters, study after study demonstrates the negative implications of Christian nationalism for racial and ethnic minorities as well as immigrants and refugees.

As Tyler shared with me, "Christian nationalism can strip Christianity of any kind of theological meaning" all in the name of cultural supremacy.[37] Such quests to privilege Christianity ostracize our neighbors who do not share our faith. We run the risk of emptying our faith tradition of its inherent power and ultimate meaning. We open up the opportunity for our faith and sacred symbols to be misused, even exploited, in service of particular political interests.

I am convinced that to resist the pull of white Christian nationalism to gain power or privilege over others, I need to seek to become a good neighbor by defending the right of all to worship, or not worship, without government interference.

Leveraging Our Power to Benefit the Marginalized

The data are clear. Despite its vast wealth, the United States exhibits higher levels of inequality across several measures than almost any other developed country.[38] Some Christians argue we should seek to help those in need through individual or organizational acts of charity or kindness. They claim it "isn't the government's job" to address inequality. Rather, they argue, we stand the best chance of reducing inequality on a one-to-one basis. Such a stance questions why Christians should ever demand those in power use their influence to reduce inequality systematically.

Providing Christian charity at the individual level is akin to seeing someone flailing in a river and pulling them out.[39] It is certainly a good deed. Moreover, the person you saved will obviously be thankful. However, when you soon see another person, and another, and yet another, you start to wonder how many people you will have to pull out. And at some point you'll be unable to help anyone else as there is only so much pulling you can do.

In such a scenario, an appropriate course of action would be to start asking questions: Why are people continuing to fall in the river upstream? What might we do to keep them from falling in? Christians can attend to both: reducing the suffering of those we meet in our day-to-day lives while seeking justice in the community at large to limit the suffering of whole groups of people. God's consistent concern for the widow and orphan throughout the Bible—and God's calling various leaders of God's people to share this concern—illustrates this dual focus and responsibility. Charity does not equate to justice.

While we can continue performing acts of charity, we can also recognize how those in power are precisely the people who can make systemic changes upstream. They can create systems that will reduce the number of people falling in the river. This means we will have to educate ourselves about how our social support systems actually operate and reevaluate the role of government in addressing large-scale social issues. The scale of the problem means we cannot rely merely on individual Christians or our congregations to meet these needs.

Given the dramatic levels of inequality in the United States across multiple dimensions, there are many groups of marginalized people for whom we can advocate. Wilson-Hartgrove encourages us to seek a wholesale "revolution of values," to begin rewiring how Christians understand their role in the world and how best to love their neighbor.[40]

Broadly, we can work to ensure that our society values all people, no matter the life stage. White American Christians can stand with the marginalized by living out a consistent pro-life ethic from womb to tomb. How might we stop equating being pro-life with focusing solely on the unborn?

A consistent pro-life ethic entails supporting (and encouraging our politicians to support) social policies that benefit mothers and children, including the unborn, with medical care and treatment. In the United States, Black women, babies, and children die at rates three times higher than do white women, babies, and children.[41] Instead of focusing solely on gaining more and more institutional power to overturn *Roe v. Wade*, for decades Christians could have sought multiple avenues through which all might experience flourishing from conception to birth and then especially after. With the fall of *Roe* in 2022, a consistent refrain was that women sensed the only lives "pro-life" Christians valued were in the womb. The person standing right in front of them didn't seem to matter.

Leveraging our power to overturn systems of oppression that crush the marginalized means opposing the death penalty and the inequality inherent in our criminal justice system. Americans from various racial and ethnic minority groups, especially men, are incarcerated and sentenced to death at dramatically higher rates than white Americans. As historian Aaron Griffith shows in his book *God's Law and Order*, white Christians have regrettably been at the forefront of arguing for more punitive criminal justice policies throughout the twentieth century.[42]

Following the lead of Bryan Stevenson, the Equal Justice Initiative (EJI), and others working in this space, white Christians can work to reform the systems that disproportionately punish minorities and the indigent. How can we begin to reform the system? We can donate to the EJI or other groups advocating for such large-scale changes and learn from them how best to leverage our time, money, and passion. We can push our political representatives—Republican and Democrat—to prioritize reforming the system. Prison ministries and their goal to reduce recidivism have their place, but they can't really address why so many marginalized folks are imprisoned in the first place. Theirs is a downstream solution.

These are just a few examples; many more exist. One group of Christians seeking to stand with the marginalized across a collection of issues is the Poor People's Campaign. Co-directed by Liz Theoharis and William Barber II, the movement seeks to reimagine and expand what our politicians and religious leaders usually identify as the moral issues that Christians should care about.[43] Where the Christian Right of the 1970s and 1980s focused on homosexuality, abortion, and divorce as the unifying issues of importance, the Poor People's Campaign seeks to direct Americans' collective attention to our neighbors marginalized in American society through racism and poverty. It is a direct continuation of the work of Dr. King that led to his assassination.

Ensuring equal access to the democratic process is one of the campaign's goals. One of the most effective ways to confront the self-interested power inherent to Christian nationalism is to work for equal access to the democratic process for *all* Americans. Americans of all political allegiances should endorse everyone having access to the vote. Committing to learn from these leaders how to advocate for the historically marginalized reframes our relationship to power and confronts white Christian nationalism.

Earlier I shared how intimately Christian nationalism is intertwined with a desire to limit who can vote. If we are interested in building a truly pluralistic democratic society where all can flourish, then we must destroy the idol of power by crucifying our desire to control access to it.

We can follow Jesus faithfully and oppose the quest for power inherent to Christian nationalism by placing ourselves alongside the marginalized—not to lead but to fall in line, follow, and serve others. Christians can provide a prophetic witness to those in positions of authority. We can demand they use their power to ensure that all Americans have equal access to our democratic systems, economic and educational opportunity, and the social safety net. The examples of Dr. King, others who participated in the civil rights movement, and the Poor People's Campaign of today show us a new way forward.

Confronting the Idol of Power

Instead of looking to exercise self-interested power over other groups, American Christians could instead leverage our power and privilege for those who have little or none. American preacher and theologian Howard Thurman wrote, "Too often the price exacted by society for security and respectability is that the Christian movement in its formal expression must be on the side of the strong against the weak. This is a matter of tremendous significance, for it reveals to what extent a religion that was born of a people acquainted with persecution and suffering has become the cornerstone of a civilization and of nations whose very position in modern life too often *has been secured by a ruthless use of power applied to defenseless people.*"[44]

Power and supremacy over others to enact our vision against the wishes and input of our neighbors is not the way of Jesus. White American Christians can lay down the desire for power and commit to service and sacrifice for those around us, be they family, friends, or enemies. The Christian religion began far from the seats of earthly power. This perspective saturates the writings of the New Testament and the witness of the early church. It is important to read it through this lens.

Jesus said we are to be "the light of the world" (Matt. 5:14). Hearing this, his listeners would most likely have imagined a candle or lamp. While a flame is necessary to give off light, we must place boundaries around it. Otherwise, a flame will greedily consume any fuel provided to it and grow in proportion. Imagine self-serving power as a kind of unrestrained fuel given to our flame. It transforms even a tiny flicker into something that not only gives off light but now also burns uncontrollably, consuming and destroying.

We can confront white Christian nationalism by seeking boundaries limiting our access to and exercise of earthly, self-interested power. Leveraging the power we have to benefit those marginalized in our society and seeking religious liberty for all are just two options. We can begin to emulate the namesake of our faith, in that we live not to be served but to serve, and to dedicate our lives in the hope of encouraging the liberation and flourishing of all.

Jesus calls us to be a light, not a wildfire.

DO NOT BE AFRAID?

On every front, the ultra-left is waging war on the values shared by everyone in this room. They are trying to silence and punish the speech of Christians and religious believers of all faiths.

—Donald Trump Sr.[1]

THE NEVER-ENDING QUEST to gain and maintain power over others is essential to white Christian nationalism. Self-interested power is the central idol. When we idolize power, fear of losing access to the idol, of power being taken away so we cannot privilege our group any longer, becomes paramount. We fear power in the hands of those over whom we used to wield it because we assume they will similarly use it to benefit only themselves.

Fear of threat is a powerful motivational tool.

Throughout American history, religious and political leaders stoked fear among Christians to convince them they needed to change the course of the nation. And the only way that could be done was through the use of power. These writings and speeches generally took the form of jeremiads.[2]

Jeremiads are political rhetorical devices that lament the loss of an idyllic past as a result of people's gradual betrayal of a sacred covenant and founding ideals. They simultaneously point listeners toward a future hope with restoration and reclamation of a covenant and promise.

Jeremiads help formulate and define a community's boundaries as well as create social cohesion. Modern jeremiads contain three basic components. First, they focus on fear and anxiety around a current crisis or the sins and actions of the people they believe are causing the crisis. Next, they contrast the current situation with an idealized vision of the past, demonstrating how turning our backs on our history is leading us down a dark path. They contend that losing sight of this history results in losing aspects of our collective identity. Finally, jeremiads call for repentance and renewal, highlighting how fear should motivate listeners to act.

Political and religious leaders frequently employ jeremiads to motivate their listeners to "protect the faith" and "defend their way of life." They remind us we must defend our power because if we do not, then others will use the same tactics against us that we used against them. In response to this fear, we have an obligation to act, and act decisively. The future of the nation's relationship with the Christian God is uncertain. The only options are blessing or destruction.

Many of the religious and political leaders committed to privileging Christianity in the public sphere make use of the jeremiad. Who or what Christians should fear changes depending on the year or decade. Sometimes jeremiads focus on a generalized sense of fear to motivate listeners to action. Before the 2020 election, Pastor Robert Jeffress of First Baptist Dallas cautioned evangelicals that the "moral and spiritual direction" of the country was at stake and that "this Christian nation" would be in jeopardy if they did not vote.[3] Franklin Graham, president and CEO of two large evangelical nonprofits, claimed in the lead-up to the 2020 election, "You're going to see Christians attacked; you're going to see churches close; you're going to see a real hatred expressed toward people of faith."[4] As we saw in the previous chapter, James Dobson's "sky is falling" responses to the last twenty years of presidential elections intertwined fear with calls to protect the future existence of the United States. Only through gaining and protecting access to power can Christians save their country.

Donald Trump's "Make America great again" campaign slogan functioned as a jeremiad. It highlighted a current crisis stoking an undercurrent of fear, contrasted the present situation with an idealized past, and called followers to chart a new path forward in response to their fear, with him leading the charge. In 2016 Trump told one crowd,

> Your values of love, charity and faith built this nation. So how can it be that our media treats people of faith so poorly? One of the reasons is that our politicians have really abandoned you, to a large extent. And Hillary Clinton, you can forget about her. So let me say this right up front: A Trump administration, our Christian heritage will be cherished, protected, defended, like you've never seen before. Believe me. . . . Imagine what our country could accomplish if we started working together as one people under one God, saluting one flag?[5]

Trump highlighted anxiety his listeners should experience given a current crisis and the bad actors he deemed responsible: the media, politicians, Clinton. He then contrasted this current situation with an idealized past. He pointed out the nation's "Christian heritage" and how Christian values "built this nation." He then provided the path forward for renewing the nation: himself.

Trump repeated this rhetorical practice well after losing the 2020 election. In 2022, he told a group of evangelical Christians, "What they're doing to religion, what they're doing to Christianity, it's a very sad, sad thing for our country. . . . They want to take your religious freedoms away. In terms of a threat, they want to take them away. . . . One of my greatest honors was fighting for religious liberty and for defending the Judeo-Christian values and principles of our nation's founding."[6] Only through supporting him again, he argued, could they once again bring this nation back on track.

Christian citizens have responded to jeremiads for centuries, from the colonial era up until today. We are primed for messages structured in this way, and Trump, among other religious and political leaders, continues to capitalize on it. It is important to acknowledge that the feelings of fear jeremiads tap into are in some cases real—it isn't as though these leaders are pulling them out of thin air (although that does happen[7]). Times of dramatic social and cultural change create unsettledness. We sense our nation is trying to determine who it is and why it exists.

Recent shifts in the demographic contours of the United States are just one example. Growing religious diversity over the past fifty years is another. White Americans, particularly white Christians, are shrinking as a share of the population and the electorate. No longer being the unquestioned and unchallenged center of social and political life is particularly fear-inducing for some and can lead to greater acceptance of white Christian nationalism.[8]

White Christian nationalism is especially potent during unsettled times. It provides a ready-made explanation for who "we" are, what "we" are all about, and how "we" should achieve a particular vision. Sadly, the influence of white Christian nationalism through the centuries has ensured that in times of social unrest and cultural change, when it seems the ground is shifting beneath us, Christians have consistently idolized fear.

Fear and Christianity in the Americas

Examining the history of fear within American Christianity from the earliest colonists up until the present day prompted historian

John Fea to point out, "We should expect anxiety-induced emotions to rise in response to social change. But evangelicals have not always managed their fears in a healthy way. Their responses have led to some dark moments in the history of American Christianity and, indeed, the nation."[9] While writing specifically about evangelicals, Fea's point applies to white Christianity in America broadly.

A fear of social and moral decline, as defined by their interpretation of the Bible, led the Puritans to execute "troublemakers" and even fellow Christians because of differences in religious beliefs. Quakers, Baptists, and Catholics were anathema. And Puritans were especially ruthless toward Native Americans. They feared that a group who did not look like them or worship like them would destroy their "City on a Hill." Here is one of the first instances in the "New World" of fear that a racialized "other" might destroy God's chosen white, Christian people.

The Puritans' desperation to cultivate a "Christian civilization" overruled the scriptural command to love their neighbors and their perceived enemies. At times, their fear motivated them more than love for God or their neighbor, resulting in a quest for power and domination leading to persecution and bloodshed. The Puritans' legacy of fear linked with their desire for a Christian society reverberates throughout history.[10] Throughout the twentieth century, the Christian Right emphatically embraced Christian nationalism, which "required an ever-present sense of threat" to motivate followers to particular political and religious ends.[11] In general, these threats revolved around race, immigration, religion, and Christian persecution.

Racial Fears

The close connection between a desire for a white Christian nation and fear of racialized "others" encouraged many Christians to commit astonishing evils against Black slaves and Black Americans throughout the centuries. While we will explore the links between Christian nationalism and racism soon, here we can note that fear surrounding the abolition of slavery, fear of the upending of cherished social norms that placed whites above Blacks, and fear of reprisal from Black Americans are a consistent presence in the fight for a Christian, and presumably white, America.

For example, Fea recounts how fears of losing the "purity" of the white race were widespread leading up to the Civil War. "One Presbyterian minister in Kentucky claimed that 'no Christian American' would allow the 'God-defying depravity of intermarriage between the white and the negro races.'"[12]

During the Jim Crow era, fears of jeopardizing a Christian America through equal opportunities for Black Americans continued. In *White Too Long: The Legacy of White Supremacy in American Christianity*, Robert Jones provides a chilling quote from an assistant to the Mississippi state attorney general: "The facts of history make it plain that the development of civilization and of Christianity itself has rested in the hands of the white race," and integration "will result in driving the white race from the earth forever, never to return."[13]

Such fears are still with us. In 2021, Fox commentator Tucker Carlson—whose nightly show reaches over four million Americans—passionately defended a version of "white replacement theory," saying that more racial minorities voting would "dilute" the political power of people like him.[14] Stephen Wolfe, the author of a pro-Christian nationalism book, claims that "interethnic" marriage is sinful in that it harms the nation.[15] Other prominent media figures like Ann Coulter echo these views. Considering such views alongside the consistent defense of Christianity by these media personalities as fundamental to American national identity, the link between Christian nationalism and fear of racial minorities is clear.

Carlson's and Coulter's stances reflect the views of the national adult population. One recent national survey showed that Ambassadors—those Americans who embrace Christian nationalism most fervently—were the most likely to report feeling afraid of the day when whites will no longer be the majority in the United States.[16] Cultivating a fear of white replacement creates a fertile ground for extremism to take root and then sprout. The eighteen-year-old who targeted a Black community in Buffalo, New York, murdering ten people at a supermarket in May 2022, wrote that he was motivated to kill because he feared a declining white population in the United States.

Immigrant Fears

Americans' fears of racialized others extend to immigrants. Highlighting cultural and religious differences, American Christians fear immigrants will chip away at the country's "Christian" foundations. As one example, James Dobson, founder of Focus on the Family, wrote an open letter about his visit to a border town in Texas. He implored his readers that a border wall must be built because "millions of illegal immigrants will continue flooding to this great land from around the world. Many of them have no marketable skills. They are illiterate and unhealthy. Some are violent criminals. Their numbers will soon overwhelm the culture as we have known it, and it could bankrupt the nation." Seemingly realizing his callousness, Dobson followed by saying, "America has been a wonderfully generous and caring country since its founding. That is our Christian nature. But in this instance, we have met a worldwide wave of poverty that will take us down if we don't deal with it. And it won't take long for the inevitable consequences to happen."[17]

Notice the words he chooses: "overwhelm the culture," "bankrupt the nation," "take us down," "inevitable consequences." Dobson highlights the threat, contrasts the current state of affairs with an idealized past, and then determines a way forward in order to save the future. To motivate his readers to action, he links Christian nationalist sentiment, immigration, and fear. We will unpack the links between Christian nationalism and xenophobia in a subsequent chapter. Central to the relationship, though, is fear.

Similarly, refugees seeking asylum in the United States are repeatedly demonized. This is especially true of refugees from the Middle East. In 2021, when President Biden withdrew American troops from Afghanistan—effectively ending the war—politicians and religious leaders who embrace Christian nationalism stoked fear around what Afghan refugees might mean for their communities. Kristi Noem, who held a Christian worship service in the South Dakota capitol rotunda on her first full day as governor in 2019, stated, "We do not want them coming here unless we know they are an ally and a friend, and that they don't want to destroy this country."[18]

Religious Fears

Fearmongering about immigrants reflects centuries-old realities. From the time of the Puritans to the latter half of the twentieth century, nativist impulses tied to fears of immigrants led many American Protestants to fear Catholics because they were thought to be subject to a foreign power, under the authority of the pope, and not sufficiently "American." White American Protestants racialized Catholic immigrants as nonwhite, underscoring the overlap between race, nationality, and religion. In the 1960s, America's most famous evangelist, Billy Graham, helped rally opposition to John F. Kennedy's presidential aspirations on account of his Catholic faith.

For the most part, conservative Protestants and Catholics have found common cause since the 1970s with the rise of the Christian Right. But even today, purveyors of Christian nationalist sentiment stoke fear surrounding Catholicism. Jeffress once claimed that Catholicism is a false religion created and used by Satan to corrupt Christianity and cause people to "miss eternal life."[19]

Consistently, fear of immigrants extends to those suspected of worshiping a god or gods outside the Christian religion. Christian and political leaders intent on defending our "Christian heritage" have long stoked fear surrounding Muslims, Hindus, Sikhs, or any other religious group that is racialized as nonwhite. Much of the fearmongering in 2021 around accepting refugees from Afghanistan centered on anti-Muslim sentiment, claiming refugees would work to institute sharia (Islamic law). The unspoken assumption is that these guiding religious principles for Muslims would supplant the "Christian principles" ensconced in the United States. Tucker Carlson declared the United States would soon see so many refugees that the numbers "may well swell to the millions," making it an "invasion."[20]

National polling over the last decade and beyond highlights how Christian nationalism stokes fears of refugees and echoes the content in Governor Noem's and James Dobson's stances. Ambassadors of Christian nationalism are more likely to fear refugees from the Middle East as a terrorist threat, state they are afraid of illegal immigration, think that recent immigrants are more reluctant to assimilate, believe that immigrants are a drain on the economy, and fear that immigrants bring diseases into the United States.[21]

Much of the Christian nationalist militant masculinity of white evangelicalism over the past century drew heavily on anti-Muslim sentiment that increased after the September 11 attacks. Capitalizing on Americans' fears of Islamic terrorism and jihad became something of a cottage industry throughout the first decade of the twenty-first century. Dozens of Christian leaders sounded the alarm that Muslims were "worse than the Nazis," "a religion of violence," and "the greatest threat America has faced since the Civil War."[22]

Sadly, entire books could be filled with quotes signaling fear that non-Christian religions will destroy our "Judeo-Christian roots." From 2010 to 2018, several states passed anti-sharia legislation on account of fears that Muslims were gaining political power. Jason Rapert, Arkansas state senator and founder of the

National Association of Christian Lawmakers, said, "Countries with Muslim leaders in control persecute Christians. Why do we want them having increasing political power in America?"[23]

It is important to note how unfounded fears about sharia are. Recent data report that Muslims represent somewhere between less than 1 percent to 1.3 percent of the United States population and under one-half of 1 percent of the population in Senator Rapert's home of Arkansas.[24] Only four Muslim Americans have ever been elected to Congress. A 2020 report counted 2,769 mosques in the United States.[25] If that sounds like a lot, it isn't. The Southern Baptist Convention, the largest Protestant denomination in the United States, has more than forty-seven thousand congregations. The Lutheran Church–Missouri Synod has more than six thousand congregations in the United States.[26] These are just two of dozens of conservative Protestant denominations. The idea that there are enough Muslims living in the United States to alter our system of laws—even if they wanted to do so—strains credulity.

Nevertheless, let us assume religious minority groups continue to grow and make up a larger portion of our population. If American Christians are truly committed to religious freedom and democracy, why are we trying to silence the voices and input of those around us?

During his time in the Oval Office, Trump whipped up support for various iterations of "Muslim bans" by equating the religion with terror, claiming that "Islam hates us," and repeating the falsehood that "thousands and thousands" of Muslims in the United States celebrated the 9/11 attacks.[27] His words surely resonated with Ambassadors of Christian nationalism, who are much more likely to fear immigration from majority-Muslim countries and fear that Muslims are more likely to be terrorists.[28]

Decision magazine, the monthly publication of the Billy Graham Evangelistic Association with a circulation of more than 450,000,[29] features a consistent theme of fear concerning Islam. Leading up to the 2016 election, Franklin Graham wrote how this was the most important election in our lifetime (again, a consistent theme every four years) because our Christian foundation and principles hung in the balance. He explicitly pointed out how those concerned with protecting our Christian heritage should be afraid that Democrats will not protect us against Islamic terrorism: "Will they [Democrats] defend our nation against Islamic terrorists who have slaughtered and killed innocents across our country in the name of their god? Will they call the enemy—radical Islam—by its name?"[30]

Fear of Islam among leaders committed to Christian nationalism exists in the broader United States population as well. Americans who embrace Christian nationalism are much more likely to fear that Muslims want to limit the personal freedoms or even endanger the physical safety of "people like me."[31] Another recent national survey shows that Ambassadors are much more likely to fear having a mosque built in their neighborhood and the possibility their child might marry a Muslim.[32]

Muslims in the United States experience real consequences because of these fears. Twenty-eight percent of mosques in the United States face "significant opposition" from the general community when they obtain permission from the local zoning board to move, expand, or build.[33] After 9/11, hate crimes against Muslims increased significantly; the number of hate crimes in 2016 surpassed that from 2001. In 2022, the Council on American-Islamic Relations (CAIR) reported over sixty-seven hundred civil rights complaints filed by American Muslims, a 9 percent increase since 2020. CAIR also reported a 28 percent increase in hate or bias incidents over that time.[34] Remember these statistics whenever you hear Christianity is "under attack" in the United States. It's worth repeating: equality feels like discrimination when you are used to privilege. Christians can instead empathize with the real discrimination and threat of bodily harm that religious minorities face and seek to protect their right to live and worship in peace.

The defense of a Christian America also routinely sparks fears about the nonreligious. Atheists, freethinkers, and other skeptics have been labeled a mortal threat to the republic from the 1700s until the present day. The election of 1800 is just one famous example, when Federalists (who supported John Adams) spread rumors that Democratic-Republicans (who generally supported Thomas Jefferson) were radical atheists who would destroy the newly formed country. In the present day, Franklin Graham carries a similar tune: "We are in deep trouble as socialist-progressives have doubled down on their efforts to turn our legislatures, schools and communities into showcases for a godless, secularist agenda that is openly hostile to the Christian faith."[35] Fear of atheists among our fellow Americans mirrors the pronouncements of these various religious and political leaders. Like Americans' fears of Muslims, increasingly higher levels of Christian nationalism correlate with much more fear of atheists. Americans who embrace Christian nationalism see atheists as a threat to their personal freedoms and even their physical safety.[36]

Fear of Christian Persecution

Political and religious leaders consistently spread fear about the persecution of American Christians, warning that we will lose our religious freedom. For instance, before the 2020 election, Trump told an Ohio crowd, "[Biden is] following the radical left agenda, take away your guns, destroy your 2nd Amendment, no religion, no anything, hurt the Bible, hurt God. He's against God. He's against guns. He's against energy, our kind of energy."[37] How exactly the Bible or God could be "hurt" remained unsaid.

In 2021, a congressional representative claimed that the Biden administration might one day aim to go door-to-door and "take your Bibles." Stoking this fear is nothing new, as Republicans used this same strategy in 2004. Over half of Ambassadors fear that a Democratic president will ban the Bible, compared to less than 10 percent who resist or reject white Christian nationalism.[38] Another survey found that 61 percent of Americans who embrace Christian nationalism fear that Democrats will curtail Christians' religious freedom.[39] In a survey conducted soon after Biden's inauguration, white Christian nationalists feared increased persecution under a Democratic president. Nearly two-thirds of this group anticipated "a lot of discrimination for both whites and Christians."[40]

Fear of persecution is a powerful component of the mythology of a Christian America. Those who embrace white Christian nationalism are likely to see themselves as the heroes of years past but also as the victims of recent cultural and political shifts. The persecution narrative has roots that extend to the ancient church. In the early days of Christianity, converting the Roman emperor to Christianity was a sign of protection from God, while being persecuted was a sign of virtue.[41] Holding these two seemingly contradictory views in tension is how Christianity flourished for hundreds of years. And this narrative is still powerful. American Christians feel victimized even though most political positions are held by self-identifying Christians.[42]

Using the threat of persecution as a rhetorical tactic remains a powerful political tool. Many white Christian Americans fear persecution is coming their way. I even hear fellow Christians who I know oppose Christian nationalism use phrases suggesting faithful Christians are "in the minority" in the United States. I trust they mean well, but such claims support a narrative of persecution and minority status that leads to fear. A constant sense of embattlement hinders us from collaborating with our neighbors.

History and social science suggest that stoking a sense of threat among an in-group, aimed at out-groups—whether racial, religious, or otherwise—is central to defending and maintaining the cultural framework of white Christian nationalism. Recent research even shows that the development of Christian nationalist views during the transition to adulthood conditions us to sense "we" are constantly under attack. It can lead to a greater reliance on stereotyping, group-centric decision-making, in-group loyalty, hierarchy, and submission to authority. This "affective condition-ing" toward fear serves as a primary justification for social and political engagement focused on defending "our way of life."[43]

Fear is useful for defining "us," the Christians this country was founded for, from "them," those who are trying to steal our na-tion.[44] And as these examples show time and again, when people, even Christians, are convinced that they should fear the "other," they can forgive themselves for any and all mistreatment of the other because ultimately they fear how the other will likely treat them (Christians) when in power. Here, the fear inherent to Chris-tian nationalism contradicts core Christian beliefs.

Political scientist Paul Djupe provides a helpful concept to de-scribe this effect of fear: the inverted golden rule. The inverted golden rule stipulates, "Expect from others what you would do unto them."[45] For many Christians, fear of losing cultural and political power makes them want to restrict other groups' civil rights precisely because they fear this is how these groups might treat them. Essentially, white Christians fear mistreatment from racial and religious monitories in a manner similar to how white Christians have historically mistreated religious and ra-cial minorities.

Here's the irony about the inverted golden rule. When Djupe compared atheists' and Christians' willingness to allow those they disagree with to give speeches in the community, teach in public schools, or run for public office, atheists were more willing to ex-tend civil liberties to Christians. Christians were much less likely to extend the same liberties to atheists.

In addition to drawing sharp boundary lines between "us" and "them," fear is also useful for consolidating power. Christian na-tionalism is ultimately concerned with acquiring and defending privileged access to power. Peddling fear is the most effective route to achieve those ends.

Consistently introducing a sense of threat leads the worried masses to want a protector. White Christian nationalism as a framework and those committed to its dominance are ready and willing to provide solutions to those threats to reduce these fears. All that those who are afraid must do is accord the right people the necessary power and privilege to enact this particular agenda.[46]

This raises the question: Should American Christians be so fearful?

Christians and Fear

In this section, I want to focus on Christians' fear of racial and ethnic minority groups, non-Christian religious groups, or secular Americans. I want us to consider Christians' fears around losing power, control, and privilege—fear at the group level. I am not speaking about all forms of fear or anxiety, such as those resulting from various anxiety disorders, loss, or trauma. Rather, I want to consider what the Bible says about fear that often leads us to circle the wagons and protect ourselves. I want us to think about our fears around being asked to make room in our communities, nation, and culture for those who do not look, talk, or worship like us. I want my fellow white American Christians to apply what the Bible says about fear to what we feel threatened by and how—as a group—we might respond to those threats and fears.

While results vary depending on translation, one concordance shows that the Christian scriptures mention variations of "fear not" and "do not be afraid" nearly one hundred times.[47] Discovering a precise number isn't the point. The point is that "fear not" is easily one of the most repeated directives in the Bible. The repetition of the command not to be afraid throughout the narrative of God's interaction with humans signals several things.

First, fear is a natural part of being human. We should expect day-to-day experiences in which fear of being "left out" will happen. Christians are not guaranteed lives of social and cultural privilege. Further, Christians are not commanded to seek such privilege. Jesus himself, on the night he was betrayed, pleaded with God to "take this cup" from him (Mark 14:36). He was afraid of what he was about to endure. If Jesus faced fear at being tasked with laying aside his privileges in order to show the world the extent of God's love, then we can and should expect to as well.

Second, the decision to embrace fear is ours to make. We can choose *not* to fear. We can respond to our sense of group threat or a personal threat by choosing to resist it. For instance, an angel of the Lord commanded Joseph, Jesus's earthly father, "*Do not be afraid* to take Mary home as your wife" (Matt. 1:20). After the resurrection, an angel of the Lord told the women at the tomb, "*Do not be afraid*. . . . Come and see the place where he lay. Then go quickly and tell his disciples." Jesus then appeared, likewise commanding them, "*Do not be afraid*. Go and tell my brothers to go to Galilee" (Matt. 28:5–10). At another time, Jesus instructed Jairus, the synagogue ruler whose daughter had died, "*Don't be afraid*; just believe" (Mark 5:36). Jesus directed Peter, who was still called Simon, "*Don't be afraid*; from now on you will fish for people" (Luke 5:10). After Paul began to experience opposition from religious leaders in Corinth, Jesus directed him, "*Do not be afraid*; keep on speaking, do not be silent" (Acts 18:9).

In each of these instances, the command not to be afraid occurs alongside an invitation to act. For Joseph, Jairus, Jesus's disciples, and Paul, not giving in to fear necessarily entailed following Jesus's command to behave in some other way. This was particularly true for Paul, who was facing certain violence from a group of religious leaders intent on controlling his actions.

This leads to a third observation: instead of choosing fear, American Christians can choose to act in opposition to fear. We confront and oppose fear by choosing to listen to and love racial and ethnic minority groups through seeking justice. We confront and oppose fear by extending hospitality and empathy toward immigrants and citizens of other nations who make their way to our shores. We confront and oppose fear by embracing and building relationships with those who worship differently than we do or who do not worship at all. We confront and oppose group-level fear when we embrace the gospel and collaborate with God in toppling oppression and suffering.

It is through such actions that we move beyond fear. We overcome fear toward those we are told to fear by living according to the example given us by our Lord. Central to his example, as we saw in the previous chapter, is to avoid seeking self-interested power over the people those in power want us to define as "others."

The kingdom of God inverts the power dynamics of the kingdoms of this world. The Son of Man did not come to be served but to serve and to give his life as a ransom for many. He commands us to give to those who ask. He commands us to give our cloak if someone asks for our tunic. He commands us to go two miles with the one who asks us to go one mile. He commands us not to fear but to respond with love to those around us—even if, and especially when, it might cost us our power, privilege, and comfort. We are to confront our fear by loving our neighbors and enemies through service and self-sacrifice, seeking the flourishing of all.

I don't know about you, but these commands scare me. I am afraid of being commanded to live according to these principles. It seems like counting ourselves among the marginalized, seeking their good, and not giving in to fear ensures that we Christians will be sidelined. It seems like a surefire way to invite others to take advantage of us. Moreover, it can seem like an inefficient way to live out the gospel and influence the world around us.

However, God does not call us to efficiency. He calls us to be faithful. Before going to the cross to give up his life in order to complete his rescue mission, Jesus was deeply afraid. Dying must not have seemed like the most effective or efficient means to achieve the end goal. His disciples certainly felt this way. Most of them embraced fear at what Jesus's sacrifice meant for them. Jesus, however, committed to trusting the upside-down nature of God's kingdom, and he transformed the world. In time, his disciples did the same.

These are difficult teachings. They do not align with the American ideals of individualism, power, comfort, safety, and security. The gospel animating Christianity is a lot more radical than most American Christians are likely to admit. It sure seems radical to me. And uncomfortable.

But it also sounds so beautiful. This vision always pulls me back in. I wish to see this expression of Christianity reflected in our organizations, in our nation, and in the world around us. Christian nationalism would have none of this sacrifice and service business. Christian nationalism demands we embrace group-level fear and threat. But by doing so, we betray the gospel.

How can we seek to live out Jesus's example in our daily lives? Rather than allowing fear to turn us inward and toward our chosen tribe, how can we turn ourselves outward, leveraging what we have in order to love those around us? Let's look at two ways to do this: thinking critically and practicing empathy.

Our media landscape tells us we should be afraid. Certain news outlets feed us a constant stream of fear and threat to induce clicks and views. These clicks and views allow them to sell more advertising, which lines the pockets of those who own and work at the media outlets. They can pressure us to buy things we don't need or demonize whole groups of people we've never met and who our faith teaches are *just like us*. Fear sells, and the promise of wealth has long motivated the embrace of white Christian nationalism.

In 2021 Russell Moore, then leader of a public theology project at *Christianity Today*, decried rhetoric he was hearing on major cable outlets such as Fox News like that in Dobson's letter from 2019. He criticized labeling refugees as "unclean," using metaphors such as rodents or insects to describe refugees, or saying that refugees are an "invasion" intent on replacing "us." Moore pointed out that "'us' almost always refer[s] to white and nominally Christian Americans." He wrote how these fears of refugees are outright lies "meant to keep us in a state of emergency that sees everyone and everything not immediately familiar to us as a threat." This state of emergency "keeps viewers tuning in to television shows, callers calling in to radio shows, donors sending in dollars to politicians and interest groups."[48] Fear is in the service of gaining and maintaining self-interested power. This is white Christian nationalism at work.

Thinking critically about our media habits is one way we can commit to living according to God's truth. This means being informed by actual evidence. Christian leaders can take the lead in modeling how to consume news and media, with a commitment to verifying claims.

Let's look at one claim, that immigrants or religious minorities coming into our communities will raise the crime rate. Who isn't afraid of increasing levels of crime? But when we sense fear, we should commit to examining whether the fear is warranted. This is where social science can serve the common good. As it turns out, quite a few studies examine this exact question. Do undocumented immigrants raise the crime rate?

Studies analyzing data across hundreds of metropolitan areas and over several decades consistently find no evidence that communities with more immigrants experience an associated increase in crime.[49] In Texas, two separate studies found that undocumented immigrants have significantly lower crime rates and fewer convictions across a number of crimes. In one study, the authors note, "Relative to undocumented immigrants, US-born citizens are over 2 times more likely to be arrested for violent crimes, 2.5 times more likely to be arrested for drug crimes, and over 4 times more likely to be arrested for property crimes."[50] This same relationship—more immigrants has no relation to increasing crime rates—appears to hold across the United States and in samples from other countries as well.[51] In fact, there is evidence that documented and undocumented immigrants make our communities safer.

Sometimes, such as with undocumented immigrants, there is no empirical evidence to support our fears. In such situations, it seems obvious we should not choose to fear. However, what about when we face situations in which the evidence suggests that we who are Christians might have to face whatever it is we are being told to fear?

As Christians, it should not matter. Christians can commit to loving and welcoming our neighbors without privileging our personal safety. We can be committed to working toward shalom—peace—wherever we are and with whoever surrounds us. Therefore, we do not have to argue with those who peddle false fear toward others. If they claim to be Christians, we can hold them to the examples from the Bible.

Afraid of undocumented immigrants? If you are a Christian, you are called to love and support them, since we are aliens of this world as well.

Afraid of Muslims, Hindus, or atheists? If you are a Christian, you are called to love and support those not in your religious group just as the Samaritan cared for the Israelite attacked on the road to Jericho.

Afraid of those highlighting the abuses faced by Black and non-white minority groups in the United States? If you are a Christian, you are called to listen to and learn from their experiences and respond with charity. The apostles—upon hearing about the plight of Grecian Jewish widows who were being systematically overlooked by the early church—listened, learned, and then worked to alleviate the inequality this minority group experienced.

We should be informed citizens thinking carefully and critically about how we consume news and how it might be forming us. We can read books and attend talks by those outside our demographic enclave. One practice to consider if you are a white, able-bodied Christian like me: read one book a month by an author who differs from you in at least one—but ideally more—of the following characteristics: race/ethnicity, ability, gender, or religion. We can broaden the scope of our experiences through more stories than simply our own.

We can also confront fear by seeking conversations with the very people we are being told to fear. We can work to rewire our plausibility structures.[52] White Christians can seek opportunities to meet with, listen to, and work alongside religious minorities, secular Americans, racial and ethnic minorities, immigrants, and refugees.

Amar Peterman, an Indian American scholar and program officer at InterFaith America, shows how practicing empathy is one way for American Christians to begin this work. We begin by placing ourselves near those communities white Christian nationalism encourages us to demonize. Only through conversations across these lines of difference can we begin to see the world through the eyes of the immigrant and refugee. Empathy, Amar shared with me, is more than just a feeling. "Empathy begins with *paying attention* to the God-ordained diversity around us."[53] This diversity is not a hindrance but a gift from God.

Recognizing this gift should lead us next into *proximity* to that difference—a nearness to those outside our native community. We should practice, Amar explained, "holy curiosity" regarding those differences and allow that curiosity to lead us into proximity. To be in proximity we must recognize we are not in control. There are differences we will have to navigate, and that can be scary. The desire for control and feeling as if we are losing our grip on it lead to much of the fear we experience.

Our proximity to people who are different from us stirs in us *humility*. Amar explained, "When we have to eat the food of another who we don't know, when we have to be in a space where our language, ideas, or the pigment of our skin is not the common or majority, that cultivates humility in us to be in those positions." We are no longer in control. We are no longer the ones calling the shots. We can begin to recognize that we have much to learn from others and, perhaps, much to offer them as well. We also begin to see how the idol of fear creates barriers the gospel intends to destroy.

Attention, proximity, and humility lead us finally to *sacrifice*. Sacrifice is rooted in Jesus's ministry. Jesus makes space for the "other," Amar said, recalling the words of theologian Miroslav Volf. "There is a space-making hospitable element of the Christian faith that calls us to meaningful sacrifice." Our commitment to make space will likely lead to consequences that demand we forfeit our comfort, control, and privileged position.

"What are we truly willing to sacrifice for our values?" Amar asked me. If we Christians claim to value the example of Jesus and his call to neighbor love, are we willing to sacrifice what Christian nationalism demands we defend? True neighbor love ultimately requires a shifting of power. We can commit to meaningful inclusion of the marginalized. We can release the fear that keeps us from living into Jesus's commands.

We can start by asking ourselves, What would we hope to receive from those in power if we were immigrants and refugees? If we found ourselves in a country that was not our own, at the mercy of those who could claim the benefits of citizenship all to themselves, how would we hope to be received?

Amar is dedicated to showing how Christians can and should "faithfully, critically, and consistently engage in the complex issues of our modern society." Showing empathy—by paying attention, practicing proximity, cultivating humility, and committing to sacrifice—can provide Christians an alternative path that forcefully confronts the group-level fear engendered by white Christian nationalism.[54]

If you are able to enact change, whether in a congregation or religious educational institution or otherwise, commit to examining the role of fear in determining organizational decisions. Consider how your organization can help those it serves to recognize when their actions and reactions are based on fear or a sense of threat. Changing individual hearts and minds is part of the work. Ultimately, though, we will fall short of society-wide change if our organizations and cultural institutions continue to operate in the same manner.

Fear Not

White Christian nationalism encourages us to live as though our power and privilege are under threat. When living and acting out of a place of fear, we tend to do whatever is necessary to protect power and privilege, even jettisoning central aspects of the Christian faith. We begin to treat others the way we fear they are going to treat us—a group that limits others' civil liberties and rights. We become what we most fear.

Focusing on fear and threat makes us bad neighbors. Our fear keeps us from living out the call of Christ. We cannot embrace a nationalist vision of Christianity that desires control and dominion over others when Jesus came to liberate all so we could freely love all. Writer Danté Stewart is right when he points out how, when fear is at the heart of our faith, harm will be the main expression of our experience.[55] Harm to ourselves, and certainly harm to others.

Jesus never promised us cultural or political power, and he never commanded us to seek such things. Rather, "Jesus knew what it meant to live in an occupied territory, knew what it meant to be from an oppressed people," knew what it meant to be threatened with bodily assault and ultimately crucifixion.[56]

When we are told to fear losing an imaginary past, or to fear religious minorities or immigrants, let us recognize why. It is to motivate us to protect the power and privilege of a certain expression of Christianity in the public sphere. Instead, we can embody a Christianity marked by indiscriminate love of neighbor and liberation for those marginalized by the powers that be. We can turn our backs on a nationalistic expression of Christianity focused on domination and control.

Before going to the cross, Jesus encouraged his disciples, "Peace I leave with you; my peace I give you. I do not give to you as the world gives. Do not let your hearts be troubled and *do not be afraid*" (John 14:27). So now let us lay down our fear, take up our crosses, and *finally* follow him.

LAY DOWN YOUR SWORD?

On Twitter, a lot of the little Twitter trolls, they like to say, "Oh, Jesus didn't need an AR-15, how many AR-15s do you think Jesus would've had?" Well, he didn't have enough to keep his government from killing him.

—Rep. Lauren Boebert[1]

IN THE SUMMER OF 2021, the unmarked graves of hundreds of Indigenous children were uncovered near a Christian boarding school in Saskatchewan, Canada. The graves contained close to eight hundred remains. This discovery came weeks after authorities discovered a mass grave near another church-run school for Indigenous children in British Columbia. One child was likely as young as three when she died.

In the United States, the Civilization Fund Act of 1819 called for the federal government to work with missionaries to establish schools in Native territories. Funded by the federal government and in many cases run by Catholic and Protestant denominations, the boarding schools existed explicitly to erase Native American culture and practices by replacing tribal practices with Christian ones.

The founder of one boarding school bluntly stated their objective: "Kill the Indian in him, and save the man." This goal was just a slight augmentation of the prevailing opinion at the advent of these schools: "The only good Indian is a dead one."[2] The law advocated that Native Americans be forcibly assimilated to what leaders considered Western Christian culture.[3] This, they surmised, would make them good citizens. For decades, Native tribes had both their land and their children taken from them. The schools were often overcrowded and hundreds of miles from their homes. The Christian leaders of the schools did not allow the children to speak their native languages, and noncompliance was met with physical beatings. Some students reported priests fathering children with Indigenous students, whose babies were then taken from them and killed.[4]

The mass graves in Canada vindicated the often-ignored claims of Native children and families devastated by these practices. These governments could no longer try to hide the violence of years past. And in some cases, these atrocities are barely even past. The US Congress did not outlaw the forced removal of Native children from their families until the late 1970s. These horrific discoveries were just another reminder of how easily efforts to inculcate Christianity via governmental decree produce violence, especially toward feared outsiders.

While recognizing the absolute tragedy of this history, some of us might still question whether a desire for privileging Christianity in the affairs of the state could lead down a similar path. Would Christians today similarly embrace violence in the service of "the greater good" of spreading Christianity to create ideal citizens via governmental force?

Consider what Declan Leary, an editor for the *American Conservative*, wrote in July 2021 in response to the discovery of the mass graves: "Whatever natural good was present in the piety and community of the pagan past is an infinitesimal fraction of the grace rendered unto those pagans' descendants who have been received into the Church of Christ. Whatever sacrifices were exacted in pursuit of that grace—the suffocation of a noble pagan culture; an increase in disease and bodily death due to government negligence; even the sundering of natural families—is *worth it*."[5] As much of the conquest of new land was led by nations baptizing their quest in the gospel, Declan argues, such genocide—if it results in more Christians and a more Christian society—is worth countless deaths of Indigenous adults and children. For centuries, such logic has provided fertile ground for the enactment of terrible violence by Christians in service of their nations.

The tragic history of Indigenous peoples in North America clearly demonstrates that any quest to protect power based on hierarchical relationships between "us" and "them"—ultimately founded on fear of "them"—will undoubtedly resort to violence.[6] Additional examples exist at various levels of social life.

Countries will proactively go to war on the basis of real or imagined fears of threats to their land, safety, or security (Iraq War, Russian invasion of Ukraine). Whole regions will enact laws to separate and segregate groups of people and turn a blind eye when one group upholds those divisions through violence (Jim Crow and the lynching of Black Americans). Governments will systematically steal land and separate families in order to force Indigenous peoples to assimilate.

At the individual level, American men move through suburban neighborhoods—whether their own or not—looking for perceived threats to what they see as their rightful space and act with deadly violence when they deem it necessary (George Zimmerman, Kyle Rittenhouse, Gregory and Travis McMichael). Repeatedly, they find and engage perceived threats with deadly force.

No matter the scale, Christian nationalism provides theological justification for violence toward enemies, making it a righteous act. At both the national and the individual level, this political theology makes space for "true" citizens to protect themselves and their country—however they see fit—from those threatening it. While distinct ethical frameworks justifying collective violence versus individual violence exist across various strains of Christian theology, Christian nationalism blurs those lines. Christian nationalism considers the use of multiple forms of violence to defend one's body, family, community, or nation to be aligned with God's will. The world is a dangerous place, and sometimes we need good guys with guns or the nation's military to restore order.

Consider some of the examples from Kristin Kobes Du Mez's influential book, *Jesus and John Wayne*. She follows the thread of militant masculinity in American Christianity, especially through the last century, showing that white Christian men looked for and repeatedly found a new threat to Christian America to confront and subdue through righteous violence. Taking cues from popular fictionalized historical figures like William Wallace, Maximus Meridius, and various on-screen characters played by John Wayne, many have believed that the defense of our Christian nation requires the use of righteous violence, both collectively and individually, when necessary.

My own experience provides one example of how Christian nationalism blurs the application of collective and individual forms of violence. Growing up, I was drawn to the exciting and oftentimes violent Bible stories in which the people on God's side were the clear victors, and the losers suffered humiliation and defeat. Among these were David picking the five smooth stones and slaying Goliath, Gideon outwitting and slaughtering the Midianites, the Red Sea crashing down on all the Egyptians, and Samson exacting his revenge. Stories like this were told and retold through felt boards, illustrated children's books, and second-tier animation.

While we were generally taught in church that hurting others is bad and should be avoided, these stories clearly demonstrated that, at certain times and for certain reasons, those on God's side (who were always people like me) could resort to violence in order to fulfill God's will. Sure, Jesus never fought back, but how realistic is that today? He is the Son of God, after all, so we can't expect to live up to his earthly example. And don't forget how Jesus is depicted in Revelation as "a prize-fighter with a tattoo down his leg, a sword in his hand and the commitment to make someone bleed."[7]

In their sermons, pastors and teachers highlighted these or other Bible stories—or depictions of violence in popular culture—in which good claimed victory over evil.[8] The corollaries were clear. I could see myself as someone engaged in a similar struggle, albeit with lower stakes and likely in the spiritual realm but all the while willing and able to fight and destroy and defend, just like any good Christian man should.

It can be a small step between fighting spiritual battles to defend your family and religious community and fighting physical battles to do the same. It is difficult to keep the examples of physical violence in the Bible solely as lessons for spiritual battle today. It is all too easy for those earnestly listening—like I was—to see how physical violence may yet be of use today, just like it was in the Bible. I mean, we all might need to braid a whip and clear the temple every now and again. And just like David, Moses, Gideon, and other Israelites, I might have to violently defend my life or the lives of my family members from threats. Similarly, I may have to engage in or support collective violence to counter threats to our way of life (Christianity) arising from those who want to destroy it (non-Christian nations and peoples).

And just like that, I was able to endorse various forms of violence if I believed it was in service of the greater good, which usually meant my immediate needs or family, my fellow white Christians, Christian morality as we defined it, and the nation that was committed to it all—the United States. Growing up white in a majority-white community largely shielded me from any personal contact with interpersonal or collective violence. Violence was something I could support from afar without ever having to reckon with its fruit. This allowed me to maintain a sense of innocence regarding individual forms of violence and America's collective use of violence both at home and abroad. It allowed me to collapse these distinct forms of violence into one. As we'll see later, survey research underscores how I am not alone in this experience. Christian nationalism is strongly associated with support for the use of violence, whether interpersonal or collective.

Violence as Idol

Some Christians forget how shedding the blood of enemies, real or imagined, to "spread the gospel" and create a more "Christian" society or people is counter to the example of Jesus. When Jesus came to make disciples and save humanity, the only blood he shed was his own.

If an idol is whatever we place our hope and trust in, rather than God, then violence is a clear idol. Christians are called to live as though the end of history is already decided, and therefore we should not act out of worry, fear, or self-interest. We are supposed to believe "God wins," or perhaps more specifically "God already won," with Jesus rescuing humanity from the destruction of sin.

Nevertheless, white Christian nationalism is comfortable with violence to achieve a desired end. Violence as an idol overlaps with the other idols of Christian nationalism. Power is the ability to get others to do what you want them to do despite their resistance. Violence is intimately intertwined with a self-interested understanding of power. The threat or actual use of violence is a surefire way to encourage people to stop resisting in order to get what you want.

When we idolize power and grow accustomed to what it brings, we abhor the possibility that it might one day slip away. We defend what power we have and pine for more.

Likewise, violence is also a natural outcome of fear. Fear highlights feelings of being out of control, alone, attacked, and under threat. We fear when it seems our power is threatened. In those situations of high anxiety, we revert to a fight-or-flight response. We want to remain in control. When we fear that control and power are being wrested away, we will resort to whatever means necessary to keep them.

Nations and other groups often resort to dehumanizing or demonizing "others" to justify violence. Christian nationalism sanctifies and legitimates the use of violence—whether historically toward Native tribes in North America or enslaved persons from Africa, or more recently toward congressional representatives on January 6, 2021—when it serves any outcome viewed as "God's plan."

We see the roots of our idolizing violence within Christianity dating back centuries. There is nothing unique about American Christianity in this sense. The United States is operating much like any other world power. Empires can exist only because they wield the power of the sword, the threat of violence. America is an empire. It is merely another example of religion and violence intertwined to serve the needs of those protecting their power and working to gain more. Particular expressions of Christianity willingly supplied both the impetus and the doctrinal defense for groups to enact violence in service of "God's will."

Several commentators trace this history back to Constantine and the Roman Empire as the first time Christianity was intertwined with the power of the state.[9] The "power of the sword" is where Christians are now able to execute their desires for the world through domination and decree rather than giving and sacrifice. The narrative highlights how, once the church had a taste of alignment with power and the ability to use "righteous" violence as a means to a desired end, it never (willingly) gave it up. Christians found it was so much more efficient to force those opposing the church and God's will to obey.

The historical evidence does little to cast doubt on this narrative. Many of the treacherous actions of Christians over the centuries are a by-product of our wielding violence in the service of protecting or expanding our own power and privilege. The Crusades. The Inquisition. The Doctrine of Discovery. Slavery. Jim Crow. Repeatedly, white Christians idolized power and violence in order to protect our own interests at the expense of those around us. This expression of Christianity fit snugly in a long and wretched history.

Many faithful Christians believe violence can be justified in certain situations. The "just war" tradition is one example. Many other faithful Christians oppose violence across a number of spheres. I won't resolve the centuries-old and still ongoing conversation around violence and nonviolence here. What I have found repeatedly, however, is that white Christian nationalism views violence as not only justifiable in certain situations but also in many ways an ultimate good and the first choice. It is this idolization of violence within the cultural framework of white Christian nationalism that we—American Christians—must wrestle with and ultimately, I believe, reject. To do otherwise is to betray the gospel.

Christian Nationalism and Collective Violence

Large, national surveys of the American public underscore the association of violence and white Christian nationalism. This includes war or other forms of violence sanctioned at the national level. In fact, war and violence were essential to the creation and refinement of white Christian nationalism in North America.

Philip Gorski and Samuel Perry demonstrate how, up until the present day, white Christian nationalism is associated with believing that violence at the national level is necessary to bring about God's plan. This belief extends all the way back to the time of the Puritans. Leaders like Cotton Mather thought the wars with the

Native tribes were both providential and apocalyptic—literal holy wars of "good" versus "evil."[10]

The French and Indian War, the Revolutionary War, and the War of 1812 played pivotal roles in further developing white Christian nationalism and Americanizing it. Each subsequent war entrenched violence and racial hierarchy within white Christian nationalism and American Christianity writ large. This relationship was even stronger in the South, where white Americans lived in fear not only of "native war bands on a distant frontier" but also "Black insurrection on local plantations."[11] The Mexican-American War in the mid-1800s expanded the racial "others" in need of control via redemptive violence. The Civil War served to deepen and revise the foundational narrative of white Christian nationalism through the Lost Cause myth—that the South was merely defending state's rights and their traditional way of life centered on honor, Christianity, and chivalry. Ultimately, the end of the 1800s saw America shifting into what Gorski and Perry identify as the period of "American Empire."[12]

In the period of American Empire, all wars were now justified as righteous uses of violence in the hopes of spreading democracy and liberating oppressed peoples. These armed conflicts were only ever viewed as noble and righteous, sacrifices made on behalf of the will of God for the blessing of the world. "When America employs violence, this argument goes, it does so to spread freedom to others," write Gorski and Perry. "On the frontier and on the plantation, violence had been used to establish and secure white freedom. Now, military violence would be used to spread the blessings of freedom throughout the world."[13]

White Christian nationalism and the period of American Empire continue to shape Americans' views of war and violence. Several studies show that Americans who embrace the narrative of Christian nationalism are much more likely to assert American innocence regarding armed conflict across the globe. In other words, the violence enacted on behalf of the United States is deemed justifiable. These same Americans excuse violence enacted toward whole groups like the Native Americans and Africans stolen as part of the transatlantic slave trade.[14]

Indeed, many Christian Americans who embrace Christian nationalism believe that expanding the power and might of the United States is akin to spreading Christianity—that wherever democracy goes, the gospel is likely to follow and be a net benefit for those cultures and places. You can see this in statements from various leaders who tie the kingdom of God to furthering democracy or other national ideals. For example, Lieutenant General William Boykin, who was the deputy undersecretary for intelligence at the Defense Department during George W. Bush's years in office, claimed that protecting Christianity was one vital aspect of the war on terror. He maintained the United States was attacked—and should subsequently defend itself through violence—because we are a Christian nation, and our enemies are Satan and the principalities of darkness. The various wars after 9/11 were, in Boykin's mind, holy wars. In 2003, he told one congregation, "Satan wants to destroy this nation, he wants to destroy us as a nation, and he wants to destroy us as a Christian army."[15] The only recourse is to fight back on behalf of the Christian God.

European Christians used a very similar logic as they colonized North America. "Christianizing" these shores was in the end a net benefit, despite the killing, enslaving, and general bloodshed their colonization precipitated. From this perspective, violence, if in service of the gospel, was sometimes necessary and generally acceptable. Declan Leary's response to the discovery of the Indigenous children's mass graves in 2021 is evidence that such views still have purchase.

This belief in national innocence encourages citizens to view all conflicts in terms of good versus evil. We begin to believe that a divine mandate allows us to use all tools at our disposal, including violence, to defend ourselves (the good) from those God does not support (the evil).

Americans who embrace Christian nationalism are more likely to praise the virtues of the US military and advocate for its dominance on the world stage. I still remember sitting in a "God and Country" service while conducting fieldwork for *Taking America Back for God* and hearing the narrator for the service say, "Any victories we claim are all because of him and his faithfulness, and in the good times and bad, *he's always been on our side*."[16] In addition, Americans who strongly embrace white Christian nationalism are much more supportive of "self-interested" military endeavors—like protecting oil supplies—and limit their veneration of the United States military and military operations unless there is a clear benefit for the United States. They are less interested in military aid that benefits other countries.[17]

In a survey gathered in 2005, Americans who embraced Christian nationalism were much more likely to say the United States was justified in declaring war on Iraq and that the US government should expand its authority to "fight terrorism." Rhetoric from President Bush and others clearly identified America as on the side of good (God's side) and terrorists on the side of evil. Five days after 9/11 Bush commented, "We've never seen this kind of evil before. But the evil-doers have never seen the American people in action before, either—and they're about to find out."[18] The statements from Bush, as well as those from Boykin, resonated with millions of Americans. Sam Perry and I found that in 2007 Americans who embraced Christian nationalism firmly believed that God requires "the faithful" to "wage wars for good."[19] Using data from 2018, Eric McDaniel and his colleagues replicated this finding.[20] There is an enduring link between Christian nationalism, militarism, and violence.

White evangelical responses to the terrorist attacks of 9/11 are a particularly poignant example, and one that many of us lived through. For some in my generation, the attacks and our nation's response to them began a journey of wrestling with the implications of being a Christian in a nation bent on war.

The memories of that day are still fresh, even all these years later. It started like any other fall Tuesday. I was in my freshman dorm room at Purdue preparing for my 9:30 a.m. class—US history from the colonial period through Reconstruction.[21] A friend down the hall burst in and asked, "You know the World Trade Center Towers in New York?"

"Yes . . . ," I answered.

"One of them is on fire. It looks like a plane hit it," he said.

We ran down to his room to watch the news coverage. I skipped my history class as well as all my other classes that day. We sat in silence, watching the second plane hit and the two towers fall. I remember watching then president Bush address the nation that evening. I remember thinking to myself how this was a moment when everything changes. What would life look like a year from now? Ten years from now?

Within weeks, the United States began airstrikes against Taliban and al-Qaeda targets in Afghanistan. A year and a half later, the United States declared war on Iraq. Like many Americans, I saw these wars through the lens of 9/11 and fully supported attacking those whom our government saw as imminent threats to national security.

Soon after the US military entered Iraq in March 2003, I attended a weekend getaway for the campus ministry I was involved in. One evening I sat at a table with two fellow students and listened in as they discussed the morality of the United States invading Iraq: we were attacked on 9/11; we deserved revenge. I remember hoping we would find it.

Two years later, I still felt the same way. At the table was one friend from a small town in Indiana like me. We were proud Americans and Christians. Fighting to defend our country and its interests was clearly within our rights. God would want us to oust evil rulers like Saddam Hussein. God would want us to spread democracy around the world because it is the greatest form of government and allows for religion—ideally Christianity—to flourish.

My other friend at the table was an exchange student from Australia. While he shared our Christian commitments, he brought a different perspective regarding how our faith should relate to war and the nation.

"Isn't it a good thing for us to take out such a bad guy like Saddam?" my Indiana friend asked. In effect, he was asking whether violence and killing in service of a greater good—ending the reign of a murderous dictator—is something Christians can and should support. Our Australian friend shook his head, questioning how Americans could assume that waging war against Saddam—or anyone else—was within their rights or supported by the Christian God, especially given the collateral damage to innocent Iraqi civilians. Back and forth they went. It was almost as if they were each speaking a dialect the other could not understand.

I honestly don't remember much more of our Australian friend's argument. My stance on the Iraq War, warfare in general, or killing did not change in that instant. However, something did shift.

In that conversation, I recognized a faithful Christian who was strongly committed to the idea that our faith does not allow us to enact violence, no matter how righteous we might consider the desired end to be—even if it was to avenge thousands of lives lost or to prevent the use of purported and ultimately nonexistent "weapons of mass destruction."

In all my years being raised in majority-white evangelical churches, such a view was not widely held or discussed. As I shared previously, in one private conversation on a youth group summer trip, my youth pastor openly questioned whether Christians could in good conscience participate in war and kill those on the opposing side. That conversation was now paired with the conversation with my friends, and I found myself questioning the larger narratives surrounding violence, Christianity, and our nation.

The commitment of my college friend intrigued me. It encouraged me to continue to question whether I could so easily support

this war. It also made me wonder why I did not sense any dissonance, as he did, between killing in war and my Christian faith.

In the years that followed, I wondered if Christians in other
countries viewed us as my Australian friend did. I began to question whether a Christianity that is always in support of violence
enacted by the United States could be a faithful witness of Jesus
Christ. I began to question whether Christianity—or any religion
for that matter—could ever consistently oppose the use and especially the abuse of violence when closely aligned with political
power and national interests.

Sure, war is hard and difficult. But if God is with us and commands us to destroy evil, then who are we to stand back and wait?
Was this truly a war between good and evil? Was the United States
clearly on God's side? Were we merely enacting God's ultimate desire for the world? White Christian nationalism provided much of
the cultural framework needed not only to make this case but also
to assuage most of the concerns held by many white Christians.

Since that evening in college, I have wrestled with the wages of
collective violence in my personal faith journey and professional
research agenda. This naturally extended to interpersonal forms
of violence.

Christian Nationalism and Interpersonal Violence

Christian nationalism is also intimately intertwined with a comfort with violence at the individual level. As we will see in an
upcoming chapter, white Americans have appealed to defending
this "Christian nation" to authorize unspeakable violence against
Black Americans. For white Americans, upholding a Christian
nation has meant defending the racial order.

Tracking letters and announcements from Citizens' Councils
throughout the 1950s and 1960s, historian J. Russell Hawkins demonstrates how scores of everyday, churchgoing Christians firmly
believed that God created different races and desired their separa-

tion.[22] The United States, in their estimation, ignored God's will in this matter at their own peril.

Historian Kelly Baker highlights how these widely held beliefs resonated in the arguments made by members of the Ku Klux Klan.[23] She shows how the ideology of protecting a "white Protestant nation" baptized the racial views and use of violence of groups like the KKK. While KKK membership and participation never held majority status, the KKK's beliefs were in no way fringe. Groups like the KKK were present in almost every single state. They counted many powerful men as friendly to their goals or even dues-paying members. This included the governors of Indiana and Colorado in the 1920s.

An association between white Christian nationalism and a comfort with racialized individual-level violence continues to this day. In a recent survey, when asked if "police officers in the United States shoot blacks more often because they are more violent than whites," close to 50 percent of white Americans who strongly embrace Christian nationalism agreed.[24]

The death penalty is another example of individual-level violence—albeit state sanctioned—strongly associated with white Christian nationalism. One report using 2007 data found that Christian nationalism was among the strongest predictors of Americans favoring use of the death penalty.[25] Recent surveys say more of the same: seven out of ten white Ambassadors agree with the statement, "The biggest problem with the death penalty is we don't use it enough."[26] One vocal supporter of Christian nationalism explicitly argued this very point.[27]

The statistics surrounding the death penalty suggest that as a society we aren't good at administering this form of justice. Since 1973 alone, 185 people wrongfully convicted and sentenced to death have been exonerated. Furthermore, the rates of minority groups being sentenced to death are disproportionately higher than those of whites.[28] As the Equal Justice Initiative so aptly states, "The question we need to ask about the death penalty in

America is not whether someone deserves to die for a crime. The question is whether we deserve to kill."[29]

Given the rate at which innocent people are sentenced to death, perhaps we Christians should consider leading the charge to stop executions. Perhaps Christians should abdicate this form of violence that white Christian nationalism is so keen to protect.

Survey data of the American public soon after the Capitol riots on January 6, 2021, demonstrate that Christian nationalism is strongly associated with support for the following beliefs regarding forms of political violence: the riots at the US Capitol building on January 6 were justified, violence is acceptable in advancing political goals, violence is acceptable when Americans want to express disagreement with the government, true American patriots may have to resort to physical violence to save our country, and violence is justified if the members of the other side act violently first.[30]

We also see a link between individual violence and white Christian nationalism in the infatuation with guns and the right to bear arms. This goes far beyond owning guns used for hunting or target practice with clay pigeons. The community I grew up in has a strong gun culture. I support the right of my friends and family members to continue to enjoy hunting trips and responsibly use and store their firearms.

Idolizing guns goes beyond personal sport. Some might remember that in 2021 Representative Thomas Massie (R-KY), an avowed Christian, posted a family Christmas photo with all seven members holding large, semiautomatic firearms.[31] The accompanying message read, "Merry Christmas! ps. Santa, please bring ammo."

Lauren Boebert, a congresswoman from Colorado, and her family were not to be outdone. Boebert has repeatedly signaled her belief in America's Christian roots. As was noted in an earlier chapter, she told one congregation that it was not the intention of our founding fathers that the church and state be separate but rather that the church should run the state.[32] Several days after the Massies distributed their photo on Twitter, she posed in front of a Christmas tree with her sons, each holding an assault-style rifle.

These tweets received considerable attention in part because Massie's tweet appeared five days after a high school shooting in Oxford, Michigan, where four students were killed and an additional seven people were injured. Given the ubiquity of school shootings in the United States, it is inevitable that tweets like this will be temporally close to another mass shooting. Nevertheless, the timing and circumstances of the 2021 Oxford school shooting cast the post in a different light: the gun of the Oxford school shooter was an early Christmas present from his parents.

Another reason for the attention was the dissonance between Christians' commonly held reasons for celebrating Christmas—rejoicing over the birth of the Prince of Peace—and the Massies and Boeberts holding weapons of warfare. These are not tools used for hunting game. These are weapons meant for killing other humans.

Violence and the tools of violence are merely part of the cultural package of being an American Christian. After a mass shooting in a small church in Texas in 2017, a pastor in Florida posted a sign on his church's doors: "Please know this is not a gun free zone—we are heavily armed—any attempt will be dealt with deadly force."[33] In early 2022, conservative candidate for governor of Georgia Kandiss Taylor debuted her tour bus featuring her slogan: "Jesus, Guns, Babies."[34] Boebert made more headlines in June 2022 at a Christian conference in Colorado Springs when, in response to a hypothetical question about how many AR-15s Jesus would own, she boasted that Jesus "didn't have enough [AR-15s] to keep his government from killing him."[35] For Taylor, the Massie and Boebert families, and millions of others like them, weapons created for warfare and violence dovetail perfectly with Christianity. It is a religion of conquerors.

In making sense of this overlap, historian Peter Manseau points to a "muscular Christianity" and how in the United States the power of God and Christ is routinely paired with the power of men with guns. In the American imagination of "taming the west," Manseau writes, "legends of pistol-packing preachers . . . permanently joined evangelism to the six-shooter."[36] Nurturing an "authentic, God-given masculinity" is intimately intertwined with gun culture.[37]

National survey research demonstrates that views like Taylor's, Massie's, and Boebert's are anything but fringe. The millions of white Americans who favor Christian nationalism support the use of firearms to enact violence when they deem it necessary. A 2021 survey showed that nine out of ten white Americans who strongly embrace Christian nationalism agree that "the best way to stop bad guys with guns is to have good guys with guns."[38]

Another 2021 survey showed that gun owners among this same group were much more likely to report that owning a gun made them feel "patriotic" and "in control of my fate."[39] It is no surprise, then, that these same Americans eschew any mention of gun control—70 percent oppose it—and actually report greater levels of fear regarding gun-control legislation.[40]

For many white Christians in the United States, to be American and Christian is to own the option of enacting violence against one's "enemies," however defined in the moment. Take, for example, Paul Gosar, who has routinely claimed we must return to America's Christian roots in order to flourish. On November 7, 2021, the Arizona representative tweeted, "Christ is king." Later that day, he tweeted out an animated video depicting him killing New York representative Alexandria Ocasio-Cortez.[41] For Gosar and many others we surveyed, there is little if any dissonance between claiming Christ as king and endorsing violence. Waging war, gun violence, the death penalty, and rioting at the Capitol are all acceptable forms of violence under the right circumstances.

The righteousness of violence is limited to those like "us," however, which naturally excludes racial and ethnic minorities. As

Danté Stewart writes, "Only white bodies are allowed to be angry in this country, even violent, and still live to tell the story."[42] Racial and ethnic minorities are viewed as an inherent threat because of their skin color. As mentioned above, embracing white Christian nationalism is strongly associated with believing police violence against Black Americans is due to their being inherently more violent than people of other races.

Despite the easy acceptance of violence within the cultural framework of white Christian nationalism, perhaps other historic and global expressions of Christianity might cause us American Christians to pause and consider the implications of idolizing violence for our worship of Jesus as king.

The Prince of Peace and Violence

Considering America an empire akin to ancient Rome alters how we might think about the role of violence in the service of the nation and what it can and should accomplish. It reframes how we think about the utility of violence in our interpersonal lives, and how we might be complicit in violence beyond our personal social spheres.

Consider the following incident in Jesus's life when violence, seemingly righteous violence, might have been a legitimate option. In the garden of Gethsemane, Jesus and his disciples are confronted by a "large crowd armed with swords and clubs" (Matt. 26:47), a "detachment of soldiers and some officials from the chief priests and the Pharisees" (John 18:3). When one of Jesus's companions (Matt. 26:51; Mark 14:47; Luke 22:49; specifically Simon Peter in John 18:10) lunges with his sword and cuts off the ear of the high priest's servant, Jesus rebukes him:

No more of this! (Luke 22:51)

Put your sword back in its place, . . . for all who draw the sword will die by the sword. Do you think I cannot call on my Father,

123

and he will at once put at my disposal more than twelve legions of angels? But how then would the Scriptures be fulfilled that say it must happen this way? (Matt. 26:52–54)

Put your sword away! Shall I not drink the cup the Father has given me? (John 18:11)

Jesus then heals the man, making him whole once again.

So, as Lisa Sharon Harper asks, "Why didn't Jesus brandish the sword as any king worth his legend would do?"[43] Or, to use a more recent example, would Jesus have brandished an AR-15? It might be easy for us to blithely move past Jesus's example here. But I cannot stop wrestling with this question.

Growing up evangelical meant I was told time and again how Jesus calls us to follow his example. I was told it would not be easy and many people would not understand the countercultural nature of being a Christian. I would likely be labeled a fool. Questioning the use of violence in the context of modern-day American Christianity shows me how true those lessons were. But the costs and pushback come almost entirely from those *inside* my faith tradition rather than outside it.

How can we so easily excuse ourselves from questioning our use of violence? If Jesus is lord over all, doesn't it make sense that he would also demand we emulate his example regarding violence? What if Jesus calls me to lay aside my desire to protect my rights or my group with violence? What if Jesus calls me to resist those who do evil with self-sacrificial love instead of violence?

In order for white American Christians to wrestle with how our faith tradition has historically idolized various expressions of violence in our embrace of white Christian nationalism, we must recognize that nonviolence in the Christian tradition is multifaceted as well. There is no one single expression. Violence appears in many forms, and so it should be no surprise that Christian responses to it are likewise multidimensional and complex.

In *A Field Guide to Christian Nonviolence,* David Cramer and Myles Werntz show that throughout history and today various strains of Christian nonviolence overlap and at times contradict one another. Christian proponents of nonviolence even draw from various strains simultaneously. Christian discipleship and Christian virtues are two of the strains Cramer and Werntz identify. In the one, Christians are called to pursue nonviolence because our nonviolent Savior calls us to Christian discipleship. In the other, Christians are called to a virtuous life no matter the external circumstances, and violence—even in the form of a just war—encourages the wrong sorts of virtues.

One example of nonviolence as an expression of Christian discipleship is the story of André Trocmé and his village of Le Chambon, France, during World War II.[44] He and his community served as a refuge for almost five thousand Jews and other refugees fleeing the Holocaust. Trocmé writes that part of Jesus's ministry was to liberate humanity from the ravages of sin, enacted sociopolitically, and to expand the way of peace through community with other Christians. Accounts of Le Chambon highlight the ordinary but subversive ways the Christians there opposed the Vichy government and the deportation of and violence toward Jews. Through consistent discipleship, Trocmé and his fellow Christians asked, "And who is my neighbor?" and were moved to create places of refuge.[45]

Several strains of nonviolence teach that choosing it will require suffering. The nonviolence of Christian mysticism teaches us that "to join in the nonviolence of Jesus is to join in the suffering of God on behalf of the world."[46] Proponents of Christian nonviolence recognize that "violence of the world is not always solved by nonviolence" and nonviolence necessarily requires suffering. "It is in suffering, as the apostle Paul writes, that our character is formed more fully into the image of Christ."[47]

Liberationist nonviolence, nonviolence as political practice, and Christian antiviolence all push us to listen to the voices of "those most affected by violence to point the way to what is needed to transform institutions—including the state—to bring about authentic, lasting peace." For white American Christians, this means looking to oppressed peoples in other nations, Black Americans and other minority racial and ethnic groups, and victims of sexual and gender-based violence.[48] In order to confront and oppose violence within white Christian nationalism, we must listen to, learn from, and follow the examples of those most likely to bear the brunt of violence.

Martin Luther King Jr. and the civil rights movement give us a clear example of nonviolence as political practice. As Cramer and Wertz show, "This stream is primarily concerned with how nonviolence—as a normative Christian practice—can be the basis for public action."[49] King and others saw the dignity of all persons—even those they were in conflict with—leading them to embrace a social witness of nonviolence. They believed nonviolence would draw attention to racial injustice and prick the consciences of their opponents, drawing out their humanity and creating coalitions where there once were none. This leads to a common vision for political life where all humanity can flourish. Christians inspired by the life and person of Jesus enter into a relationship with all others to help create a beloved community regardless of whether we share particular theological convictions. In living out the gospel, which includes the realignment of the power structures of society, those in the civil rights movement saw the idol of violence for what it was: a chief tool of white Christian nationalism.

We can learn how to consistently wrestle with the use of violence, whether interpersonal or between nations. We can explore how violence distances us from a Christian practice that mirrors Jesus and instead draws us toward an empire-building expression of Christianity comfortable with self-interested power. How can we expect to participate in the kingdom of God, a kingdom the Bible teaches is characterized by nonviolence, if we consistently turn to violence as the means to achieve what we believe to be God's will?

Lisa Sharon Harper answers her own question from above, pointing out how "God beat the power of human empire not with a sword but with the power of the Resurrection."[50] Death is not the final act. Resurrection is. Jesus's power—and by extension ours—lies not in exerting power over others through violence but in giving our lives, trusting in the power of God to bring new life out of death.

Living according to this truth could be what makes Christians both good and bad citizens, simultaneously. We are willing to give of ourselves to our fellow citizens in order that they may flourish. We are not willing, however, to take the lives of those deemed our enemies based on nationality. All empires require both forms of sacrifice. Good citizens in the eyes of empire—those who embrace white Christian nationalism—will sacrifice lives for the empire if necessary, their own and *especially* those of their enemies. Expressions of Christianity that confront white Christian nationalism can fulfill only the former.

For years, I blithely accepted the narrative embraced by white Christian nationalism that violence is a natural part of our individual and collective survival and success. While grateful for those who sacrificed their lives for my country, I thought little about those from other nations who were caught up in the cycles of war. I was never forced to grapple with the ravages of interpersonal and institutional violence in other communities around the country. White Christian nationalism teaches that the only way to protect Christianity is to protect the United States. And the only way to ensure that a nation of this world continues to exist is to exert the power of the sword.

I am convinced now more than ever that the idolization of violence alongside power and fear inherent to white Christian nationalism serves only empire and results in the further marginalization and suffering of minority groups. It does not lead us to emulate the example set by Jesus. It causes us to betray the gospel.

White American Christians can begin to look to and learn from the expressions of Christianity among the marginalized throughout history to find a new way forward, one that does not rely on violence in order to protect power over others and assuage the fear of losing what we consider ours.

Jesus was clear on the day of his death that his kingdom is not of this world and does not depend on violence for its defense or expansion (John 18:36). He refused to pick up the sword and rather chose to take up a cross—the violent instrument of *his own* death, not that of his enemies. "Jesus did not stand with state or religious authorities being violent against bodies and marginalized bodies. Jesus stands as one who knew the economic, political, and religious violence but also as one who formed people in the way of resistance, dignity, power, justice, and love," writes Danté Stewart.[51] Such a move defies the logic of white Christian nationalism.

Let us consider how we might embody the example set by Jesus and collectively lay down our swords.

MAY YOUR KINGDOM COME, ON EARTH AS IT IS IN HEAVEN?

Individually, Christian people in the South—white and black—through the years have been able to work together and to understand each other. But now a world of outside agitation has been started, and people are coming in the name of piety, but it is a false piety, and are endeavoring to disturb God's established order; and we are having turmoil all over America. This disturbing movement is not of God. It is not in line with the Bible. It is Satanic. Now, listen and understand this. Do not let people lead you astray.

—Bob Jones[1]

I CAN STILL REMEMBER HEARING Randall Balmer, a distinguished historian of American religion, share how it was race—not abortion, divorce, or homosexuality—that served as a catalyst for the Christian Right in the 1970s. Balmer was presenting at Baylor University in Waco, Texas. This was before Chip and Joanna Gaines and their *Fixer Upper* empire shiplapped Waco into the American cultural mainstream. I was just beginning my graduate studies and still trying to find my way in academia as a first-generation college student.

Growing up in the late 1980s and early 1990s, when the Christian Right had been a political and social force for the past decade or so, I assumed I knew the originating myth of this powerful voting bloc. Evangelicals like me were concerned with the moral direction of this country. We believed divorces were on the rise. We fretted about how sex permeated the culture. We felt disgust at how homosexuality was becoming more widely accepted. And, most important, we were horrified that abortion was legal.

Our pastors, echoing leaders of the Christian Right, told us how each of these was a stain on our country and its religious heritage. The United States was clearly a nation favored by God—how else does one explain its global dominance?—but this status was in jeopardy. If we continued to slide down this path of unrepentant sin, we would violate our covenant. God would then be forced to withdraw his blessing, his hand of protection, and our nation—this Christian nation—would collapse.

We had to enforce our moral vision on the country to ensure that our nation could and would flourish. The only way to do that was to enter the political sphere and "vote for our values." Getting the "right" people in the "right" places of power to enact the "right" policies was paramount. The idols of self-interested power and fear were in full effect.

Much of white Christianity's concern for morality—defined at that time as opposition to abortion, homosexuality, and divorce—demanded we become politically active. We cared about the United States. Its success was ours. When you got down to it, we really had no choice but to strive for positions of influence and power. We alone had the answers to what ailed the nation.

By the time I heard Balmer speak, I had already begun to jettison aspects of this framework. The "founding myth" of the Christian Right, however, was still firmly in place. While I no longer identified with the Christian Right's interpretation of what was wrong with the United States or with the methods through which the Christian Right argued Christians were supposed to solve the country's problems, I still believed these particular moral issues united and motived the Christian Right.

I was not aware of the racial context surrounding the formation of the Christian Right. Again, growing up in white evangelicalism, race wasn't something I had to worry about. Throughout my elementary, middle, and high school years, the number of minority students in the schools I attended could likely be counted on one hand. Not just my grade—the entire school. In 2019, my community was around 90 percent white according to the US Census, an almost identical figure for the county in 1990.[2]

By the time I was old enough to hear and internalize the messages of my religious tradition, the centrality of race to our religio-political movement was hidden—purposefully or otherwise. It was as if there was a mist swirling around, obscuring and refracting what I could see. Balmer's lecture was like piercing sunlight on a foggy morning—the surrounding landscape pops suddenly into clear view. I could now see what had always been there.

Absent among those "right" policies was any mention of continuing racial inequality. I just assumed the civil rights movement had fixed everything. Since slavery had been outlawed over a hundred years ago, the ongoing concerns of Black Americans were not given much, if any, thought. After spending my entire childhood, teenage years, and time as an undergraduate in the pew on Sunday mornings, I can't remember a single message focused on racial inequality. Not one.

This was likely no accident. Jerry Falwell and other Christian Right leaders had previously opposed Christians engaging in politics, particularly in response to Black ministers taking an active role in the civil rights movement. Falwell himself proclaimed, "Preachers are not called to be politicians but soul winners."[3]

Equality for Black Americans (or any minority racial or ethnic group) was not a moral issue for most white American Christians. Rather, we regarded racial issues as political distractions. Christians like us focused solely on "preaching the pure saving gospel of Jesus Christ" and saving souls.[4] Groups like the Moral Majority signaled their concern for the morality of America, but they ignored race. Congregations like those I grew up in followed suit. The moral issues threatening the country were abortion, homosexuality, and divorce, but not racial inequality. As historian Anthea Butler points out, this "color-blind conservatism" and specifically defined "morality politics" functioned as a shield, creating "new political alliances and creating organizations . . . that would promote their favored issues while continuing to embrace racist practices and strategies to consolidate economic and political power."[5]

Recounting personal conversations with Paul Weyrich, one of the key political operatives intent on bringing white Christians into the Republican Party, Balmer reported how Weyrich claimed it was opposition to the IRS mandating desegregation of Christian schools, like Bob Jones University (founded by the same man whose quote began this chapter), that motivated the formation of the Christian Right. Weyrich confirmed that the Christian Right formed in opposition to a federal government mandate that organizations receiving federal funds must not endorse racially discriminatory policies.[6] They wanted to be able legally to segregate their white children from Black children in schools.

During that time, Weyrich was looking for other issues around which he hoped to unify and motivate conservative voters. He had no success. Pornography, school prayer, the Equal Rights Amendment, and even abortion yielded no fruit.[7] In Weyrich's own words, "I was trying to get those people [evangelicals] interested in those issues and I utterly failed. What changed their mind was Jimmy Carter's intervention against the Christian schools, trying to deny them tax-exempt status on the basis of so-called de facto segregation." It was the IRS threat against segregated Christian academies, not abortion or some other issue, that Weyrich said "enraged the Christian community."[8]

Moreover, it isn't just Weyrich who attests to the ways racial segregation animated the early Christian Right. Ed Dobson, Grover Norquist, Richard Viguerie, and even administrators at Bob Jones University corroborate it was "government intrusion into private education"—to ensure racial equality—that kicked the hornets' nest and brought the Christian Right into politics.[9]

To be sure, Balmer's argument is not the whole story.[10] Catholics and some Protestants had publicly opposed abortion for years. Grassroots activists had already built strong anti-abortion networks that were folded into the Christian Right's mobilization into the political arena. Homosexuality, gender, school prayer—each of these was part of the constellation of "moral" issues the Christian Right wanted to highlight. However, these accounts and that of Balmer's *do* align in that racism and racist ideas played an integral role in shaping a political realignment that brought conservative white Christians into the Republican Party fold. Therefore, the key is not that it was *only* racism that united the Christian Right, as Balmer argues. The key is that racism was rendered so consistently invisible alongside other "moral" issues the Christian Right highlighted. Balmer's thesis, while oversimplified, does bring the importance of race into clear view.

As I sat listening to Balmer speak, I felt bewildered. How could a movement intent on ensuring that an entire nation represented their "pro-life" views share a commitment to such a despicable stance? It raised questions about the other "moral issues" that were deal breakers to being a good American Christian. How might these have directly and indirectly been shaped by racism and racist ideology?[11]

As I was finally starting to learn, by then decades into my Christian journey, the sin and stain of racism within white Christian nationalism is but another piece of rotten fruit from a long-diseased tree. It is in this history that we see how white supremacy is—and always has been—intimately intertwined with idolizing power, fear, and violence in the calls to make the United States a Christian nation.

Calls for a Christian Nation and Racism

After hearing Balmer's lecture, I began to follow my interests in the literature surrounding civil religion, Christianity, and politics. I wanted to know more about what social scientists were finding about the overlap of religion, race, and politics.

In the intervening fifteen years, dozens of new studies demonstrated how a quest to make America more Christian is strongly linked to racially discriminatory attitudes. The evidence from social scientists examining racism and Americans' embrace of Christian nationalism shows that desires for a "Christian" nation are closely linked to comfort with or outright advocation of racially discriminatory policies and values. The more we embrace Christian nationalism, the more likely we are to hold racist attitudes and beliefs.

These findings underscore how the desire to define the United States as a "Christian" nation is intertwined with ideals of whiteness. Just like the earliest colonists, Americans today who argue that America must be more Christian are also signaling—even if unintended or unstated—beliefs about who the country belongs to and what sorts of issues should be most important.

Studies show that embracing Christian nationalism predicts opposition toward both interracial marriage and transracial adoption. White Americans who embrace Christian nationalism are much more likely to attribute racial inequality experienced by Black Americans to their personal or individual shortcomings rather than to structural explanations like the ongoing effects of Jim Crow or hundreds of years of slavery.[12]

One study shows that embracing Christian nationalism leads Americans to be much less supportive of welfare spending and more supportive of border spending and spending to reduce crime—all policy areas that are generally racially coded. For policy areas that are not as racially coded, Christian nationalism plays little to no role.[13]

Christian nationalism is also strongly predictive of believing that deadly force by police toward Black Americans—such as George Floyd, Philando Castile, and Eric Garner—happens more often because "they [Blacks] are more violent than whites." The same Americans who embrace Christian nationalism are also more likely to say that Black and white Americans receive the same treatment from police.[14]

White Christian nationalism is also strongly linked to greater political tolerance of Americans who explicitly tout racist ideas. Using data from the late 1990s and then from 2014, one study shows that whites who embrace Christian nationalism are more tolerant of racists than they are of other stigmatized groups like atheists, communists, militarists, or homosexuals.[15]

Recent studies also show that white Americans who embrace Christian nationalism are much more willing to deny racial minorities access to the democratic process. These Americans believe that voter suppression is rare (despite evidence to the contrary) and that voter fraud is widespread (despite evidence to the contrary). Generally, white Americans who embrace Christian nationalism believe that only those "worthy" of engaging in the democratic process should be allowed to do so. Given our nation's history of voter suppression, "those who are worthy" has ultimately meant white, natural-born citizens.[16]

White Christian nationalism is strongly associated with racist views of the COVID-19 pandemic. Americans who embrace Christian nationalism are much more likely to disagree that it is "racist to call COVID-19 'the Chinese Virus' " and that "higher minority infections are symptoms of an unjust society." They are more likely to agree that Black Americans are infected at higher rates because they are more irresponsible, that Black Americans may be biologically susceptible to COVID-19, and that COVID-19 spreading among prisoners is "the least of our concerns," and further that its toll on the incarcerated could be the result of "divine justice."[17]

In summary, calls for a more "Christian" nation are really calls for a nation where white Americans maintain a privileged position in the social hierarchy. Racial inequality is legitimized as the result of individual shortcomings within minority groups. Our racialized culture and society, where distinct differences in wealth, health, and opportunities across racial and ethnic groups are present, are often viewed as natural, perhaps even God-ordained. White Christian nationalism obscures the structural and systemic causes of racial inequality in service of upholding a narrative that the United States has a special relationship with the Christian God.

In the face of this overwhelming evidence, I find it hard to reconcile my Christian belief that all humans equally bear the image of the living God with a desire for the United States to privilege Christianity, when Christian nationalism is so strongly associated with racially insensitive—and in some cases repugnant—beliefs. We cannot have both. In order to align ourselves with expressions of Christianity that encourage the flourishing of all people, we have to dispense with our quest to privilege Christianity in social and cultural spheres. From the beginning, the mission to make a "Christian nation" has served to create and maintain a racial hierarchy. The Christian Right was just singing the same old song.

These strong and consistent relationships raise the question, How did we get here? To make sense of these findings, we need to examine the historical record linking Christianity with race and racism.

Christianity and the History of Racism in the United States

As we have explored thus far, white Christian nationalism focuses on gaining and maintaining privileged access to power. Fear is one of the primary tools Christian nationalism uses to motivate action and prop up a fusion between Christianity and national identity. Generally, fear is used to distinguish between "us" and "them"—those committed to a "Christian" nation and those who are not. Violence is a natural response, used to demarcate and defend these boundaries. Power, fear, and violence are the three main idols of Christian nationalism.

The use of religion and Christianity to delineate those who are with "us" from those who are not is common throughout history. Over the centuries, popes, priests, kings, and other rulers have baptized their desire for economic and geographic gains in the will of God, assuring themselves and their people that those they conquered deserved to be conquered. It was no accident that skin color became a straightforward way to determine whom God desired them to conquer.

As early as the mid-1400s, the first instances of anti-Black racism appear in the accounts of the inauguration of the western European slave trade. Tied to the denigration of darker-skinned people were religious justifications for kidnapping and enslaving them. Europeans labeled those taken as slaves as "barbarians" in desperate need of salvation. Quickly, whiteness and Christianity stood in sharp relief to blackness and "heathen."[18]

Official orders from the church likewise baptized the "discovery" of new lands and the displacement of Indigenous populations, as well as their capture and enslavement, through the Doctrine of Discovery. Yet again, church and state leaders considered all people outside European Christendom—who were almost exclusively racialized as nonwhite—as deserving of domination in service to the "true people of God."[19]

These justifications were imported to the United States, where the very first boundaries around "us" (Christians) versus "them" (non-Christians) were fundamentally intertwined with whiteness and race. Racial categories developed alongside religious categories. Colonists in North America debated whether Indigenous tribes or African slaves could become Christians, because they believed religious identities—like physical characteristics—were passed down through generations. Thus, as historian Jemar Tisby writes in his best-selling book *The Color of Compromise,* "European meant 'Christian' and Native American or African meant 'heathen.' Over time, these categories simplified and hardened into racial designations."[20] We could now identify true Christians via visual cues.

Repeatedly, those who claimed to be Christians were also the ones creating and spreading racist ideologies. Christians used Scripture to formalize theologies baptizing racial segregation and race-based chattel slavery. Used in this way, Christianity colonized the physical and social worlds it encountered. European Christians imagined themselves at the top of a racialized hierarchy, instituted by God.[21]

The earliest European colonists of North America likewise imported the Doctrine of Discovery—believing the Christian God fully supported their quest to "discover," capture, and dominate new lands and peoples—in service to the "City on a Hill" they hoped to inaugurate. Mark Charles and Soong-Chan Rah show in their book *Unsettling Truths* how John Winthrop and other Puritan leaders sought repeatedly to highlight their divine destiny. The consequences of this "dysfunctional social and theological imagination" were terrifying. "Winthrop's assertion of a special status for the Puritans in the New World justified the resulting genocide of the existing population in the American continent. . . . The Doctrine of Discovery allowed Native genocide to be understood as a holy act of claiming the promised land for European settlers."[22]

From the moment Europeans stepped onto North American soil, they drew sharp racial and religious boundaries to separate themselves from the dark-skinned slaves and brown-skinned Native Americans in their midst. The distribution of resources and opportunities in the "New World" adhered to this hierarchy, with white European men firmly situated at the top. Christian theologies were constructed to serve their economic interests.[23]

For the next several centuries, those on top—white men and their families—continued to make the case as to why slavery was not only tolerable but actually God's design and a fundamental good that should be protected and extended. Preachers, theologians, and rank-and-file Americans even drew directly from their Christian faith to argue that enslaved Africans should be *thankful* for American slavery, as it was part of God's ordering of the cosmos and brought them under the auspices of a good Christian nation.

The links between white Christian nationalism and racial terror did not end with slavery. Racism merely adapted. From Reconstruction until the civil rights era in the 1960s, Christians in both the North and the South perpetuated terrorist violence against Black Americans through lynching. Growing up in a majority-white community in northern Indiana, I learned in school that lynching was part of our country's history. However, I had a mostly sanitized and detached knowledge of the practice. That changed when I read the account of Jesse Washington and "the Waco Horror" while I was in graduate school at Baylor. Jesse's lynching in the city in which I resided brought home just how barbaric a practice it was—one that white Christians like me enthusiastically participated in just a couple of generations prior.

On May 8, 1916, illiterate and possibly mentally disabled seventeen-year-old Jesse Washington was arrested for killing Lucy Fryer, who was found dead earlier that day. While in police custody, he confessed to raping and murdering her.[24] At Jesse's trial seven days later, a jury of twelve white men found him guilty and sentenced him to death after four minutes of deliberation. Thousands of Wacoans surrounded the courthouse that day, and officials worried mob violence might ensue.

After the sentence was read, spectators grabbed Jesse and dragged him outside. The white mob, numbering over ten thousand people at one point, chained Jesse by the neck, dragged him toward city hall, stripped him naked, and repeatedly stabbed and beat him. They then stacked wood next to a tree in front of the building, where they doused him with oil and set him on fire. Semiconscious, Jesse tried to climb the chain but couldn't because the crowd had cut off his fingers—in addition to his toes and genitals. They repeatedly raised and lowered him over the flames for two hours. The *Waco Times-Herald* reported that when his body began to burn, "shouts of delight went up from the thousands of throats."[25] By the end, all that remained of Jesse was his skull, torso, and limb stumps. Bystanders collected souvenirs, including Jesse's bones. A local photographer captured the violence and sold the images on postcards and prints.

In all, white Americans murdered more than forty-four hundred Black Americans on the lynching tree. Just imagine the horror of Jesse's murder repeated thousands of times throughout the United States and the terror this instilled in minority communities. Imagine the thousands of "sundown towns," where the threat of this violence extended to any Black American out too late into the evening. The Equal Justice Initiative offers a map of where lynchings occurred. I counted the number of reported lynchings in the counties in which I have lived.[26] In those six counties, there are twenty-two reported lynchings. In all likelihood there were more.

Examples abound of white Christians actively participating in lynchings. Sometimes the mobs carried out lynchings after services on Sundays near or around churches, which ensured a sizable crowd, as in the lynchings of Harris Tunstal, Samuel Thomas Wilkes, and Luther and Mary Holbert.[27] Just as harmfully, most white Christians failed to actively oppose this evil. This includes some famous progressive theologians like Reinhold Niebuhr.[28] They instead maintained silence in the face of brutality, tacitly supporting the color line and its accompanying racial violence.

Collectively, Tisby points out, many white Christians' silence about the terror of lynching suggests that the white-supremacist, nationalistic Christianity fomented by the KKK, intent on excluding anyone who was not Protestant, white, and a natural-born citizen, was more mainstream than we would like to believe. The KKK was intent on defending a white, Christian America through terror and violence. Do a simple Google Images search for "KKK Jesus Saves." While some white Christians might have blanched at the methods used by the KKK, for many, such a vision of the nation sounded good, even if they did not personally participate in or promote such methods.

Many white Christians also directly opposed desegregation. Looking back, some of us believe white Christians did so *despite* their Christian beliefs. We like to believe they were somehow repressing or ignoring or misreading their Bibles in order to maintain their segregationist beliefs. In other words, their misdeeds were a result of a failure to live out their Christian convictions. However, the historical record is clear: white Christians opposed desegregation *because* of their Christian convictions.[29] Famous preachers like W. A. Criswell demanded that all ministers oppose federally mandated desegregation efforts "because it is a denial of ALL that we believe in."[30] Bob Jones believed efforts to outlaw segregation central to the civil rights movement were "endeavoring to disturb God's established order." In an Easter message, he claimed, "This disturbing movement is not of God. It is not in line with the Bible. It is Satanic. Now, listen and understand this. Do not let people lead you astray."[31] At a meeting of fellow ministers with President John F. Kennedy to discuss the need for a civil rights law, one Florida preacher stood up and addressed the president directly, stating as fact that many white Christians "held a 'strong moral conviction' that 'racial integration . . . is against the will of their Creator.'"[32]

Christian opposition to desegregation and full inclusion of Black Americans into civic life was not limited to the South. For instance, Christian churches, Catholic parishes, as well as Christian colleges, universities, and seminaries—in both the North and the South—supported racially discriminatory housing practices like redlining and restrictive community covenants that forbade homeowners from selling to Black buyers. Clergy even went door-to-door to collect signatures in support of maintaining residential segregation based on race.[33]

White Christians also played a pivotal role in the "law and order" and "tough on crime" politics that dominated the second half of the twentieth century. Repeatedly, Christians supported more punitive practices, pushing for harsher sentencing, policing, and prosecution. The US criminal justice system, however, disproportionately touches and subsequently harms racial minorities, especially Black Americans. Stigma related to having a criminal record dramatically limits access to jobs, housing, health care, and participation in civil society.[34] This language about "law and order" finds its roots in the horrific practices of racial terrorism and lynching.

This legacy of racism is one of the original sins of the United States, and American Christianity was complicit in it. White Christian nationalism played and continues to play an integral role in the perpetuation of racism throughout our society. As we have seen, recent scholarship clearly demonstrates this ongoing connection.

What has this legacy of white Christian nationalism and racism wrought? Consider the systemic inequalities Black Americans, Native Americans, and other racial and ethnic minority groups face in the United States:

- The net worth of a typical white family is close to ten times greater than that of a typical Black family. This gap has increased since 2000.

- Native Americans have the highest poverty rate among all minority groups (24.9 percent), closely followed by Black Americans (23 percent) and Hispanic Americans (19.6 percent). The poverty rate for white Americans, however, is 9.6 percent.
- Native and Black American unemployment rates in 2018 were 6.6 percent and 6.5 percent, respectively. White Americans' unemployment rate was 3.5 percent.
- The 2019 US Census estimates show 15.0 percent of Native Americans and 21.6 percent of Black Americans have a bachelor's degree or higher. Around twice as many White Americans (35.8 percent) can say the same.
- The 2019 American Community Survey estimates show just under 6 percent of white Americans do not have health insurance. Over 10 percent of Black Americans and over 19 percent of Native Americans are uninsured.
- The 2021 American Community Survey estimates show only 44 percent of Black Americans and 51 percent of Native Americans own their homes, compared to 74 percent of white Americans.
- In 2018, the prison incarceration rate for Black men is almost six times the rate for white men. The rate for Hispanic men is over two and a half times the rate for white men.[35]

How can we read these statistics and in good faith disagree with the claim that racial and ethnic minorities face a distinctly different set of hurdles than do white Americans?

These differences do not just happen by chance. They are the result of decades and even centuries of limiting minority racial and ethnic groups access to social and cultural opportunities in the United States. Throughout that time, white Christian nationalism played an integral role in creating and sustaining the policies and ideologies that produce widespread racial inequalities in the United States.

However, despite the evidence demonstrating pervasive racial terror and enduring structural inequality in the United States, there are significant gaps in white Christians' acknowledgment of these realities compared to racial and ethnic minorities. The legacy of this inequality lives on today in the form of forgetting or outright ignorance.

In 2020, when the country was grappling with the murder of George Floyd at the hands of police officer Derek Chauvin, the Public Religion Research Institute polled Americans, asking if recent killings of Black men were isolated incidents. Seventy-two percent of white evangelical Protestants agreed that the recent killings were isolated incidents.[36] Compare this to 30 percent of white religiously unaffiliated Americans who said the same. Again, this is despite evidence from the Bureau of Justice Statistics showing that people of color, and particularly Black Americans, are much more likely to experience the use of force when they come into contact with police.[37]

These same patterns hold when white evangelicals are asked if discrimination against whites is as problematic as discrimination against Black Americans. Compared to the unaffiliated, white evangelicals are more likely to believe that discrimination against whites is an equally large problem. White evangelicals are more likely to disagree that generations of slavery and discrimination have held Black Americans back from achieving equality. In addition, white evangelicals are more likely to agree that the Confederate flag or Confederate monuments are symbols of Southern pride rather than monuments to racism.

Taken together, the legacy of white Christians upholding white supremacy and the current manifestations of white Christian ignorance about racial inequality lead researcher Robert P. Jones to succinctly state, "American Christianity's theological core has been thoroughly structured by an interest in protecting white supremacy."[38] It is this desire for supremacy, this pining for self-interested power and privilege, that betrayed the gospel with an expression of the Christian faith in service of evil ends. To make a nation and a people, racism was baptized in Christian waters.

As Ida B. Wells, the person most responsible for making white Americans face the horrors of lynching, asked, "Why is mob murder permitted by a Christian nation? The nation cannot profess Christianity which makes the golden rule its foundation stone, and continue to deny equal opportunity for life, liberty and the pursuit of happiness to the black race."[39]

Now, some may say, Christians did not *have* to embrace racism throughout history. Some expressions of Christianity avoided and even confronted racism! Yes, this is true. Those expressions of Christianity did and still do exist, and in white communities as well. While most white Christians throughout US history either actively embraced racism or failed to confront it, there were white Christians who did do this necessary and difficult work.

This brings me to a key finding of our work on Christian nationalism: white Christians who reject or resist Christian nationalism are much less likely to embrace racist attitudes and beliefs. This suggests that embracing Christianity does not always result in more racist attitudes. The key is whether we actively embrace white Christian nationalism.

White Christian nationalism is not primarily a theological category but a cultural framework intent on privileging a conservative ethno-cultural and political orientation—one draped in religious rhetoric. A key element of this conservative ethno-cultural and political orientation is demanding strict ethno-racial boundaries around who is considered truly American. National membership, full participation in civic life, and social belonging are predicated on whether someone is "like us," which, again, stands for white folks.

A common response to this growing collection of evidence is that "correlation doesn't equal causation." Most often this claim is an attempt to say that just because Christian nationalism and racist attitudes and beliefs are strongly linked, one does not necessarily cause the other. This is true—many of these studies cannot (and do not) say that Christian nationalism "causes" one to be racist. However, what these studies *do* show is that Christian nationalism and racist attitudes are irrevocably linked, even when we account for an assortment of other possible explanations (political attitudes or sociodemographic measures like age, racial identification, or gender).

It does not matter whether Christian nationalism encourages us to become racist or whether those with racist beliefs are drawn toward Christian nationalism. What's clear is that if someone embodies one, they are much more likely to embody the other. Both possibilities are bad. Either way, given the connection between Christian nationalism and racism, we should think critically about whether we should be advocating for Christian nationalism.

Does Christianity Have Anything to Offer Regarding Racial Injustice?

White Americans have long used Christian theology to perpetuate racism in service of hoarding power and fomenting fear.[40] This raises a question for white Christians today: How could self-identified Christians create and sustain social systems that upheld white supremacy? For James Cone, the answer is simple: "Self-interest and power corrupted their understanding of the Christian gospel."[41]

This thirst for self-interested power is fundamental to Christian nationalism. The desire to maintain power and privilege required our ancestors to do whatever was necessary to keep themselves on top economically, whether it was benefiting from slavery, stealing Indigenous lands, endorsing segregation, or ignoring pleas from Black Americans for equality. This fact led Robert Jones to ask if Christian theology and practice as they developed in North

America and the United States are corrupt to their core by the stain of racism and white supremacy.[42] As he powerfully argues in the book *White Too Long*, white Christianity and its assorted theologies and moral claims have functioned to blind white American Christians to the suffering of Black Americans. These theologies and moral claims silently and invisibly protect the social, cultural, and economic privileges white American Christians enjoy. My experiences growing up in white evangelicalism attest to this.

I advocated and voted for systemic pro-life policies intent on protecting the lives of the unborn while never deeply considering similarly systemic policies intent on improving the lives of those already born. I was completely ignorant of the ongoing effects of America's history of racial discrimination in housing, education, criminal justice, and health care. My actions implicitly supported the idea that the United States was indeed a meritocracy where all could create a better life for themselves—and God would bless them—if they would only try hard enough. Therefore, the blessings I and those like me enjoyed were due to God's good grace that allowed our hard work to bear fruit. If other groups faced a crisis, it was likely due to several issues, including a lack of hard work, which God would never commend. We could try to help them, but ultimately it was up to them to do what was necessary. The system was not to blame.

Can Christianity—complicit in the maintenance of white supremacy for centuries now—offer us anything of use regarding racial injustice? Here again Cone provides an answer. Speaking specifically about the horrors of lynching, but applicable beyond, he shares that while the cross allowed him to make sense of the brutal history of lynching in the United States, the lynching tree also helped him understand much more deeply the "tragic meaning" of the cross.

The terror experienced by Black Americans over the centuries through slavery, Jim Crow, and lynching mirrors the terror experienced by Jesus. Both Jesus and African Americans were victims of mob hysteria and violence at the hands of Romans or white Americans. The central paradox of the Christian story, Cone tells us, is a crucified Savior—one who dies to rescue a suffering humanity. According to Cone, the entirety of the gospel—Jesus's life, death, and teachings—brings to life "God's protest against the exploitation of the weak by the strong."[43] Kat Armas argues similarly when she asserts that God sides with the marginalized, stands in opposition to the power of empire and its quest to destroy the frail, and "is for the liberation of those on the margins."[44]

What does Christianity have to offer us given this legacy of white supremacy and the denial of Black humanity? It is worth quoting Cone in full:

> It was not easy for blacks to find a language to talk about Christianity publicly because the Jesus they embraced was also, at least in name, embraced by whites who lynched black people. Indeed, it was white slaveholders, segregationists, and lynchers who defined the content of the Christian gospel. They wrote hundreds of books about Christianity, founded seminaries to train scholars and preachers, and thereby controlled nearly two thousand years of Christian tradition. Cut off from their African religious traditions, black slaves were left trying to carve out a religious meaning for their lives with white Christianity as the only resource to work with. They ignored white theology, which did not affirm their humanity, and went straight to stories in the Bible, interpreting them as stories of God siding with little people just like them. They identified God's liberation of the poor as the central message of the Bible.[45]

Echoing Cone, Tisby shows us that Christianity can be a part of rectifying that sordid and evil past. In his book *How to Fight Racism*, he writes, "Christianity must be a part of the conversation about racial justice because, in the context of the United States, white Christians often have been the ones responsible for racial injustice." Tisby goes further, however. Christianity, he claims, can also show us *why* racial justice is important and provide the "moral and spiritual resources to rebel against racism and white supremacy."[46]

Beyond the narrative of God siding with the oppressed, Tisby explains how the doctrine that all humans bear the image and likeness of God is another resource that Christianity provides. Every single person is an image-bearer, displaying particular characteristics of and similarities with God. All are created to exercise dominion and stewardship.[47] Because all humans equally share this character, they therefore "possess incalculable and inviolable value."[48]

The centuries-long history of colonialism and racism—race-based chattel slavery, the Doctrine of Discovery, the horrors of lynching, Jim Crow, mass incarceration, and the "war on drugs"—stands in opposition to the Christian doctrine that all humans bear the image of God, are created for stewardship, and are equally valuable. The reality that Christians used their religion to support each of these travesties can signal to us how careful we must be as we look to live out our faith in the public sphere.

Growing up, I heard "there but for the grace of God go I" repeatedly in church. We applied this phrase individually, thinking about only our own personal sins. Perhaps we Christians today should use this phrase in relation to our history, recognizing how white Christians—like us—repeatedly denied the God-given value of others in service of gaining and maintaining economic and political power. Repeatedly, our desire to make and defend our "Christian" nation has led us to embrace politics that deny the basic humanity of both our fellow citizens and our brothers and sisters of different nationalities, races, and religions from throughout the world.

White Christians can begin to acknowledge the harm Christianity played in creating and sustaining racism. We can begin to interrogate the legacy of various Christian theologies commonly highlighted as ways to solve racism—such as individual heart changes, reconciled relationships, and appeals to colorblindness—as "tools fashioned and utilized by their segregationist forebears precisely to avoid the racial justice" we now seek.[49] We can follow the lead of Christians who have gone before and drawn on their faith in the fight for racial justice. We can imitate those who reckon with their own religious journeys and consider how race has shaped our experiences of the Christian faith. As Cone teaches us, "Until we can see the cross and the lynching tree together, until we can identify Christ with a 'recrucified' black body hanging from a lynching tree, there can be no genuine understanding of Christian identity in America, and no deliverance from the brutal legacy of slavery and white supremacy."[50]

One way to begin to dismantle the distorted theologies and politics of race that white Christian nationalism handed us is to read, follow, and listen to our Black brothers and sisters. For centuries, they have been busy charting a way forward for Christians in the United States. Sociologist and social critic W. E. B. Du Bois wrote of the Black church that "there has run in the heart of black folk the greatest of human achievements, love and sympathy, even for their enemies, for those who despised them and hurt them and did them nameless ill. . . . They have been good and true and pitiful to the bad and false and pitiless, and in this lies the real grandeur of their simple religion, the mightiest gift of black to white America."[51] They help us imagine and explore theologies unencumbered by the weight of white Christian nationalism that do not idolize self-interested power, violence, and fear. We can begin to listen to them and allow them to take the lead. As Tisby said on an NPR podcast, "We need to widen the aperture of Christianity. The entire story is not white Christians or Christian nationalists. The Black church has always seen a connection of faith and politics, but to achieve much different ends."[52]

A number of resources can help white Christians take definitive steps toward confronting and opposing the racial injustice perpetuated by white Christian nationalism and dismantling its distorted theology. I have already cited several books throughout this chapter. Read those histories and theological reflections.

In *How to Fight Racism*, Tisby guides us through a three-part process of Awareness, Relationships, and Commitment, the ARC of racial justice. The ARC asks us to continue to educate ourselves, commit to creating diverse communities and social networks, and leverage our political and social capital in service to racial justice.

In their book *Faithful Antiracism*, Christina Edmondson and Chad Brennan clearly and concisely outline how Christians can draw on their faith tradition to confront and oppose systemic racism.[53] They provide concrete and reproducible action steps drawing from both Scripture and the wisdom of Christians in the past. Edmondson and Brennan help readers think through how their congregations or organizations can actively work toward and effectively measure racial progress.

To confront and oppose white Christian nationalism, we will need to proactively push resources and decision-making power in different directions. We can make numerous changes—changes to what we preach, how we preach, where we spend money, where we go for theological training, and the books we assign or quote or stock in the congregational bookstore.

It will take a concerted effort in our individual choices and especially at the organizational level. This is a key insight from the field of sociology. Organizations are not merely accumulations of the people making up that organization. Rather, organizations—our congregations, denominations, seminaries, and colleges—operate according to logics and rules that continue without needing the ongoing explicit support of the people living and working within them. They are "racialized organizations" that can perpetuate inequality by influencing how various resources are distributed, the ideas (like Christian nationalism) that people use to make sense of their social worlds, and the structure of relationships among people, like creating physical distance between racial groups by moving congregations to whiter neighborhoods.[54]

Think of it like compounding interest on your retirement savings. At first you diligently save money. Small amounts of interest are added over time, but for the first decade or so, most of the money in the account is what you put in. However, over time you begin to earn more and more interest until one day the scales tip and what you are putting in pales in comparison to the interest earned on the account. In a similar way, many of our congregations, seminaries, and other organizations were formed and guided by Christians who made decisions to accommodate Christian nationalism. They privileged the myths, narratives, and value systems of white Christian nationalism day after day, year after year. After decades of deposits, the compounding interest is now doing much of the work.

There is no single response that organizations can make to move away from continuing to encourage white Christian nationalism. There are no silver bullets. Merely changing the leader or pastor, or the views of some of the congregants or members, or even the mission statement will not be enough to turn the tide. In order for white Christianity to begin to embrace other expressions of Christianity in opposition to white Christian nationalism, our organizations and congregations will need to consider how to leverage their power and privilege in their communities and in the public sphere.

What are some steps white Christian organizations can take to abdicate some of the power and economic privilege they have accumulated over the decades because of white Christian nationalism?

First, they can recognize that the individual wealth gaps so apparent across racial and ethnic groups in the United States obviously influence the wealth and income gaps present at the organizational level. For instance, Black businesses, Black congregations, and Black colleges, universities, and seminaries are dramatically underfunded compared to majority-white businesses, congregations, and schools. The historic differences in wealth due to legal discrimination will not disappear just because the people populating the white congregations or denominations are now rejecters of Christian nationalism.

White Christian denominations, schools, and congregations—especially those with more than several hundred members or congregants—can commit to consistently giving away portions of their wealth to minority denominations, schools, and congregations. Confronting the idols of power, fear, and violence of Christian nationalism necessitates reckoning with historic economic racial inequalities. Shalom Community Church's project called A Reparative Act is one such example.[55]

During the civil rights movement, John Powell and others urged the Mennonite denomination to create a fund to serve urban poor and minorities. The denomination committed to raise millions of dollars to give away but ultimately raised $160,000 and failed to follow through. Decades later, the folks at Shalom wanted to learn from this history.[56] After reading Jennifer Harvey's *Dear White Christians*, they recognized that institutions oftentimes delay taking action around justice. They also realized they must work toward racial justice but in ways over which they (white Christians) were not in control.

I talked with Trevor Bechtel, who was in a book club at Shalom where some of the conversations around A Reparative Act began.[57] After the murder of George Floyd, the church's anti-racism work took on a new urgency. Learning from the Mennonite denominational failure from the 1960s and Harvey's book, Shalom knew that relinquishing control, alongside acting immediately, was vital to the reparative work. Remembering the tendency of white congregations to delay action, Trevor shared in this moment, "There's got to be a time where Christians act first and don't think about it."

To act now and relinquish control, Shalom decided to bypass denominational approval and to gather money and pass it on. Trevor shared how, in conversations with another Mennonite congregation interested in Shalom's reparative act, the questions surrounding where and how the money would be spent came fast and hard. While such questions may seem well-intentioned, the urge to require reporting or to offer thoughts on how monetary gifts like this are spent is really an effort to exert control. In this reparative act, a first step in this congregation's journey, it was important for them as white Christians to give their money and give up control.

Shalom collected monetary gifts for one year, which they turned over to a disbursement committee chaired by Powell and other Black religious and community leaders—no strings attached and with no expectations of reports on exactly when and how it was disbursed. Trevor shared how this process reoriented him as he considered racial inequality, poverty, and white Christianity. "The joy of giving up control and learning what that feels like has been useful to me in my own daily life," he said, as he strives to live out the gospel and love and serve those marginalized in our culture.

What if white Christian congregations and other organizations freely donated funds without a word or inquiry into how it will be used? The Scriptures teach us that where our treasure is our hearts will be also. Might this be true at the organizational level as well as the individual? What if more congregations shared their wealth with congregations who never had a fair chance on account of our history of discrimination in the United States? What if majority-white Christian churches sacrificed the opportunity to expand their size and influence and instead invested their wealth in other community and religious organizations?

Second, charity and giving will not be enough. In fact, these can sometimes serve to *perpetuate* the color line.[58] Social contact that fosters engagement and interaction and learning is equally important. Majority-white congregations and organizations will need to develop true bonds of relationship. Some congregations are already doing this work.[59]

Third, these same organizations can advocate for redressing racial inequalities in health, wealth, and educational opportunity at the state and federal levels through various social policies. The scale of the problem is too large for religious Americans or their congregations and organizations to redress. This is a key way Christians and their congregations can side with the marginalized. Vote for policies and support politicians committed to this work

Fourth, faith communities can commit to consistently and firmly opposing white Christian nationalism in their programming and built environment. We can broaden our gazes to include expressions of Christianity from racial and ethnic minorities or Christian brothers and sisters from outside the United States. By listening to these voices, we can gain perspective on our particular cultural expression of Christianity. We can then cultivate faith expressions that are less triumphalist or focused on domination and control and that focus instead on love and liberation for the historically oppressed.

During the protests over the murder of George Floyd by a white police officer, Franklin Graham was asked if evangelicalism has a "race problem." Graham said, "No." He went on to say, "When we get to heaven, a white-skinned person like myself is going to probably be in the minority, but we're going to be there to worship the king of kings and our skin color is just so many cells thick."[60] Graham's remarks echoed those of his father. During the civil rights movement, when asked about addressing the country's racial inequalities, Billy Graham said, "Only when Christ comes again will little white children of Alabama walk hand in hand with little black children."[61] Turning conversations from this life to the next is common among white Christians faced with uncomfortable racial and social realities. Rather than confront and rectify racial inequality here on earth, both Billy Graham and Franklin Graham pointed to the life to come, where one group will not be lifted above another.

Growing up in white Christian spaces, I heard and employed this same rhetorical practice. Because we (white Christians) largely benefit from the status quo, we do not look too hard at why we benefit. Chalk it up to God's blessing. Point toward the hope that is to come in heaven, where all will be made right.[62] Our gospel is one focused on personal spiritual realities. It misses the practical aspect where justice for the oppressed is realized in the here and now.

As Danté Stewart points out, Christians must "dismantle a world where we believe God wants black people to enjoy the best things in heaven while white people enjoy the best things on earth." White Christians do not have to settle for a world where we ignore the needs of those around us in the present by pointing those who are suffering toward a hope of God's "perfect" blessings in the future.[63]

Seeking to make the United States a Christian nation has for centuries been tied with creating and maintaining social systems that benefit white Americans and disproportionately harm Black and Native Americans. The current systems in place within white American Christianity will continue to produce what they were designed to produce. And by their fruit we can see that they are producing and reproducing white supremacy and racial inequality. White Christian nationalism's quest for power, motivated by fear and enacted through violence, perpetuates these racial inequalities.

Christians today have only one choice: to no longer merely stand still and be carried along by the same historical currents that sustain racial inequality. Instead, we can choose to actively push against the currents carrying us along.

Perhaps we can start this journey by resisting the idea that only certain issues are "moral" issues. We can repent when we fail to organize a collective response to racial inequality while we rally institutional and organizational responses toward other social ills.

These were some of the first dominoes to fall as I began to reckon with the legacy of white Christian nationalism in my life. We can expand our imaginations such that the gospel we embrace includes not only individual salvation but also abundant life for all around us (John 10:10). This should include economic and racial equality. We can embrace the gospel of Jesus that realigns the power structures of society that crush those on the margins, a gospel that disrupts systems of oppression and their destructive effects on human relationships. We can embrace the gospel that Jesus came so we *all* might have life abundant.

I hope for the day when American Christians advocate just as vehemently for racial reforms to the housing, education, poverty, health care, and criminal justice systems as we have for the sanctity of life for the unborn.

Many white Christians, like me growing up, seem to forget that Jesus taught his followers to pray for God's kingdom to come *on earth as it is in heaven*. It is not enough to believe that all God's children will be equal in heaven. Perhaps we should take Jesus's prayer seriously and participate in the ongoing work of reflecting God's kingdom—a racially and economically just kingdom—here on earth.

Not just in the future. Today.

AND WHO IS MY NEIGHBOR?

If you want to come in you need to honor God, you need
to honor our flag, and you need to learn to speak English.

—Charles Herbster[1]

GOING ON A SHORT-TERM MISSION TRIP to another
country is a rite of passage for many young evangelicals.
The youth group I attended sent teams of teenagers out
every summer. We took the Great Commission seriously. We felt
called to take our faith to all nations.

I went on two such mission trips during high school, both to
Peru—Lima, the capital, my first time, and later to a village in the
mountains. These trips were exciting for kids like me from small,
rural communities surrounded by cornfields. We were able to see
a different part of the world and invest in what we believed was
God's work in those nations.

My second time in Peru, I experienced some sort of allergic re-
action. Huge blisters appeared on the soles of my feet, relegating

159

me to bed for a day. We also had to navigate an agricultural strike on that trip, leaving our bus and belongings and walking through checkpoints to get back to Lima to catch our flight home. I likely experienced more excitement during those couple of weeks than I did most years in northern Indiana.

We prepared for a couple of months leading up to each trip. Learning short skits set to music with no speaking to overcome the language barrier. Memorizing Scripture. Creating all sorts of crafts and games for the local children. Sending out support letters to our friends and family, asking them to send money to pay for our plane tickets and lodging.

While there, we would usually spend part of the day going door-to-door, asking folks, through an interpreter, if they knew where they would spend eternity when they died. We would hold a Vacation Bible School for the children. At an evening service, we performed our skits. On the first trip we performed a service project too, helping to pour concrete for a new building. We desperately wanted to be the hands and feet of Jesus.

I saw myself as a conduit for the goodness of God to the people of Peru. I felt as though I was sacrificing a week or so of my summer to bless those who were less fortunate. I had the secret of the gospel, and I was desperate to share it with them. I wanted to let my light shine.

I am grateful for the opportunities these two short-term mission trips provided. I was exposed to another part of the world. I was able to gain firsthand experience of another culture and diverse expressions of the Christian faith. Only through being there could I come to realize our many similarities. Such trips can be transformative for religious young people. One nationally representative survey of young people showed that taking a short-term mission trip increased the likelihood of young people engaging in different forms of civic activity, though mainly religious.[2] For many young Christians like me, our earnest desire to go and serve was due to a literal reading of the Great Commission.

While good can come from short-term trips, oftentimes the outcomes are mixed; in some cases, they harm. Short-term missions can veer into a paternalistic posture, one result of a culture that sees itself as a special fulfillment of God's design for the world: as American Christians, we are blessed by God to be a blessing; it is our duty to share what we know and enjoy with the world.

Looking back, I now wrestle with how, for much of our visit, those we were supposed to be serving were doing so much more to serve us. Our hosts were planning and preparing meals, feeding us and cleaning up after us, finding activities for us, and coordinating portions of our time and travel. The Christians we interacted with in Peru were incredibly hospitable, constantly thinking of what we might like to do, see, or experience, and making room in their lives for us to take up space—and we took up so much space.

I am not the first to question the motives and utility of short-term mission trips or of the historical record of colonialism intertwined with white Christian missions. There are plenty who have produced incredible work helping us sort through the pitfalls and promises of short-term missions.

What stands out to me now, though, is how willing we are to sacrifice a bit of time and wealth to go to other people's communities and insert ourselves, how we feel called by God to take our religion and culture to them, with the understanding that, having been hospitably received, we will then leave. And I am struck by how opposed white Christians can be to showing similar levels of hospitality to fellow human beings from different countries—even fellow Christians—who make their way to our country.

When they come to our communities, we are much less willing to sacrifice our time, energy, and resources to serve them. We are much less willing to welcome them to share in what we have always believed are God's blessings on us. We seem to be much less willing to act on a literal reading of the Great Commandment as we are our literal reading of the Great Commission. The greatness of our Christian nation, it seems, is only for us. Not for them.

So while social science research shows that the consequences of short-term mission trips like those I took in high school are mixed, it is the posture American Christians take toward those coming to our shores that suggests white Christian nationalism is influencing us more than the Scriptures telling us to love the immigrant and stranger in our midst.

When I see how white Christian nationalism relates to opposition to immigrants and refugees, I wonder how we might respond to Jesus if he asked us about our love for our neighbors. I have the sense that we might echo the lawyer's reply to Jesus in the Gospel of Luke, seeking to justify ourselves in the face of our inaction: "And who is my neighbor?" (10:29).

Christian Fear of Immigrants and Refugees

Fear of immigrants and refugees has a long and sordid history in North America. Many Christians placed themselves squarely against any group they viewed as a threat to a white, Christian America. In the discussion of fear in chapter 4, I discussed how, from the earliest colonists to the present day, religious rhetoric intertwined with nativist impulses, motivating white Christian Americans to fear and oppose any group they felt might pose a threat to the United States' "Christian" foundations.

Again, Christian nationalism focuses on gaining and protecting political and cultural power. This translates to opposing immigrants and refugees through a variety of means. The language (cultural power) Christians use and the political policies (political power) they support are two of the most frequent avenues of resistance to loving and welcoming immigrants and refugees.

Let us begin with language. Many Americans—and many Christians as well—routinely associate immigrants and immigration with lawbreaking. One way this happens is through the labels we use. Calling undocumented immigrants *illegal* immigrants suggests an inherent criminality; only through physically leaving our nation would such immigrants cease to be criminals in our eyes. However, undocumented presence in the United States is a civil, not criminal, offense.[3]

As many others have pointed out, criminalizing undocumented presence is ironic given that the ancestors of white Americans were originally immigrants to the shores of North America. Just because some of us have been here longer than more recent immigrants makes this no less true. This reality escapes us, however, and we continue to consider ourselves "true Americans" who have a God-given right not only to reside here but also to limit who else can move to these shores.

Language suffused with worries and fears from Christian leaders, broadcast through their various media outlets, serves to encourage opposition toward immigrants and refugees. For instance, in an article in *Decision* magazine—the official publication of the Billy Graham Evangelistic Association—a writer criticizes the progressive politics of the state of California. After claiming that "secularism and hostility toward Christian values seems to be at an all-time high," she pivots to criticizing sanctuary laws, alleging they "limit police cooperation with federal immigration authorities and often prevent prosecution of crimes committed by illegal immigrants."[4]

The writer elevates fear of immigrants to a chief concern of Christians nationwide, particularly focusing on the assumed criminal tendencies of immigrants. Remember from the earlier discussion on fear how there is no empirical support for such a view. She considers not being able to sufficiently control and prosecute this population a threat to a biblical worldview. This is astounding. Where Jesus calls Christians to serve and sacrifice for those in need, the writer argues that being unable to prosecute those in need is the real threat. This is a betrayal of the gospel.

James Dobson's newsletter about the state of the US border in the summer of 2019—reaching millions of his subscribers—provides another troubling illustration.[5] Dobson alternates between assuring his readers of his concern for those detained at the border and calling them "aliens," "illegals," "hardened criminals," and "drug runners." At times he places "refugees" in quotes, signaling a dissatisfaction with the term. Apparently, "refugees" does not paint these human beings—who Christianity teaches are made in the image of God—in a sufficiently negative light.

Let me reiterate the sentiment provided earlier about what Dobson believes is at stake: "Millions of illegal immigrants will continue flooding to this great land from around the world. Many of them have no marketable skills. They are illiterate and unhealthy. Some are violent criminals. Their numbers will soon overwhelm the culture as we have known it, and it could bankrupt the nation."[6] In his view, immigrants and refugees are a dire threat to the nation, both physically and culturally.

We should be troubled by how these assumed deficiencies of immigrants do not move Dobson and our fellow Christians to action informed by empathy. The deficits Dobson claims immigrants face do not encourage him to consider how we might help meet their needs. There is no mention of how we might mobilize to house, train, educate, or provide health care. Dobson is also ignorant of the fact that immigrants, regardless of status, "contribute approximately $80,000 more in taxes than government services used over their lifetime."[7] Rather, he is concerned with protecting what he views as most important: the nation and its "Christian" culture. And the only way to protect them is to foment fear in order to garner support for detaining and deporting immigrants.

It is safe to assume that messages like these from Dobson and *Decision* magazine are both reflecting and shaping their target audience. In 2019, the Public Research Religion Institute found that the groups most likely to agree that immigrants "threaten traditional American customs and values" and are "invading our country and replacing our cultural and ethnic background" were white evangelical Protestants, white mainline Protestants, white Catholics, and other Christians.[8] Nonwhite and non-Christian groups were much less likely to agree with such statements.

A fundamental aspect of this discourse is predicated on fear. As we discussed previously, fear is integral to the tribal mentality of Christian nationalism—delineating an "us" versus "them." Again, the evidence suggests these fears are unfounded, but no matter. The demonization of entire groups works wonderfully to achieve a very specific outcome, providing a semblance of control and certainty while delineating who is part of the in-group and who is not.[9] One of the main functions of the cultural framework of Christian nationalism is to define the boundaries of who "we" are and who "they" are to ensure a strong in-group identity.

Dehumanizing language and negative discourse surrounding immigrants and refugees translate to policy agendas supported by many white Christians. Charles Herbster, who ran for governor in Nebraska in 2022, explicitly declared, "If you want to come in you need to honor God, you need to honor our flag, and you need to learn to speak English."[10] Herbster's stance earned Trump's endorsement, and these policy goals reflect the stances of many white Christians nationwide. In national polling, white Christians are more supportive of restrictive immigration policies than any other group.[11]

For instance, white Christians are more likely than any other religious group to agree that all immigrants living in the United States without proper documentation should be deported. White evangelicals and white Catholics are the least likely to agree that undocumented immigrants or any children brought to the United States without proper documentation should be given a path to legal citizenship. White Christians are also more likely to support family separation policies at the US border.

Sadly, white evangelicals were the only religious group in which a majority (55 percent) supported passing a law that prevents all refugees from entering the United States. Not just some. *All* refugees. Only slim majorities of white mainline Protestants (59 percent) and white Catholics (56 percent) opposed the idea of such a policy.

Why are white American Christians so uniformly opposed to immigrants and refugees fleeing persecution and violence and seeking a better future in the United States? Study after study identifies white Christian nationalism as the cultural framework fostering much of the antipathy American Christians report toward immigrants and refugees.

Christian Nationalism and Xenophobia

Americans who embrace Christian nationalism consistently hold more xenophobic views. Those who believe the United States must be distinctively Christian see immigrants and refugees as a threat to our national identity.

Christian nationalism distinguishes between "desirable" immigrants, generally white and from western European countries, and "undesirable" immigrants, anyone from countries assumed to be non-Christian or nonwhite.[12] Americans who embrace Christian nationalism suppose that immigrants and refugees are likely bringing with them non-Christian or nonreligious sensibilities, thereby undermining a Christian national identity.

A common talking point regarding why immigrants and refugees are a threat is how they will not accept "American culture." As an evangelical pastor claimed regarding a South Carolina bill to limit refugee resettlement in the state: "Adherents to the Muslim culture does [*sic*] not have any desire to assimilate to the United States, and refugees want to take advantage of the country, not take part in the culture."[13] In his mind, one must be Christian in order to properly "assimilate."

Political commentator Dennis Prager espouses similar views. He claimed that non-Christians coming to the United States and participating in public life might "undermine American civilization" because the Bible is "the only relevant religious text in the United States."[14] In Prager's opinion, taking part in the broader culture of the United States requires assenting to Christianity and the cultural baggage that comes with it.

These views are not fringe. Almost half (42 percent) of Americans who believe either the United States has always been a Christian nation or was once a Christian nation but is not anymore—which together represent 80 percent of the population—believe that immigrants are a threat to "traditional American customs and values." These same Americans are also much more likely to see immigrants as "invaders" who will replace "our cultural and ethnic background" (40 percent).[15]

Across several other national surveys, Americans who strongly embrace the narrative that the United States has a covenantal relationship with God were much more likely to oppose the resettlement of Syrian refugees and support the "Muslim Ban" and border wall of then president Donald Trump. They were even more supportive of the controversial family separation policies implemented by the Department of Homeland Security in the fall of 2017.[16]

During the same public testimony heard during the bid to pass the South Carolina refugee resettlement bill, Americans who embraced white Christian nationalism also signaled that immigrants and refugees might pose a threat to their economic opportunities. Researchers Breanne Leigh Grace and Katie Heins highlight how white Christians emphasized that "refugees would also be 'welfare queens' or a 'drain on the American welfare system' while simultaneously claiming that this would be a burden to *us* 'good, hard-working Americans.'"[17]

As we've discussed, the national identity proffered by white Christian nationalism is one that tightly intertwines Christianity as the preferred religion and whiteness as the superior racial category. Included with this is the importance of being a natural-born citizen. White, Christian, American citizens redefine "refugee" and "immigrant" as referents for Black or Brown (nonwhite), Muslim, terrorist, and Third World. They juxtapose this redefinition with a preferred identity of white, Christian, and "civilized."[18]

Essentially, Christian nationalism focuses on preserving a particular culture over and above caring for or welcoming those who are not "from here." Embracing Christian nationalism is consistently associated with affirming a wide range of negative statements toward immigrants and refugees, which include the following:

- Immigrants are a burden.
- Immigrants make government services worse.
- Immigrants take (wanted) jobs away.
- Immigrants do not pay their fair share.
- Immigrants are less likely to adapt.
- Newcomers threaten traditional American values.
- Recent immigrants do not share my vision of American society.
- Immigrants increase crime in local communities.
- Refugees from the Middle East pose a terrorist threat to the United States.
- Immigration has increased the tax burdens on Americans.
- The values and beliefs of immigrants regarding moral and religious issues are not compatible with the beliefs and values of most Americans.[19]

White Christian nationalism routinely holds immigrants responsible for various societal troubles. Whether it comes to economic issues or terrorist threats, refugees and immigrants are easy targets for blame—and this even though refugees undergo screening from a handful of government agencies, including the

FBI, the Department of Defense, the Department of Homeland Security, and the State Department, and almost two-thirds are under the age of fourteen or women.

The COVID-19 pandemic provides another example of targeting refugees and immigrants for blame. White Christian nationalism is associated with support for immigration restrictions to protect Americans from the virus, believing our "lax immigration laws are partly to blame for the COVID-19 crisis," and supporting building a wall on our southern border to protect us from future pandemics.[20]

The anti-immigrant and anti-refugee views of Americans who embrace Christian nationalism bleed over into distrust and fear of religious minorities. Various scholars find that white Christian nationalism and nativism lead to a desire to restrict the civil rights of Muslims in the United States. In fact, believing America is a Christian nation is equally strongly related to anti-immigrant attitudes (believing immigrants commit more crime and immigrants bring diseases) and Islamophobia (believing Muslims are more likely to be terrorists and Muslims hold anti-American values; being uncomfortable with a mosque in your neighborhood).[21] White Christian nationalism encourages a fear of Muslims as a threat to our bodies, our culture, and our values.[22] For many, "Muslim" is merely another word for "terrorist," someone hell-bent on inflicting incalculable harm on innocent, white Americans.

Some politicians and commentators claim that religious minorities are "infiltrating" the United States through immigration and refugee resettlement. In 2006, Representative Virgil Goode (R-VA) claimed their goal is to "mold the United States into the image of their religion, rather than working within the Judeo-Christian principles" that founded our country.[23] In an almost unbelievable quote, one man speaking during public testimony in support of the 2016 South Carolina anti-refugee resettlement bill—which became a model for eighty-six other proposed anti-refugee bills—claimed that allowing refugee resettlement "would destroy our children and subject our females to be raped, and our males to be slaughtered, and our Christian beliefs to be totally annihilated."[24] It is important to pay attention to whom this man is referring to as "our." For him, refugees—whom he likely conceptualizes as non-white and non-Christian—fall outside the boundaries of American national identity. There is no way they are included in his "our."

The influence of white Christian nationalism is so strong that it even predisposes American Christians to resist immigrants and refugees who share the same religious identity. This is "because immigrant newcomers' religious identities are only part of a broader national narrative positing that moral and religious values—defined by White Christian Protestantism—make some groups assimilable to America's culture, whereas others are deemed fundamentally incompatible with what it means to be American."[25] White Christian nationalism prevents American Christians from accepting the immigrant and stranger even when they are fellow Christians and especially if they are not.

These findings are distressing. It is impossible to detect any ethic of love toward immigrants and refugees. It is all about protecting our power and privilege. It is a betrayal of the gospel. However, there is a silver lining of sorts. Knowing what the exact problem is allows us to be much more precise in our response. By consistently and firmly challenging the assumptions of white Christian nationalism and advocating for the care of all who come to our shores seeking relief, American Christians can effectively shift the trajectory of our nation and the view of our religious tradition toward immigrants and refugees.

Christian Love toward Immigrants and Refugees

White Christian nationalism advocates for tight boundaries around who can receive the benefits of living in the United States. Should American Christians welcome immigrants and refugees? Or are American Christians absolved of this responsibility?

In his 2021 book, *Christians against Christianity*, religion scholar Obery Hendricks Jr. provides example after example from the Bible of the importance of welcoming and caring for the immigrant and refugee. Caring for refugees and immigrants is actually "one of the Bible's highest ethics," and "refusing hospitality to immigrant strangers is among its major sins."[26]

Throughout the Old Testament (the only sacred scriptures Jesus of Nazareth would have known, as Hendricks reminds us), God signaled his concern for the immigrant and alien to his people. Hendricks translates God's declaration in Malachi 3:5 as follows: "I will be swift to bear witness . . . against those who thrust aside the immigrant, and do not fear me." Hendricks also draws from Deuteronomy 10:17–19, where God tells his people that he "loves the immigrants" and that they should "also love the immigrant, for you were immigrants in the land of Egypt."[27]

God taught his people that caring for immigrants is ethical and just. It had the added effect of serving as a reminder that the people of God were once in that same situation. As Leviticus 19:34 commands, "The foreigner residing among you must be treated as your native-born. Love them as yourself, for you were foreigners in Egypt. I am the Lord your God."

The Bible commands God's people not only to care for immigrants but also to take actionable steps to protect them. In Hendricks's translation of Exodus 23:12–13, we see God command the Israelites to "not exploit a hired worker who is poor and needy, whether that worker is a fellow Israelite or an immigrant residing in one of your towns." God commands the Israelites to provide an inheritance to the immigrants residing among them (Ezek. 47:22–23) and to include immigrants in their tithe to the Levites and the fatherless and the widow (Deut. 26:12).

The Bible also encourages Christians (in the New Testament) to consider themselves as "aliens" and "strangers" in this world. Jesus himself tells his listeners not to refuse service to anyone, especially those who seem like they are not "from here" (Matt.

25:44–46). Doing so, Hendricks points out, is evidence we are not one of his followers.

The irony, of course, is that so many Americans who embrace Christian nationalism read the Bible regularly (59 percent say weekly or more) and read the Bible literally (50 percent) or consider the Bible to be the inspired Word of God (39 percent). It seems, though, that white Christian nationalism does more to shape their response toward immigration and immigrants than reading the Bible does. They neglect the vital aspects of the gospel like loving your neighbor, seeking justice, and caring for orphans and widows.

Here Hendricks makes the connection between white Christian nationalism and the xenophobic tendencies of evangelicals, though his point applies to the broader white American Christian church. He speaks plainly: "It is difficult to reach any other conclusion, for the Bible's teachings on this subject are much too clear and straightforward to be misread. It seems much more likely that evangelicals *purposely* misinterpret the Bible in this way because it suits their white supremacist biases and Christian nationalist aspirations."[28]

We accept these misinterpretations because the nativism inherent to white Christian nationalism lies to us about our past—pining with nostalgia for a time when American culture was largely under the unquestioned and unchallenged control of white Christians—and encourages us to disregard the teachings of Jesus to welcome the stranger. It keeps us from fulfilling the call to love. The toxic stew of Christian nationalism and xenophobia subverts the heart of faith.[29]

For Hendricks and some American Christians, Scripture is clear about our responsibility to immigrants and refugees in our midst. This leads to the following questions: How do American Christians go about welcoming immigrants and refugees? How might we set aside our idols of power, fear, and violence to fulfill the Bible's teachings? How do we manifest this ethic of neighbor love in our neighborhoods and communities?

First, the modern-day issues surrounding immigration and the displacement of millions of people because of war, famine, and persecution are extremely complicated. There will be no easy and straightforward political answer. This is equally true for confronting power, fear, violence, and racial injustice. However, Americans should not forget that the United States bears some responsibility for many people's displacement. Our country's various military and economic quests have led us to pursue policies that impoverished and, in some cases, destroyed the native lands of those coming to our shores. Acknowledging our complicity in that history is vital, and it can lead us to take more seriously our responsibility to follow the commands to love and serve the immigrant and refugee among us.

Moreover, it is unreasonable to suggest that the Bible—written thousands of years ago by dozens of people with dramatically different audiences facing radically distinct social worlds—can give us *explicit* instructions on how to craft immigration policy for a country with over 330 million citizens. The Bible was not written for that purpose. This applies equally to those wanting to proof-text in support of "building a wall" or "open borders." Rather, the Bible clearly shows the *values* we should hold dear— neighbor love, welcoming the immigrant and stranger. Hendricks highlights these values above. How we end up living out these values depends on the situation at hand and happens in conversation with our neighbors, Christian or otherwise.

For this reason, theologian and ethicist Lee Camp argues that faithful Christian social engagement should be ad hoc. As he writes in his book *Scandalous Witness*, there is no ideologically pure social arrangement that one political party has sole rights to.[30] Christians must work out together, in conversation with those on the margins being crushed by the weight of social structures, what it means to create a more just and equitable world.

It deserves repeating: fulfilling an ethic of love must include listening to immigrants and refugees themselves. Most of us have not experienced what it is like to be forced to leave behind everything we know and love out of fear, threat, or despair and to move to an entirely new country. The stories of families who braved the journey to come to our shores and built new lives out of little or nothing—like those told by author and theologian Kat Armas in *Abuelita Faith*—can help us orient ourselves in a new direction. She writes how "thinking *with* the marginalized rather than thinking *about* them" is vital; "we listen not to consume, to take, or to appropriate but to hold sacred space, to learn, and to make room for the holy."[31] Here we might begin to recognize how limited our understanding is. We can begin to recognize and resist the temptation toward power, control, and domination in how we interact with and respond to the needs of the immigrant and refugee.

When we begin to listen to what our neighbors need and to recognize how systems and structures around them create unfair barriers, a clear path forward appears if we are committed to loving and serving our neighbor, as Jesus commanded. Walking this path will require we lay aside the idols of white Christian nationalism: power focused on benefiting our own; fear of losing that power to those outside our group; the violence necessary to assuage fear and protect power.

Solidarity with those on the margins brings the structural and systemic barriers into sharp relief. Confronting white Christian nationalism means we will be forced to take a side. As Jemar Tisby reminds us, justice takes sides.[32] Attempts to abstain from involvement signal we're operating from a place of privilege. Those being crushed under the weight of these systems do not have the option to opt out. Their very lives and livelihoods depend on navigating these barriers and surviving the systems.

I love how my friend Andrea Cramer puts it: "No relationship is apolitical." Andrea is the executive director of Neighbor to Neighbor, a nonprofit operating in northern Indiana focused on creating "mutual relationships among [the] immigrant and non-immigrant population, through meaningful friendships and community networking."[33]

Several years ago, a fifty-year-old woman from Lebanon asked Andrea to help her improve her English. Through this relationship, Andrea was able to consider the barriers that her friend and others in her community faced in their day-to-day lives. It was obvious language was a barrier. Transportation was another. Given how dependent American culture is on personal vehicles, so many recent immigrants and refugees lack the independence and freedom that come with a driver's license. Andrea's Lebanese friend asked if she would help her pass the Indiana driver's education test to earn her license. Only later did Andrea learn that her friend had taken and failed the driving test almost a dozen times already.

It soon became clear why Andrea's friend had struggled to pass this test. It was not because she did not have the innate ability or the desire to achieve. It was not because she did not put in the necessary work. What Andrea discovered was that while the *test* was offered in fourteen languages in Indiana, at that time the *manual* was offered only in English. Andrea's friend could take the driver's test in her native language, but she was prevented from studying for the test in her native language.

Andrea and her nonprofit could have spent hundreds of hours teaching each individual immigrant English so they could study the manual in preparation for their driver's test. Or they could choose to leverage their privilege and focus "upstream" to reduce or eliminate barriers for whole groups of people. Andrea and her colleagues decided to do the latter.

Partnering with the ACLU, Neighbor to Neighbor represented the immigrant communities throughout Indiana being denied equal access to driver's training materials. The Bureau of Motor Vehicles ultimately settled the lawsuit and translated the training manual into five additional languages, with a continual review of requests for new languages each year.

Being a neighbor means being in contact with folks, recognizing their needs, and then doing something to address those needs. "If I care and love them, then I can do something. Don't just say you care and then go about your life," Andrea told me.[34]

I was curious why Andrea started Neighbor to Neighbor. She shared how several experiences set her on this path. Years ago, she had relocated to central Texas with her husband and young child. Andrea quickly realized how different a place can feel, even if it is only another state in the same nation. She recalled how a fellow Midwesterner took the time to offer tips for navigating the local scene. Andrea felt seen and understood. It was the first time she was able to experience welcome.

Several years later, her oldest child saw a cover for *Time* magazine picturing refugee children and began asking questions. This forced Andrea to begin educating herself on what refugees faced when relocated to the United States. Her family began volunteering close to the Texas border with Mexico, placing themselves in proximity to newly arriving people. It was then she realized this was what she wanted to do—work with displaced people.

You see, Andrea grew up in the same community I did, attended the same church, and even went to Peru for short-term mission trips in high school like I did. For us, the heroes of the faith growing up were always missionaries who gave up everything to go to other nations. However, Andrea had a similar experience to mine. She began to sense that when the people in those same countries came to our shores, we Christians seemed to act as if we did not really want them. We were fine with limited interaction, as long as it was on our terms and the immigrants stayed "over there." We were intent on taking our culture and religion to them but not nearly as interested in the possibility of their presence reshaping our culture, communities, and religious experiences.

Andrea shared with me how the mission trips and Romans Road gospel tracts of our upbringing failed to fully embody the breadth and depth of what the gospel includes. She now embraces a fuller vision of the gospel. This vision acknowledges Jesus's claim in Luke 4 that he fulfills the promise in Isaiah, the promise of the Year of Jubilee: freedom from oppression, healing from sickness, freedom for the captives—essentially, a fundamental realignment of the power structures operating in society.

Leveraging your power to benefit the marginalized—being a neighbor as the Bible calls us to be and realizing that no friendship is apolitical—is a revolutionary act. It could mean voting for a political candidate who would enact policies that benefit a historically marginalized group more than your own. It might mean donating your time or money to organizations focused on ensuring that immigrants and refugees can live and work in peace rather than fear for their safety. Or, as in Andrea's case, it might mean collaborating with the ACLU to sue your state's Bureau of Motor Vehicles. We can begin to look for where and how we can listen and learn and then stand with those on the margins.

Instead of protecting power and privilege for our own benefit in a Christian nation, Christians can set such things aside to count ourselves among those being crushed. We can remember that the Savior we worship was a Middle Eastern man who lived as a religious minority and whose family members were once refugees. We can commit to listen to our friends' and neighbors' experiences and stand in solidarity with them. We can be there to learn, support, and serve. We can commit to taking a back seat in these interactions.

I believe Andrea and Neighbor to Neighbor illustrate the practice of empathy so clearly. They pay attention, embrace proximity, cultivate humility, and commit to sacrificing their power and privilege to ensure that those in need flourish in their community. Christians can find an alternative path that confronts the xenophobia and racism encouraged by white Christian nationalism. This can lead us to collaborate with anyone and everyone who shares these commitments of neighbor love and common flourishing, whether they are Christians or not.

With a commitment to empathy and to placing ourselves in situations of diversity, we can begin to train ourselves to respond not with fear and a sense of threat, grasping at power and privilege, but with a sense of "holy curiosity." We can begin to see the value and beauty in the diversity and difference surrounding us and how those we are told to fear can offer so much if we would only receive it.

With this attitude, we might begin to see with new eyes the true nature of our shared circumstances: a system placing us on one end of a continuum of affluence and power with immigrants and refugees on the other. While love might move us toward acts of charity, sometimes they are short-sighted or insufficient for addressing the roots of poverty, inequality, and, in this case, an unfair immigration and refugee asylum system. We can commit to looking upstream to break down the barriers that limit entire groups from participating in American culture and society.

Fear, hatred, and a lack of empathy toward immigrants and refugees are not faithful representations of the love of God. They are, however, faithful representations of the desire for power and privilege inherent to Christian nationalism.

This is not to say that American Christians who fear immigrants and demonize refugees are not "true" Christians; they most definitely are. All Christians, including those of us who oppose such actions, must own all the parts of our tradition, the good, bad, and ugly. We can, however, call those actions what they are—sin—and implore our fellow Christians to lay down the idol of their national identity and the comfort and power it promises. We can turn from our idols of power, fear, and violence. We can commit to viewing everyone—whether immigrant or refugee—as fellow travelers deserving of any privileges our American citizenship might provide.

Only then can we stop betraying and begin to fulfill the gospel command to love our neighbors. *All* our neighbors.

REMAKING AMERICAN
CHRISTIANITY

O VER YEARS OF ACADEMIC STUDY and personal faith
journey, I have become convinced that white Christian nationalism in the United States is fundamentally opposed to
the ethics and teachings of Jesus. Through idolizing power, fear,
and violence, white Christian nationalism betrays the gospel, in
which Jesus's sacrifice liberates us from our enslavement to sin *as
well as* the destruction it causes through systems of oppression. It
betrays the gospel that realigned the power structures of society.

In the United States, the idols of white Christian nationalism
have for centuries actively encouraged—even demanded—the
marginalization, oppression, and dehumanization of racial and
ethnic minorities as well as the immigrant and refugee. Both history and current polling overwhelmingly demonstrate that racism and xenophobia are strongly associated with white Christian
nationalism.

White Christian nationalism creates disciples who are more concerned with advancing their own kingdom of this world through acquiring and defending self-interested power than with advancing the kingdom of God through service—a kingdom where everyone can flourish. Instead of being willing to serve for the sake of the King, Christian nationalism demands we amass power over others for the sake of an earthly kingdom that benefits only "us."

White Christian nationalism encourages disciples to live in a near-constant state of fear about losing privilege, power, and prosperity. Instead of cultivating lives marked by trust, hope, and faith in a Savior whose kingdom is not of this world, white Christian nationalism cultivates a fear of loss to mobilize us Christians against anyone deemed a threat to our affluence and cultural dominance.

It creates disciples more concerned with who is "in" and who is "out," who is "right" and who should be silenced, than with welcoming and accepting all. Instead of breaking down all dividing walls of hostility, white Christian nationalism glories in building them up.

It creates disciples comfortable with using violence to subdue enemies. Instead of promoting giving up one's life for an enemy, white Christian nationalism insists on attacking enemies to defend one's life.

It creates disciples who are more concerned with ensuring they control the center of the culture than standing with those on the margins. Instead of advocating being counted among the lowly, white Christian nationalism requires stepping on the lowly in order to be counted.

It creates disciples focused on ensuring flourishing for "us," even if "our" flourishing is at the expense of "them." Instead of proclaiming all humans as image-bearers and listening to how we can work toward a collective prosperity, white Christian nationalism elevates some as favored and blessed by God above others.

White Christian nationalism devalues racial and ethnic minorities as inherently faulty, broken, and deserving of whatever hardships come their way. It blesses the use of authoritarian measures and violence to control minority groups. It sanctifies the slave auction, consecrates the lynching tree, and pardons those standing over the bodies of Black Americans lying in the street.

It causes us to perceive refugees and immigrants—those the Christian Bible explicitly demands we value—as deserving of skepticism if not outright disdain. It sees them as threats, burdens, disease-ridden harbingers of the downfall of Western civilization. It demands that Christians in the United States look after their own, ignoring their complicity in the suffering of those in nations around the world.

White Christian nationalism produces Christians who see the "other" lying broken and bloodied on the side of the road and cross to the other side—Christians who seek to justify themselves, asking Jesus, "And who is my neighbor?" while ignoring the cries of pain and injustice rising all around them.

White Christian nationalism fundamentally sorts the world in terms of "us" versus "them," with stark boundaries. It cannot and will not ever embrace expressions of Christianity that advocate "us" *for* "them."

White Christian nationalism produces Christians who bear little resemblance to a Savior who, being in the very nature God, humbled himself, made himself nothing, becoming a servant to all. A Savior who humbled himself to the point of giving up his life for his enemies rather than overpowering them. A Savior who chose faithfulness to the point of death (Phil. 2:6–11).

It fosters in us a desire only to win. It does not and cannot abide anything perceived as a loss. It does not cede ground. It only takes it. It does not share power. It only wields it. It looks at the cross with disgust, seeing it as folly, offended by the thought of Christians dying for their enemies. It would crucify rather than be crucified. It views self-sacrifice as the path of a fool in this era of culture-warring. It does not encourage us to serve our enemies, let alone consider them groups worthy of good-faith interaction. It scoffs at the idea of sacrificing for our adversaries. It demands we pick up the sword and fight.

When I look at white Christian nationalism, I cannot find Christ. When I look at the cultural-warring Christianity inherent to white Christian nationalism in the United States of the past fifty years, I cannot find Christ. When I look at the Christianity of white Christian nationalism that desires power, control, domination, and ultimately subjugation of those defined as our enemies, I cannot find Christ.

The Christianity of white Christian nationalism leaves only death and destruction in its wake. It does not encourage abundant life. But will American Christians turn from this expression of Christianity and move toward a Christianity in which all image-bearers flourish and find love, liberation, and abundant life?

Recalibrating Our Christianity

Throughout the preceding chapters, I highlighted stories and expressions of Christianity that can help us confront and oppose white Christian nationalism. These examples can inspire us and ignite our imaginations.

We can imitate Amanda Tyler and commit to being Christians against Christian nationalism by defending religious liberty for all Americans—whether of faith or no faith at all—rather than weaponizing religious liberty to benefit Christians alone.

We can emulate Amar Peterman and embrace empathy within our relationships and social networks. We can pay attention to the needs of our neighbors, practice proximity, cultivate humility in our interactions, and commit to sacrifice our tendency toward group-level fear of sharing power in a pluralistic democratic society.

We can listen to and learn from the strains of the Christian tradition that confront and oppose violence in its many forms,

both individual and collective. We can listen to those most affected by violence to point us forward to expressions of Christianity that help us realign our hearts and institutions toward
being peacemakers.

We can follow the example of Shalom Community Church
and begin the work of reckoning with the history of racism and
white supremacy in our denominations and congregations. We
can commit to taking the next step, no matter how big or small,
and continue on our journey of reparative acts.

We can collaborate with those like Andrea Cramer and Neighbor to Neighbor who commit to living out the commands of neigh-
borly love toward those who find themselves in a strange land. We
can recognize that no friendship is apolitical. We can internalize
the biblical truth that we are all visitors and aliens. That no land
or nation is "ours." Through our relationships with those marginalized by systems of power, we can leverage our power and
privilege *for others.*

Recognizing the idols of white Christian nationalism in our
midst will be the first step as we work to faithfully respond. Power,
fear, and violence have for centuries created relationships and
systems that privilege white Christians. History and social science clearly demonstrate how these idols lead to expressions of
Christianity content to work in partnership with empires that
crush those on the margins.

One repeated theme in the stories shared is that reevaluating
our expressions of the Christian faith from the perspective of the
marginalized and oppressed helps us recognize these three idols
of white Christians nationalism. Through their eyes, we can begin
to see the work of God more clearly in this world through Jesus,
and what his life, teachings, death on the cross, and resurrection
mean. Take a moment to read the first ten verses of Matthew 5.
Empire is not at the center of God's story.

As James Cone writes, "The real scandal of the gospel is this:
humanity's salvation is revealed in the cross of the condemned

criminal Jesus, and humanity's salvation is available *only* through our solidarity with the crucified people in our midst."[1] Cone and others teach us how viewing the cross from the perspective of Black Americans terrorized by the lynching tree reminds us of the reality of suffering in this life and how God is embodied in it. We are reminded the cross is not abstract. It is real. It has implications for us today in how we live with one another. Through this lens, we can rescue the cross from becoming a weak and ineffectual symbol of personal virtue. We can embrace the full reality of the gospel, one that frees humanity from the destructive systems of oppression and sin *as well as* our personal spiritual needs.

The Christian story is one of a God empathizing with the plight of humanity and identifying with us. Seeking relationship with us and with the outcast despite fear. Sacrificing himself at the hands of the violent rather than employing violence. Jesus, the perfect representation of God (Heb. 1:3), the author and perfecter of our faith (12:2), scorned fear, violence, and the self-interested employment of power that would benefit only him or his followers. I believe we must too.

Does confronting white Christian nationalism and the idols of power, fear, and violence mean Christians should not participate in American civil society or the political process? No. It does not. Of course Christians should participate. The key is *how* we participate and to whose benefit. The gospel empowers us to seek the flourishing of all. Politics is one way we can faithfully fulfill that calling.[2] It is one avenue through which we can oppose the principalities and powers that oppress humanity through systems of destruction like racism, xenophobia, patriarchy, and economic inequality.

As Lisa Sharon Harper tells us, "It is . . . necessary for all people of faith to draw from our principles to help us engage the world in a way that moves our nation and world toward God's very goodness. If the flourishing of the image of God and all the relationships in creation is our goal, then we will become partners with God."[3]

Christians can remember that we participate in a pluralistic democracy alongside neighbors with different commitments, beliefs, and desires. Neighbors we are called to love. Neighbors we are to collaborate with in order that all may flourish. In this sense, the gospel is going to be political. There is no way around it. The gospel has something to say about how to structure society.

The key here, though, is that it is not partisan. No one political party can speak to the diversity and depth of the Christian tradition and the gospel Jesus inaugurated with his life, teachings, death, and resurrection.

For too long, white Christian nationalism encouraged us to seek the good of our own tribe at the expense of others. To do so is to idolize power, fear, and violence. Jesus and the gospel call us to a different way. We should read our Bibles with the needs and burdens of our neighbors in mind, allowing the practice to alter our perspectives.[4]

As you listen to politicians, religious leaders, or political commentators, pay attention to what they are directing you to do or wanting you to feel. Consider the actions they recommend or the feelings their words bring up. Do they motivate you to expand the boundaries of who benefits from a policy? Or are you compelled to secure your own rights and privileges over others who, you're told, conspire to steal them away?

Consider whether you are tempted to embrace fear of loss, where others are benefiting more than you think they should. Consider whether these actions and feelings in some way allow for violence, or the threat of violence, in order to "restore law and order," defend the status quo, or return us to a previous period they claim we have lost. Consider whether this supposed previous period was better for everyone or just "us."

If one or more of these is true, perhaps the directives you are receiving are more in line with a dominating vision of Christianity embraced by Christian nationalism than with an expression of

Christianity that loves, serves, and empowers others to experience abundant life.

If you are a pastor or leader, invite others to help you review your recent messages and determine whether you tend to embrace a hermeneutic of fear, control, or even withdrawal. Consider where and how you can begin to listen to and learn from the biblical interpretations of those marginalized by power. Commit to faithfully socializing your congregation into an expression of the Christian faith that is incompatible with white Christian nationalism, one that equips them to recognize and question the theologies that undergird it.[5]

No part of the gospel directs Christians to defend their privileged access to political power and control to receive most of the benefits. Instead, we are to seek the flourishing of all through giving, sacrifice, and service. God calls us to participate in building the kingdom, inaugurated with Jesus, where the fundamental power structures of society are realigned. We can and should work alongside our neighbors so that everyone has access to all the benefits of citizenship.

Sadly, the idolization of self-serving power inherent to the white Christian nationalism embraced by most American Christians for the past fifty years means that many of our non-Christian neighbors know us by anything *but* love and service. All they have seen is a group of people intent on ensuring its privilege at the expense of everyone else. Instead of defending ourselves by pointing out all the good we think we have achieved, let us humble ourselves and begin to listen and respond to what we hear.

While writing this book, I kept returning to the stories of Reinhold Niebuhr and Dietrich Bonhoeffer. In some ways, I think they provide a useful contrast for white American Christians in this moment. Niebuhr was an American theologian and ethicist who taught at Union Theological Seminary. Bonhoeffer was a German pastor and theologian who was ultimately martyred for his opposition to the Nazi regime.

Living and writing in the first half of the twentieth century, both men recognized America's heinous history of racial violence. However, as James Cone notes, Niebuhr stopped short of publicly advocating for justice. After identifying how badly Black Americans were treated, in the next breath Niebuhr would call for gradualism and patience when overturning Jim Crow or integrating public schools. Niebuhr believed it wise to allow Southern whites "time to adjust."

The irony, Cone shows us, is that Niebuhr clearly saw the cross as God flipping the script on humanity's obsession with power and control over others. Through the cross, God condemned self-interested grasps at power. God revealed to us that true goodness and grace are found through "sacrificial, vicarious suffering."[6] Still, Niebuhr was unable to connect this theological insight to the context surrounding him.

Cone remarked how Niebuhr sounded like a "southern moderate more concerned about not challenging the cultural traditions of the white South than achieving justice for black people."[7] As Martin Luther King Jr. pointed out, "It is hardly a moral act to encourage others patiently to accept injustice which he himself does not endure."[8]

Niebuhr remained largely silent about the atrocities of lynching, never taking a consistent public stand against them. He identified the cross as the fullest and final representation of God's character and purpose, fundamentally altering the dynamic of how we should relate to the world *intellectually*. Despite this, Cone shows how Niebuhr did not have the imagination necessary to see the lynching tree as the "most obvious symbolic re-enactment of the crucifixion in his own time."[9]

Why did Niebuhr fail to make this connection? Cone and others suggest that Niebuhr recognized racial inequality but he did not *embody* this knowledge by siding with Black brothers and sisters marginalized in our society. He did not see how calls for patience were essentially calls to perpetuate injustice. "Niebuhr had 'eyes to see' black suffering, but lacked the 'heart to feel' it as his own."[10]

Bonhoeffer, however, did not miss the lessons on Christianity provided by those marginalized by systems of power and violence in the United States. He acknowledged how white Christians in the United States stopped well short of truly loving Black Americans. He saw how the creation and maintenance of "second-class citizens" in the United States—and the role of Christianity in this work of the state—was also happening in Germany. Historians document how Hitler and the Nazi Party patterned their own actions using the history of race and the treatment of Black Americans by white Americans in the United States as a guide.[11]

Bonhoeffer grasped that a more faithful expression of Christianity demands we count ourselves among those on the margins. As Reggie Williams forcefully shows us in his book *Bonhoeffer's Black Jesus*, Bonhoeffer's writings and opposition to the Nazi regime in Germany were fundamentally shaped by his experiences in Harlem. "For Bonhoeffer, Christians must see society from the perspective of the marginalized people since faithful Christianity is calibrated from the perspective of suffering rather than from dominance. This is costly yet crucial to true Christian discipleship."[12] Again, empire is not at the center of God's story.

Bonhoeffer's embodiment of Christ's siding with the marginalized led to his twentieth-century martyrdom. His life and actions continue to serve as inspiration for those who hope to collaborate with Christ to see a world where justice rolls down like mighty waters (see Amos 5:24). Again, Williams reminds us that Bonhoeffer's experiences in Black Harlem were central to learning this perspective. Or, using the symbolism of James Cone, Bonhoeffer saw the cross in the lynching tree.

In this juxtaposition, we glimpse an example of how we might express our Christian faith in opposition to white Christian nationalism. As Williams and others note, we must try to follow Bonhoeffer's example, listening to and learning from our brothers and sisters on the margins of society, those systematically denied access to the centers of power and privilege. Through their lives and experiences, we can begin to locate ourselves nearer the life and experiences of our Savior, who lived, suffered, died, and rose again in the midst—and under the sword—of empire.

When we remove ourselves from the seat of honor at the table, when we quit striving to be the loudest voice in the room, we recalibrate our Christianity. We begin to turn away from expressions aligned with white Christian nationalism and toward expressions that teach us to unite with Christ and his love for the world through collaboration, cooperation, humility, and vulnerability *with* all our neighbors rather than through domination and control of our neighbors.

We will discover those on the margins are at the center of God's story. That is where I want to be found.

Parting Words for the Journey

My hope and prayer is that you commit to the ongoing work of turning from the idols of white Christian nationalism and receive Christ Jesus as Lord, continuing to live your life in him, rooted and built up in him, strengthened in the faith as you were taught, and overflowing with thankfulness. No longer allow yourself or your faith community to be taken captive by this hollow and deceptive philosophy, which depends on human tradition and the basic principles of this world rather than on Christ.

Rather, recognize that in Christ all the fullness of the deity lives in bodily form, and in Christ you have been given this fullness. Jesus claimed to fulfill the promise of good news to the poor, freedom for the prisoners, recovery of sight for the blind, and deliverance for the oppressed. And the word of God, the glorious mystery, is *Christ in us*, the hope of glory. Through us, Christ continues that work. God has disarmed the powers and authorities of this present world, the powers and principalities of darkness. For our battle is not against flesh and blood but against the sin-soaked systems of oppression that crush and tyrannize our neighbors.

Because of Christ's work on the cross, we can live into his example of service and sacrifice *for* others, resulting in abundant life for all, rather than control and domination *of* others (see Col. 2:6–15; Eph. 6:12).

American Christianity and the Christian nationalism so deeply intertwined with it have produced unimaginable pain and suffering for so many groups. For white American Christians as a whole, Christian nationalism has produced privilege, comfort, and affluence built on the suffering of others.[13] Is there any wonder so many are leaving the Christian church and never looking back? But as Danté Stewart writes, "I have learned that many of us have not given up on the faith, just the way our faith has been used to oppress others. We have not given up on the Bible, just the way it has been used to marginalize others. We have not given up on Jesus, we just know he ain't a blue-eyed Republican. . . . In reality, [people leaving churches] have given up on the white supremacist brand of Christianity that cares more about power than Jesus."[14]

To oppose white Christian nationalism is not to give up on Christianity. Christianity can be marked by sacrifice, hope, grace, service, faith, and, of course, love. Christians can disentangle our faith from Christian nationalism and thus more closely embody the life and teachings of Jesus, the gospel, in our congregations and communities. We can tell better stories. We can provide better narratives than those we have been handed. We can take part in the good work of the gospel that Jesus inaugurated, rescuing us all from the oppression of sin in our personal worlds and in the systems and structures of society.

This collective work will not be easy. Idols are not easily destroyed. Institutions, organizations, and powerful positions depend on the continued alliance between Christianity and the power of the state. There is money to be made, and there are elections to be won. Congregations, friendships, and even families have been and will continue to be torn apart over a commitment to white Christian nationalism. It will not be easy for you. It has not been easy for me. As Kat Armas poignantly states, "It's a surprising pain that often comes when we dig up the skeletons from the ground, when we realize the dirt we stand on is tainted and the reality we've been fed is curated."[15]

We may look around us and say, "I don't want all this pain, oppression, and suffering." And my point isn't that any one person consciously or explicitly wants these things. It is that white Christian nationalism undergirds the systems producing these outcomes, and we are all implicated in this broader reality—one that forms our interactions and us, whether we like it or not.

It is only when we name it that we can begin to reckon with how our faith tradition and its theologies have been used and abused. This is uncomfortable work. People close to you will question whether you are even a Christian any longer. This has happened to me. This struggle, however, is sacred. God is present within it.[16]

It will be an ongoing journey. We never "arrive." Confronting white Christian nationalism will be less like an amputation— where we just cut off the unhealthy appendage. It will be more like flossing. A routine we, and the groups we inhabit, commit to every day. No one will do it perfectly, either. I appreciate the wisdom of Christina Edmondson and Chad Brennan when they write, "No one's life is completely for or against justice," but we can and should acknowledge where we fall short because "we do not need to be perfect in order to stand for justice."[17] I hope you will join me and continue this journey for years to come.

I am told hope is a spiritual discipline. When facing a chasm of the unknown, a darkness, it is so easy to let fear grip us and allow despair to take hold. It is important we face the darkness, feel the despair, and clearly declare all is not as it should be. Only then can we begin to imagine something new. Only then can we begin to hope, to commit to living as though a different future is truly possible. For hope is "a radical act of faith and courage, an embodiment of the Kingdom, and vital to our work for justice."[18]

We may not even enjoy this future ourselves. As with planting trees, we're doing the work of hope, expecting that what we do today will reverberate in unknown ways, making real an alternate reality, providing a healing shade for those who come after.

Writing to her son in a time when all seemed hopeless, the Reverend Kelly Brown Douglas provides a poignant example of such a commitment to hope. During the George Floyd protests in 2020, she recounted the enormity of darkness Black women and men suffering under the evils of various forms of systemic racism faced day after day for centuries in the United States.[19] Millions never saw the freedom for which they were hoping. Millions lived and died without stepping foot in the promised land. Despite this, so many never surrendered their commitment to realizing a more just society for everyone, Black or white.

They practiced hope and remade the world anyway. Their example instructs us. No matter the height of this mountain, the depth of this sea, we are to hold tight to hope and move forward with the expectation that we can and will remake American Christianity to look a lot more like Christ than a servant of empire.

Sometimes, the bravest thing we have is hope.

NOTES

Preface

1. My goal in using "we" is to encourage us all to take ownership and responsibility for the current context we find ourselves in, acknowledging that what happened in the past still resonates today. However, "we" is doing a lot of work. I use it to refer to the United States as a whole—all of us who make up this nation. Clearly, Native American and Black readers are part of the "we" but are primarily on the receiving end of the harms perpetrated by the United States throughout its history and into the present day. White readers might balk at accepting any sort of responsibility for the United States' destructive practices in its history. For those like me who grew up and still find themselves in white Christian spaces, I hope the use of "we" gives us an opportunity to sit and ponder why it makes us feel uncomfortable and what this might require of us.

2. I am not the first and won't be the last to make this point. See Greg Boyd, *The Myth of a Christian Nation: How the Quest for Political Power Is Destroying the Church* (Grand Rapids: Zondervan, 2005), 11; Paul Miller, *The Religion of American Greatness: What's Wrong with Christian Nationalism* (Downers Grove, IL: InterVarsity, 2022), 6–7, 137–42; and Kaitlyn Schiess, *The Liturgy of Politics: Spiritual Formation for the Sake of Our Neighbor* (Downers Grove, IL: IVP Academic, 2020), 35–36. See also David A. Ritchie, *Why Do the Nations Rage: The Demonic Origin of Nationalism* (Eugene, OR: Wipf & Stock, 2022), for an argument that nationalism is not only idolatrous but also demonic—the powers and principalities referenced in the apostle Paul's writings. Ritchie argues that nationalism offers a set of corresponding but contrary doctrines to Christianity.

3. See Philip S. Gorski and Samuel L. Perry, *The Flag and the Cross: White Christian Nationalism and the Threat to American Democracy* (New York: Oxford University Press, 2022); and Miles T. Armaly, David T. Buckley, and Adam M. Enders, "Christian Nationalism and Political Violence: Victimhood, Racial Identity, Conspiracy, and Support for the Capitol Attacks," *Political Behavior* 44 (January 2022): 937–60.

4. Miller, *Religion of American Greatness*, 14–15; and Schiess, *Liturgy of Politics*, chap. 4.

Chapter 1 A Hollow and Deceptive Philosophy

1. The band was Five Iron Frenzy. This song, "The Old West," appears on their first album, *Upbeats and Beatdowns*. In a podcast interview, lead singer Reese Roper shared how their label strongly urged them to cut this song because it "wouldn't play well in the Midwest," clearly referring to the thousands of church kids and youth groups just like mine who might balk at the band telling the truth. The band not only disagreed but even placed the song first on the album. "Anthem" and "Beautiful America" were two other songs on the same album that similarly pierced the veil. "Reese Roper: Five Iron Frenzy," *The Black Sheep Podcast*, February 2, 2021, https://hmmagazine.com/podcast/reese-roper-five-iron-frenzy/.

2. Frank Lambert's books on religion, the founding fathers, and politics are excellent. See *The Founding Fathers and the Place of Religion in America* (2003), *Religion in American Politics* (2008), and *Separation of Church and State* (2014), among others. Lambert was also a punter for the Pittsburgh Steelers in the 1960s.

3. In the years since I encountered Boyd's writing, folks from historically marginalized communities have taught me how the language of "power under" can be problematic when it implies passivity in the face of unjust and oppressive power structures. As I describe later in this chapter and throughout this book, rejecting the impulse to wield "power over" others is not about sacrificing power. Rather, it is about leveraging power for the common good. I am grateful to Boyd for setting me on a trajectory toward better understanding the social and political dimensions of the kingdom of God, even as my understanding of how the kingdom of God intersects with society continues to develop. It should be noted that Boyd's understanding of these issues has evolved since 2005 as well.

4. See Andrew L. Whitehead and Samuel L. Perry, *Taking America Back for God: Christian Nationalism in the United States* (New York: Oxford University Press, 2020), 163.

5. See Lisa Sharon Harper, *The Very Good Gospel: How Everything Wrong Can Be Made Right* (Colorado Springs: WaterBrook, 2016); Kaitlyn Schiess, *The Liturgy of Politics: Spiritual Formation for the Sake of Our Neighbor* (Downers Grove, IL: IVP Academic, 2020); and Sarah Bessey, *Out of Sorts* (New York: Howard Books, 2015), especially chap. 11. Each author shares a similar experience in which the faith they were raised in limited the work and definition of the gospel, and each provides moving reflections on the importance of justice to the gospel.

6. Scott Coley is a philosopher and ethicist and worth following on Twitter. Personal correspondence, July 23, 2022.

7. Kat Armas, *Abuelita Faith: What Women on the Margins Teach Us about Wisdom, Persistence, and Strength* (Grand Rapids: Brazos, 2021), 35.

8. Kaitlyn Schiess writes, "So the gospel comes with an ethical imperative to love our neighbor, and Scripture is clear that loving our neighbor means opposing social and political barriers to their flourishing." *Liturgy of Politics*, 71.

9. Schiess, *Liturgy of Politics*, 76.

10. Harper, *Very Good Gospel*, 7.

11. Schiess, *Liturgy of Politics*, 59.

12. Barbara Rossing, *The Rapture Exposed: The Message of Hope in the Book of Revelation* (Boulder: Westview, 2004).

13. Robert P. Jones, *White Too Long: The Legacy of White Supremacy in American Christianity* (New York: Simon & Schuster, 2020), 73–106; and Paul Miller, *The Religion of American Greatness: What's Wrong with Christian Nationalism* (Downers Grove, IL: InterVarsity, 2022), 191–94.

14. Bessey, *Out of Sorts*, 197.

15. See Dominique DuBois Gilliard, *Subversive Witness: Scripture's Call to Leverage Privilege* (Grand Rapids: Zondervan, 2021).

16. Harper, *Very Good Gospel*, 42.

17. Martin Luther King Jr., "Letter from a Birmingham Jail," April 16, 1963, https://kinginstitute.stanford.edu/sites/mlk/files/letterfrombirmingham_wwcw _0.pdf.

18. Jonathan Wilson-Hartgrove, *Revolution of Values: Reclaiming Public Faith for the Common Good* (Downers Grove, IL: InterVarsity, 2019), 20.

19. For additional definitions and explanations of white Christian nationalism, see Whitehead and Perry, *Taking America Back for God*; and Philip S. Gorski and Samuel L. Perry, *The Flag and the Cross: White Christian Nationalism and the Threat to American Democracy* (New York: Oxford University Press, 2022).

20. Schiess, *Liturgy of Politics*, 35–36.

21. Drew Strait, "Political Idolatry and White Christian Nationalism: Toward a Pastoral Hermeneutic of Resistance," *Mennonite Quarterly Review* 96 (January 2022): 47–72.

22. For exceptional histories, see Kristin Kobes Du Mez, *Jesus and John Wayne: How White Evangelicals Corrupted a Faith and Fractured a Nation* (New York: Liveright, 2020); Frances Fitzgerald, *The Evangelicals: The Struggle to Shape America* (New York: Simon & Schuster, 2017); Tony Keddie, *Republican Jesus: How the Right Has Rewritten the Gospels* (Oakland: University of California Press, 2020); Kevin Kruse, *One Nation Under God: How Corporate America Invented Christian America* (New York: Basic Books, 2015); Matthew Avery Sutton, *American Apocalypse: A History of Modern Evangelicalism* (Cambridge, MA: Harvard University Press, 2014); and Daniel K. Williams, *God's Own Party: The Making of the Christian Right* (New York: Oxford University Press, 2012).

23. These statistics are drawn from the following sources: Joseph Baker and Buster Smith, *American Secularism: Cultural Contours of Nonreligious Belief Systems* (New York: New York University Press, 2015); Ruth Braunstein, "A Theory of Political Backlash: Assessing the Religious Right's Effects on the Religious Field," *Sociology of Religion* 83, no. 3 (Autumn 2022): 293–323; Michael Hout and Claude S. Fischer, "Why More Americans Have No Religious Preference: Politics and Generations," *American Sociological Review* 67, no. 2 (April 2002): 165–90; Michael Hout and Claude S. Fischer, "Explaining Why More Americans Have No Religious Preference: Political Backlash and Generational Succession, 1987–2012," *Sociological Science* 1 (2014): 423–47; and Samuel Perry (@profsamperry), "But if you wanna see a receipt here's one. In 2021, when non-evangelicals are asked which group wants to physically harm them, nearly 30% said conservative Xtians. Only 19% said Muslims, and 9% said atheists. Suggests to me non-evangelicals don't see conservative Xtians as loving." Twitter, June 16, 2021, 7:44 p.m., https://twitter.com/profsamperry/status /1405310392092479491?s=20&t=n6Vp5Con_g_6f5bA_d1xyw.

24. Jemar Tisby, *The Color of Compromise: The Truth about the American Church's Complicity in Racism* (Grand Rapids: Zondervan, 2019), 18–19.

25. New Testament professor Drew Strait recommends a "pastoral hermeneutic of resistance," which means "faithfully showing up week after week to socialize congregants into a theo-political worldview that is incompatible with Christian nationalism." By doing so, we all reproduce resistance through our networks and equip one another to "name and interrogate theologies of oppression." See Strait, "Political Idolatry," 65.

Chapter 2 What Is Christian Nationalism?

1. Jenny Cudd participated in the January 6 Capitol insurrection. See her quote (p. 36) and more in the report *Christian Nationalism and the January 6, 2021 Insurrection* (February 9, 2022), a joint project of the Baptist Joint Committee and the Freedom from Religion Foundation, available here: https://bjconline.org/jan6report/.

2. Twitter banned Trump on January 8, 2021. You can find Trump's tweets at thetrumparchive.com. Tweets referenced in this paragraph were sent on December 18, 2020, at 9:14:32 a.m. EST; December 19, 2020, at 1:42:42 a.m. EST; and December 19, 2020, at 9:41:03 a.m. EST. Toward the end of writing this book, the Select Committee to Investigate the January 6th Attack on the United States Capitol televised several hearings. The facts and evidence they shared continue to reshape our understanding of what happened that day. This includes what then president Trump knew when he sent this now-infamous tweet. Given the fast-changing nature of our public understanding of all these events while I was completing this book, I had to focus this section on that day in 2021 and the next year to year and a half.

3. Franklin Graham, Facebook post, January 6, 2021, https://www.facebook .com/permalink.php?story_fbid=4023059261083558&id=131201286936061.

4. See Wyatte Grantham-Philips, "Pastor Paula White Calls on Angels from Africa and South America to Bring Trump Victory," *USA Today*, November 5, 2020. This is the same prayer service where she called on "angelic reinforcement" from Africa and South America.

5. Bob Smietana, "Eric Metaxas, Christian Radio Host, Tells Trump, 'Jesus Is with Us in This Fight,'" *Religion News Service*, November 30, 2020, https://religion news.com/2020/11/30/eric-metaxas-christian-radio-host-offers-to-lay-down-his -life-for-trump-election-triumph/.

6. Byron Tau and Sara Randazzo, "Trump Cries Voter Fraud. In Court, His Lawyers Don't," *Wall Street Journal*, November 13, 2020, https://www.wsj.com/articles /trump-cries-election-fraud-in-court-his-lawyers-dont-11605271267.

7. See the report *Christian Nationalism and the January 6, 2021 Insurrection*, cited above.

8. See Emma Green, "A Christian Insurrection," *The Atlantic*, January 8, 2021, https://www.theatlantic.com/politics/archive/2021/01/evangelicals-catholics -jericho-march-capitol/617591/; Peter Manseau, "Some Capitol Rioters Believed They Answered God's Call, Not Just Trump," *Washington Post*, February 11, 2021, https://www.washingtonpost.com/outlook/2021/02/11/christian-religion-insurrec tion-capitol-trump/; Elizabeth Dias and Ruth Graham, "How White Evangelical Christians Fused with Trump Extremism," *New York Times*, January 11, 2021, https:// www.nytimes.com/2021/01/11/us/how-white-evangelical-christians-fused-with -trump-extremism.html; Jack Jenkins, "For Insurrectionists, a Violent Faith Brewed from Nationalism, Conspiracies and Jesus," *Religion News Service*, January 12, 2021, https://religionnews.com/2021/01/12/the-faith-of-the-insurrectionists/; and Tom Gjelten, "Militant Christian Nationalists Remain a Potent Force, Even after the Capitol Riot," NPR, January 19, 2021, https://www.npr.org/2021/01/19/958159202 /militant-christian-nationalists-remain-a-potent-force.

9. Russell Moore, "The Roman Road from Insurrection," *Russell Moore Newsletter*, January 11, 2021, https://www.russellmoore.com/2021/01/11/the-roman-road -from-insurrection/.

10. Russell Moore, "The Capitol Attack Signaled a Post-Christian Church, Not Merely a Post-Christian Culture," *Christianity Today*, January 5, 2022, https://www

.christianitytoday.com/ct/2022/january-web-only/january-6-attack-russell-moore -post-christian-church.html.

11. Albert Mohler, "What Is Christian Nationalism and What Is the Danger?," *The Briefing*, January 13, 2021, https://albertmohler.com/2021/01/13/briefing-1-13-21.

12. R. Albert Mohler Jr., "One Year After Jan. 6," *World*, January 6, 2022, https:// wng.org/opinions/one-year-after-jan-6-1641475924.

13. 2021 Baylor Religion Survey (https://www.baylor.edu/baylorreligionsurvey/), specifically "Accommodators" and "Ambassadors," measuring Christian nation alism according to the scale used in Andrew L. Whitehead and Samuel L. Perry, *Taking America Back for God: Christian Nationalism in the United States* (New York: Oxford University Press, 2020).

14. Stephanie Martin, "Albert Mohler to Join DeSantis, Hawley, and Rubio at Up-coming National Conservatism Conference," *Church Leaders*, August 17, 2022, https:// churchleaders.com/news/432138-albert-mohler-desantis-hawley-rubio-national -conservatism-conference.html.

15. Annika Brockschmidt and Thomas Lecaque, "White Christian Nationalism, Out in the Open," *The Bulwark*, August 22, 2022, https://www.thebulwark.com/white -christian-nationalism-out-in-the-open/. See also Samuel L. Perry and Andrew L. Whitehead, "Who Is a Christian Nationalist?," *Dallas Morning News*, November 8, 2022, https://www.dallasnews.com/opinion/commentary/2022/11/08/coming-out -of-the-christian-nationalist-closet/.

16. Samuel L. Perry, Andrew L. Whitehead, and Joshua B. Grubbs, "'I Don't Want Everybody to Vote': Christian Nationalism and Restricting Voter Access in the United States," *Sociological Forum* 37, no. 1 (March 2022): 4–26.

17. See Philip S. Gorski and Samuel L. Perry, *The Flag and the Cross: White Christian Nationalism and the Threat to American Democracy* (New York: Oxford University Press, 2022).

18. Peter Berger, *The Sacred Canopy: Elements of a Sociological Theory of Religion* (New York: Anchor Books, 1967).

19. It is also important to recognize that there is no "pure" or sui generis Chris-tianity distinct from the particular sets of cultural baggage present in American Christian nationalism. Even those expressions of Christianity that confront Chris-tian nationalism are products of their cultural context.

20. See chap. 2 of Gorski and Perry, *The Flag and the Cross*.

21. Anthea Butler, *White Evangelical Racism: The Politics of Morality in America* (Chapel Hill: University of North Carolina Press, 2021); Jemar Tisby, *The Color of Compromise: The Truth about the American Church's Complicity in Racism* (Grand Rapids: Zondervan, 2019).

22. See Gorski and Perry, *The Flag and the Cross*.

23. See Randall Balmer, *Bad Faith: Race and the Rise of the Religious Right* (Grand Rapids: Eerdmans, 2021).

24. See J. Russell Hawkins, *The Bible Told Them So: How Southern Evangelicals Fought to Preserve White Supremacy* (New York: Oxford University Press, 2021).

25. Samuel L. Perry, Ryon J. Cobb, Andrew L. Whitehead, and Joshua B. Grubbs, "Divided by Faith (in Christian America): Christian Nationalism, Race, and Diver-gent Perceptions of Racial Injustice," *Social Forces* (2021), https://doi.org/10.1093 /sf/soab134.

26. Gorski and Perry, *The Flag and the Cross*; Samuel L. Perry and Andrew L. Whitehead, "Christian America in Black and White: Racial Identity, Religious-National Group Boundaries, and Explanations for Racial Inequality," *Sociology of Religion* 80, no. 3 (Autumn 2019): 277–98; and Perry et al., "Divided by Faith."

27. Paul Miller, *The Religion of American Greatness: What's Wrong with Christian Nationalism* (Downers Grove, IL: InterVarsity, 2022), 108.

28. For more on the data that underscore these five basic facts about Christian nationalism across the US population, see Whitehead and Perry, *Taking America Back for God*, chap. 1, "Four Americans."

29. Whitehead and Perry, *Taking America Back for God*, 34.

30. Gregory A. Smith, Michael Rotolo, and Patricia Tevington, "45% of Americans Say U.S. Should Be a 'Christian Nation,'" *Pew Research Center*, October 27, 2022, https://www.pewresearch.org/religion/2022/10/27/45-of-americans-say-u-s -should-be-a-christian-nation/.

31. 2021 Baylor Religion Survey.

32. See especially section VI in the report *Christian Nationalism and the January 6, 2021 Insurrection.*

33. For more on the four orientations toward Christian nationalism, Ambassadors, Accommodators, Resisters, and Rejecters, see Whitehead and Perry, *Taking America Back for God*, chap. 1.

34. For more on the importance of building coalitions beyond our natural allies in the service of protecting democracy, see Steven Levitsky and Daniel Ziblatt, *How Democracies Die* (New York: Crown, 2018).

35. Whitehead and Perry, *Taking America Back for God*; Andrew Whitehead and Samuel Perry, "Is Christian Nationalism Growing or Declining? Both.," *Washington Post*, October 25, 2022, https://www.washingtonpost.com/politics/2022/10/25 /republicans-christian-nationalism-midterms/.

36. In 2006, the National Congregations Study found that 60.4 percent of congregations answered yes to the prompt "Does your congregation display an American flag in your main sanctuary or worship space?" The results of this poll are available from the Association of Religion Data Archives: https://www.thearda.com/data-ar chive?fid=NCSIVED&tab=4&vName=DISPFLAG.

37. See the response that Angela Denker and her co-pastors received for removing only some of the American flag bunting in her congregation's sanctuary for their Fourth of July worship service: Angela Denker, *Red State Christians: Understanding the Voters Who Elected Donald Trump* (Minneapolis: Fortress, 2019), 14.

38. See Whitehead and Perry, *Taking America Back for God*; and Denker, *Red State Christians.*

39. See Miller, *Religion of American Greatness*, 124–33. Second Chronicles 7:14 and Psalm 33:12 are two well-worn biblical justifications for Christian nationalism. But as Miller writes, the Bible does not require Christians to "make our cultural and political borders correspond" (133).

40. David Barton and his organization WallBuilders are the chief purveyors of inaccuracies and outright lies concerning the religiosity of the founding fathers and the foundational documents. Barton's book on Thomas Jefferson was pulled by its publisher, conservative Christian press Thomas Nelson, because of its many historical inaccuracies. See Elise Hu, "Publisher Pulls Controversial Thomas Jefferson Book, Citing Loss of Confidence," NPR, August 9, 2012, https://www.npr.org /sections/thetwo-way/2012/08/09/158510648/publisher-pulls-controversial-thomas -jefferson-book-citing-loss-of-confidence.

41. See John Fea, *Was America Founded as a Christian Nation? A Historical Introduction* (Louisville: Westminster John Knox, 2011); David L. Holmes, *The Faiths of the Founding Fathers* (New York: Oxford University Press, 2006); Frank Lambert, *The Founding Fathers and the Place of Religion in America* (Princeton: Princeton University Press, 2003); Lambert, *Religion in American Politics* (Princeton: Princeton

University Press, 2008); Lambert, *Separation of Church and State* (Macon, GA: Mercer University Press, 2014); and Andrew L. Seidel, *The Founding Myth: Why Christian Nationalism Is Un-American* (New York: Sterling, 2019).

42. Miller, *Religion of American Greatness*, 27–28.

43. Kat Armas, *Abuelita Faith: What Women on the Margins Teach Us about Wisdom, Persistence, and Strength* (Grand Rapids: Brazos, 2021), 72.

44. Kaitlyn Schiess, *The Liturgy of Politics: Spiritual Formation for the Sake of Our Neighbor* (Downers Grove, IL: IVP Academic, 2020), 166.

45. Samuel L. Perry and Andrew Whitehead, "January 6th May Have Been Only the First Wave of Christian Nationalist Violence," *Time*, January 4, 2022, https://time.com/6132591/january-6th-christian-nationalism/.

Chapter 3 Turn the Other Cheek?

1. See Peter Wehner, "The Gospel of Donald Trump Jr.," *The Atlantic*, December 26, 2021, https://www.theatlantic.com/ideas/archive/2021/12/gospel-donald-trump-jr/621122/.

2. See "White Christian Nationalism in the United States" (session 2), YouTube, August 30, 2021, https://www.youtube.com/watch?v=8hzFamNEAX4.

3. Philip S. Gorski and Samuel L. Perry (*The Flag and the Cross: White Christian Nationalism and the Threat to American Democracy* [New York: Oxford University Press, 2022], 4) borrow this idea from sociologist Arlie Russell Hochschild's *Strangers in Their Own Land* (New York: The New Press, 2016) and apply it to white Christian nationalism.

4. "We" equals "Christians." But remember, these audiences are and were overwhelmingly white. This underscores the racialized nature of Christian nationalism. We identify as Christians, but our experiences and desires are fundamentally organized around our social location as white Americans.

5. From the PBS documentary *Billy Graham*, May 17, 2021, https://www.pbs.org/wgbh/americanexperience/films/billy-graham/.

6. See Kevin Kruse, *One Nation Under God: How Corporate America Invented Christian America* (New York: Basic Books, 2015).

7. "TV Ads Attack Moral Majority, Other Groups for 'Intolerance,' " *Washington Post* archive, accessed July 28, 2022, https://www.washingtonpost.com/archive/local/1982/10/09/tv-ads-attack-moral-majority-other-groups-for-intolerance/60255fd6-b1cf-4af7-aa88-e95b1764c75d/.

8. Michael Foust, "Dobson Urges Listeners to Vote; Much Is 'On the Line,' He Says," *Baptist Press*, November 1, 2004, https://www.baptistpress.com/resource-library/news/dobson-urges-listeners-to-vote-much-is-on-the-line-he-says/.

9. James Dobson, "Letter from 2012 in Obama's America," *WND*, October 23, 2008, https://www.wnd.com/wp-content/uploads/Focusletter.pdf.

10. CT Editors, "James Dobson: Why I Am Voting for Donald Trump," *Christianity Today*, September 23, 2016, https://www.christianitytoday.com/ct/2016/october/james-dobson-why-i-am-voting-for-donald-trump.html.

11. James Dobson, "America's Civil Wars—Then and Now," *Dr. James Dobson Family Institute Newsletter*, August 2020, https://www.drjamesdobson.org/newsletters/august-newsletter-2020-americas-civil-wars-then-and-now.

12. Colin Campbell, "Trump: If I'm President, 'Christianity Will Have Power' in the US," Yahoo, January 23, 2016, https://www.yahoo.com/entertainment/trump-im-president-christianity-power-195834887.html (emphasis added).

13. Benjamin Fearnow, "Pastor Robert Jeffress, White House Ally, Warns Evangelicals Not Voting Is 'Sin against God,'" *Newsweek*, November 1, 2020, https://www.newsweek.com/pastor-robert-jeffress-white-house-ally-warns-evangelicals-not-voting-sin-against-god-1543871.

14. Oliver Willis, "Lauren Boebert Suggests Her Election Was Ordained by God," *American Independent*, June 22, 2021, https://americanindependent.com/lauren-boebert-donald-trump-tony-perkins-signs-wonders-bible-qanon-evangelicals/.

15. Adela Suliman and Timothy Bella, "GOP Rep. Boebert: 'I'm Tired of This Separation of Church and State Junk,'" *Washington Post*, June 28, 2022, https://www.washingtonpost.com/politics/2022/06/28/lauren-boebert-church-state-colorado/.

16. It is important to note that Eisenhower signed a law declaring "In God we trust" the nation's official motto on July 30, 1956. One year earlier a joint resolution from Congress, approved by Eisenhower, placed the motto on all US currency.

17. Frederick Clarkson, a researcher who first identified and publicized Project Blitz, reports that in 2020, ninety-two such bills were introduced across the fifty states, with eight passing. And just midway through 2021, seventy-four bills were introduced, with fourteen passing. See Paul Rosenberg, "The Christian Nationalist Assault on Democracy Goes Stealth—but the Pushback Is Working," *Salon*, July 24, 2021, https://www.salon.com/2021/07/24/the-christian-nationalist-assault-on-democracy-goes-stealth--but-the-pushback-is-working/.

18. Mya Jaradat, "How This New Group for Christian Lawmakers Will Try to Remake American Politics," *Deseret News*, July 9, 2021, https://www.deseret.com/faith/2021/7/9/22566116/meet-the-new-conservative-faith-based-organization-that-will-make-a-big-impact-on-american-politics.

19. Jaradat, "How This New Group for Christian Lawmakers."

20. See Katherine Stewart's recent book, *The Power Worshippers: Inside the Dangerous Rise of Religious Nationalism* (New York: Bloomsbury, 2019); Anne Nelson's *The Shadow Network: Media, Money, and the Secret Hub of the Radical Right* (New York: Bloomsbury, 2019); and Sarah Posner's *Unholy: Why White Evangelicals Worship at the Altar of Donald Trump* (New York: Random House, 2020).

21. Edward-Isaac Dovere, "Tony Perkins: Trump Gets 'a Mulligan' on Life, Stormy Daniels," *Politico*, January 23, 2018, https://www.politico.com/magazine/story/2018/01/23/tony-perkins-evangelicals-donald-trump-stormy-daniels-216498/.

22. Obery M. Hendricks Jr., *Christians against Christianity: How Right-Wing Evangelicals Are Destroying Our Nation and Our Faith* (Boston: Beacon, 2021), 2.

23. See Samuel L. Perry, Andrew L. Whitehead, and Joshua B. Grubbs, "'I Don't Want Everybody to Vote': Christian Nationalism and Restricting Voter Access in the United States," *Sociological Forum* 37, no. 1 (March 2022): 4–26.

24. See Gorski and Perry, *The Flag and the Cross*, 97.

25. See Andrew L. Whitehead and Samuel L. Perry, *Taking America Back for God: Christian Nationalism in the United States* (New York: Oxford University Press, 2020), 77–80.

26. Robert P. Jones, *The End of White Christian America* (New York: Simon & Schuster, 2016), 144–45.

27. Samuel L. Perry, Landon Schnabel, and Joshua B. Grubbs, "Christian Nationalism, Perceived anti-Christian Discrimination, and Prioritising 'Religious Freedom' in the 2020 Presidential Election," *Nations and Nationalism* 28, no. 2 (April 2022): 714–25.

28. Gorski and Perry, *The Flag and the Cross*, 91.

29. See David Bentley Hart, *The Story of Christianity: A History of 2,000 Years of the Christian Faith* (London: Quercus, 2013), 47.

30. 2018 Chapman University Survey of American Fears, https://thearda.com/Archive/Files/Analysis/CSAF2018/CSAF2018_Var5_1.asp.

31. Kat Armas, *Abuelita Faith: What Women on the Margins Teach Us about Wisdom, Persistence, and Strength* (Grand Rapids: Brazos, 2021), 9.

32. James H. Cone, *The Cross and the Lynching Tree* (Maryknoll, NY: Orbis Books, 2013), 2, 35.

33. Author interview, January 25, 2022.

34. You can find the following examples, quotes, and more on the BJC's "Baptist Roots" page. See https://bjconline.org/mission-history-baptist-heritage/.

35. Martin Luther King Jr., "A Knock at Midnight," June 11, 1967, sermon posted by CNN.com, January 18, 1999, http://www.cnn.com/books/beginnings/9901/knock.midnight/.

36. You can view and sign the statement here: https://www.christiansagainst christiannationalism.org/statement.

37. Author interview, January 25, 2022.

38. *Wealth and income*: Anshu Siripurapu, "The U.S. Inequality Debate," Council on Foreign Relations, updated April 20, 2022, https://www.cfr.org/backgrounder/us-inequality-debate. *Health*: Nambi Ndugga and Samantha Artiga, "Disparities in Health and Health Care: 5 Key Questions and Answers," KFF, May 11, 2021, https://www.kff.org/racial-equity-and-health-policy/issue-brief/disparities-in-health-and-health-care-5-key-question-and-answers/. *Criminal justice system*: "Report to the United Nations on Racial Disparities in the U.S. Criminal Justice System," The Sentencing Project, April 19, 2018, https://www.sentencingproject.org/publications/un-report-on-racial-disparities/. *Education*: Emma García and Elaine Weiss, "Education Inequalities at the School Starting Gate," Economic Policy Institute, September 27, 2017, https://www.epi.org/publication/education-inequalities-at-the-school-starting-gate/. *Democratic access*: "The Consequences of Political Inequality and Voter Suppression for U.S. Economic Inequality and Growth," Washington Center for Equitable Growth, February 3, 2021, https://equitablegrowth.org/research-paper/the-consequences-of-political-inequality-and-voter-suppression-for-u-s-economic-inequality-and-growth/.

39. It's hard to track down who used the "thinking upstream" metaphor first. J. B. McKinlay used it in a 1979 presentation to the American Heart Association. Patricia Butterfield furthered the concept of thinking upstream in the field of nursing, primarily making the case that improving population health demands reducing inequalities in broad social, economic, political, and environmental pathways. Essentially, this metaphor illustrates how it is imperative to focus on the systems that produce the negative outcomes rather than seeking to only heal or attend to the negative outcomes at the individual level. See Patricia G. Butterfield, "Thinking Upstream: A 25-Year Retrospective and Conceptual Model Aimed at Reducing Health Inequalities," *Advances in Nursing Science* 40, no. 1 (2017): 2–11.

40. Jonathan Wilson-Hartgrove, *Revolution of Values: Reclaiming Public Faith for the Common Good* (Downers Grove, IL: InterVarsity, 2019).

41. The pregnancy-related mortality rate for Black women is over three times higher than the rate for white women. The infant mortality rate—death of an infant within the first year of life—for infants born to Black women is over two times higher than the rate for infants born to white women. See Samantha Artiga, Olivia Pham, Kendal Orgera, and Usha Ranji, "Racial Disparities in Maternal and Infant Health: An Overview," November 10, 2020, from the nonprofit and nonpartisan Kaiser Family Foundation, https://www.kff.org/report-section/racial-disparities-in-maternal-and-infant-health-an-overview-issue-brief/.

42. See Aaron Griffith, *God's Law and Order: The Politics of Punishment in Evangelical America* (Cambridge, MA: Harvard University Press, 2021).

43. Jack Jenkins, *American Prophets: The Religious Roots of Progressive Politics and the Ongoing Fight for the Soul of the Country* (New York: HarperOne, 2020); and Wilson-Hartgrove, *Revolution of Values.*

44. Howard Thurman, *Jesus and the Disinherited* (Boston: Beacon, 1976), 1–2 (emphasis added).

Chapter 4 Do Not Be Afraid?

1. Cited in Philip Bump, "The Trump Administration Fans Out to Defend Christianity across the Political Spectrum," *Washington Post,* October14, 2019, https://www.washingtonpost.com/politics/2019/10/14/trump-administration-fans-out -defend-christianity-across-political-spectrum/.

2. Andrew R. Murphy, *Prodigal Nation: Moral Decline and Divine Punishment from New England to 9/11* (New York: Oxford University Press, 2009).

3. Benjamin Fearnow, "Pastor Robert Jeffress, White House Ally, Warns Evangelicals Not Voting Is 'Sin against God,'" *Newsweek,* November 1, 2020, https://www .newsweek.com/pastor-robert-jeffress-white-house-ally-warns-evangelicals-not -voting-sin-against-god-1543871.

4. David Brody, "Exclusive: Franklin Graham Tells CBN News He Thinks Democratic Party Is 'Opposed to Faith,'" CBN News, August 28, 2020, https://www.cbn .com/cbnnews/2020/august/exclusive-franklin-graham-tells-news-he-thinks-dem ocrats-are-opposed-to-faith.

5. For a full transcript of Donald Trump's remarks, see Politico Staff, "Full Text: Trump Values Voter Summit Remarks," Politico, September 9, 2016, https://www.politico.com/story/2016/09/full-text-trump-values-voter-summit-remarks-22 7977.

6. Renzo Downey, "Donald Trump Recalls Defending 'Judeo-Christian Values,' Says Religion Is Under Attack," Florida Politics, September 2, 2021, https://florida politics.com/archives/454979-donald-trump-recalls-defending-judeo-christian -values-says-religion-is-under-attack/.

7. An example is QAnon and the rise of other conspiratorial beliefs and their prevalence among Christians. See Ian Huff, "QAnon Beliefs Have Increased Since 2021 as Americans Are Less Likely to Reject Conspiracies," PRRI, June 24, 2022, https://www.prri.org/spotlight/qanon-beliefs-have-increased-since-2021-as-americans -are-less-likely-to-reject-conspiracies/.

8. Robert P. Jones, *The End of White Christian America* (New York: Simon & Schuster, 2016); and Rosemary L. Al-Kire, Michael H. Pasek, Jo-Ann Tsang, and Wade C. Rowatt, "Christian No More: Christian Americans Are Threatened by Their Impending Minority Status," *Journal of Experimental Social Psychology* 97 (November 2021): article 104233.

9. See John Fea, *Believe Me: The Evangelical Road to Donald Trump* (Grand Rapids: Eerdmans, 2018), 76.

10. See Kai T. Erikson, *Wayward Puritans: A Study in the Sociology of Deviance* (Boston: Allyn and Bacon, 2004).

11. Kristin Kobes Du Mez, *Jesus and John Wayne: How White Evangelicals Corrupted a Faith and Fractured a Nation* (New York: Liveright, 2020).

12. Fea, *Believe Me,* 103.

13. Robert P. Jones, *White Too Long: The Legacy of White Supremacy in American Christianity* (New York: Simon & Schuster, 2020), 42.

14. "Tucker Carlson Gives Passionate Defense of 'White Replacement Theory,'" *Media Matters for America*, April 28, 2021, https://www.mediamatters.org/fox-news /tucker-carlson-gives-passionate-defense-white-replacement-theory.

15. For a helpful collection of screenshots, see Bradly Mason (@AlsoACarpen ter), "Presbyterian and author of *The Case for Christian Nationalism*. If you were wondering if this is what Christian Nationalism is all about, wonder no longer," Twitter, October 16, 2022, 8:55 p.m., https://twitter.com/AlsoACarpenter/status /1581811101947154433.

16. See Andrew L. Whitehead and Samuel L. Perry, *Taking America Back for God: Christian Nationalism in the United States* (New York: Oxford University Press, 2020), chap. 1, "Four Americans," for a description of the four orientations toward Christian nationalism present in the US population: Ambassadors, Accommodators, Resisters, and Rejecters. Fifty percent of Ambassadors report being slightly afraid, afraid, or very afraid of whites no longer being the majority in the United States. See "2019 Chapman University Survey of American Fears," https://www.chapman .edu/wilkinson/research-centers/babbie-center/survey-american-fears.aspx.

17. This newsletter from Dobson is no longer available in the Focus on the Family archives. Helpfully, it was reproduced in full on various other websites such as the following: James Dobson, "Dr. Dobson's Visit to the Border: An Open Letter," *The Stream*, July 1, 2019, https://stream.org/dr-dobsons-visit-to-the-border -an-open-letter/.

18. Stephen Groves, "South Dakota Is 1 of 4 States Not Resettling Afghan Evacuees," *AP News*, September 16, 2021, https://apnews.com/article/south-dakota-sd-state -wire-district-of-columbia-social-services-956ec00e633f9bd5d8605f13bb6da5e2.

19. Eugene Scott, "A Look at Robert Jeffress, the Controversial Figure Giving the Prayer at the U.S. Embassy in Jerusalem Today," *Washington Post*, May 14, 2018, https://www.washingtonpost.com/news/the-fix/wp/2018/05/14/a-look-at-robert -jeffress-the-controversial-figure-giving-the-prayer-at-the-u-s-embassy-in-jeru salem-today/.

20. Paul Waldman, "The Right Unleashes a New Wave of Fear-Mongering over Refugees," *Washington Post*, August 17, 2021, https://www.washingtonpost.com /opinions/2021/08/17/right-unleashes-new-wave-fear-mongering-over-refugees/.

21. For refugee data, see Whitehead and Perry, *Taking America Back for God*, 83; and Samuel Perry (@profsamperry), "Here's an example: Look at these attitudes across, say, belief that the US should declare itself a Christian nation. Pretty much a linear trend accept for one: Christian refugees. So part of the white evangelical bump is they're more likely to think USA is by/for Christians," Twitter, August 18, 2021, 9:30 a.m., https://twitter.com/socofthesacred/status/142798631681014 5797?s=20. Seventy-seven percent of Ambassadors say they are slightly afraid, afraid, or very afraid of illegal immigration. See also "2019 Chapman University Survey of American Fears."

22. See Du Mez, *Jesus and John Wayne*, 219–32.

23. Dustin Gardiner and Mark Olalde, "These Copycat Bills on Sharia Law and Terrorism Have No Effect. Why Do States Keep Passing Them?," *USA Today News*, July 17, 2019, https://www.usatoday.com/in-depth/news/investigations/2019/07 /17/islam-sharia-law-how-far-right-group-gets-model-bills-passed/1636199001/.

24. See the Public Religion Research Institute's American Values Atlas: http:// ava.prri.org/#religious/2020/States/religion/13. See also Yonat Shimron, "Religious Groups with Immigrant Members Grew Fastest over Past Decade," *Religion News Service*, November 11, 2022, https://religionnews.com/2022/11/11/religious-groups -with-immigrant-members-grew-fastest-over-past-decade/.

25. Ihsan Bagby, "The American Mosque 2020: Growing and Evolving," Institute for Social Policy and Understanding, June 2, 2020, https://www.ispu.org/public-policy/mosque-survey/.

26. "About Us," The Lutheran Church–Missouri Synod, accessed July 28, 2022, https://www.lcms.org/about; and Dalia Fahmy, "7 Facts about Southern Baptists," Pew Research Center, June 7, 2019, https://www.pewresearch.org/fact-tank/2019/06/07/7-facts-about-southern-baptists/.

27. David J. Bier, "A Dozen Times Trump Equated His Travel Ban with a Muslim Ban," CATO Institute, August 14, 2017, https://www.cato.org/blog/dozen-times-trump-equated-travel-ban-muslim-ban.

28. "2019 Chapman University Survey of American Fears."

29. Given the ministry itself reports this figure, it should probably be taken with a grain of salt. See "Ministry Facts," Billy Graham Evangelistic Association, accessed October 11, 2022, https://billygraham.org/news/media-resources/electronic-press-kit/ministry-facts/.

30. Franklin Graham, "The Most Important Election of Our Lifetime," *Decision*, September 20, 2016, https://decisionmagazine.com/most-important-election-lifetime/.

31. Whitehead and Perry, *Taking America Back for God*, 111–12.

32. "2019 Chapman University Survey of American Fears."

33. Bagby, "American Mosque 2020."

34. Katayoun Kishi, "Assaults against Muslims in U.S. Surpass 2001 Level," Pew Research Center, November 15, 2017, https://www.pewresearch.org/fact-tank/2017/11/15/assaults-against-muslims-in-u-s-surpass-2001-level/; and Ismail Allison, "CAIR Issues New Report Detailing 6,700+ Civil Rights Complaints, Highest Number Ever Recorded," CAIR, April 25, 2022, https://www.cair.com/press_releases/cair-issues-new-report-detailing-6700-civil-rights-complaints-highest-number-ever-recorded/.

35. Franklin Graham, "Steadfast for the Gospel," *Decision*, May 1, 2018, https://decisionmagazine.com/steadfast-for-gospel/.

36. Whitehead and Perry, *Taking America Back for God*, 111–12.

37. Jonathan Lemire, "Playing Electoral Defense, Trump Claims Biden Opposes God," *AP News*, August 6, 2020, https://apnews.com/article/virus-outbreak-election-2020-global-trade-ap-top-news-religion-a3c57cdcf8e44755d15930b29c660e36.

38. Blake Montgomery, "Rep. Madison Cawthorn Suggest Biden's Vax Outreach Is a Plot to Steal Bibles," *Daily Beast*, July 9, 2021, https://www.thedailybeast.com/rep-madison-cawthorn-bidens-vaccine-outreach-is-a-plot-to-steal-bibles; David D. Kirkpatrick, "Republicans Admit Mailing Campaign Literature Saying Liberals Will Ban the Bible," *New York Times*, September 24, 2004, https://www.nytimes.com/2004/09/24/politics/campaign/republicans-admit-mailing-campaign-literature-saying.html; and Paul A. Djupe and Ryan P. Burge, "One in Five Americans Believe That a Democrat Will Ban the Bible," *Religion in Public*, June 2, 2020, https://religioninpublic.blog/2020/06/02/one-in-five-americans-believe-that-a-democrat-will-ban-the-bible/.

39. Taylor Mooney, "Is America a Christian Nation? Pastors at Odds about Fusion of Faith and Politics," CBS News, March 4, 2021, https://www.cbsnews.com/news/america-christian-nation-religious-right/; and Djupe and Burge, "One in Five Americans."

40. Philip S. Gorski and Samuel L. Perry, *The Flag and the Cross: White Christian Nationalism and the Threat to American Democracy* (New York: Oxford University Press, 2022), 111.

41. "Trump and the Christian Persecution Complex," *On the Media*, WNYC Studios, June 3, 2020, https://www.wnycstudios.org/podcasts/otm/episodes/trumps -age-old-christian-persecution-complex.

42. For instance, the 117th Congress is 88.1 percent Christian (55 percent Protestant, 30 percent Catholic, with small percentages of Mormons and Orthodox Christians). Compare this to the general population, in which 65 percent of Americans are Christian and 43 percent are Protestant and 20 percent are Catholic. See "Faith on the Hill," Pew Research Center, January 4, 2021, https://www.pewresearch.org /religion/2021/01/04/faith-on-the-hill-2021/.

43. See Michael Rotolo, "Fight-or-Flight for America: The Affective Conditioning of Christian Nationalist Ideological Views during the Transition to Adulthood," *Sociological Forum* 37, no. 3 (September 2022): 812–35, https://doi.org/10.1111/socf .12827. Also important is the role of childhood trauma in the development of the Christian nationalism toolkit.

44. One recent study shows Americans increasingly embraced Christian nationalism when reminded of changes in demographic and religious shifts. See Al-Kire et al., "Christian No More."

45. Paul A. Djupe, "The Inverted Golden Rule: Are Atheists as Intolerant as Evangelicals Think They Are?," *Religion in Public*, December 23, 2019, https://reli gioninpublic.blog/2019/12/23/the-inverted-golden-rule-are-atheists-as-intolerant -as-evangelicals-think-they-are/.

46. See Fea's *Believe Me*, Du Mez's *Jesus and John Wayne*, and Dave Verhaagen's *How White Evangelicals Think* (Eugene, OR: Cascade Books, 2022) for excellent discussions on the centrality of fear to the political and religious consolidation of power around Christian nationalism.

47. I used the free online NIV concordance on Bible Gateway.

48. Russell Moore, "Let the Afghan Refugees Come unto Me," *Christianity Today*, August 30, 2021, https://www.christianitytoday.com/ct/2021/august-web-only/af ghanistan-refugees-resettlement-let-come-to-me.html.

49. "Immigration and Crime: What Does the Research Say?," The Conversation, February 1, 2017, https://theconversation.com/immigration-and-crime-what-does -the-research-say-72176.

50. Michael T. Light, Jingying He, and Jason P. Robey, "Comparing Crime Rates between Undocumented Immigrants, Legal Immigrants, and Native-Born US Citizens in Texas," *PNAS* 117, no. 51 (December 2020): 32340–47; and Alex Nowrasteh, "New Research on Illegal Immigration and Crime," CATO Institute, October 13, 2020, https://www.cato.org/blog/new-research-illegal-immigration-crime-0.

51. Aaron J. Chalfin, "Do Mexican Immigrants 'Cause' Crime?," Department of Criminology, University of Pennsylvania, accessed July 28, 2022, https://crim .sas.upenn.edu/fact-check/do-mexican-immigrants-cause-crime; and Mauricio Leiva, Felipe Vasquez-Lavín, and Roberto D. Ponce Oliva, "Do Immigrants Increase Crime? Spatial Analysis in a Middle-Income Country," *World Development* 126 (February 2020): article 104728.

52. Peter Berger, in his book *The Sacred Canopy: Elements of a Sociological Theory of Religion* (New York: Anchor Books, 1967), describes plausibility structures as the social arrangements that support meaning and belief systems. Plausibility structures are the relationships within which our view of the world is supported and maintained. Imagine yourself at the center of a broad web where you are connected to all your friends, family, acquaintances, and even strangers by a small strand of connective tissue. All your beliefs and values are in some way the result of these connective tissues. If all of those at the end of those connective strands

believe and value the same things as you, the web is strong. You are unlikely to let go of those beliefs and values, because everyone around you sees the world the same way you do. Now, imagine that at the end of several of the connective strands—not all, but just a few—are people who perhaps hold different beliefs and values. Your web is no longer quite as strong. Some of the connective strands are no longer supporting you in the same way. The degree to which your web is weakened depends on how close these several people are to you. If it is a thin strand from someone far away, the likelihood you reconsider deeply held beliefs and values is low. From someone close to you with a thick connective strand—the likelihood increases significantly.

As I look back over my own journey, I can see the power of the plausibility structures that provided support for my meaning and belief systems. Almost everyone around me saw the world in a similar way, and there was little reason for me to question those views. However, as I built and maintained relationships with others, some becoming close while others were somewhat further away, I could no longer *not* evaluate the myths, traditions, narratives, and symbols of white Christian nationalism. Ultimately, I could have come to the decision to hold on to them. But against the weight of evidence, those beliefs and values could not be maintained. Those of us who have walked away from white Christian nationalism to varying degrees will need to kindly, gently, but firmly serve as credible connections in the plausibility structures of our neighbors, family members, and friends, enabling them to question these deeply held beliefs and meaning systems.

53. Author interview, January 21, 2022. Quotations from Amar that follow are from this interview.

54. See Amar D. Peterman, "The Great American Potluck," *Sojourners*, October 11, 2021, https://sojo.net/articles/great-american-potluck. Follow Amar's work here: www.amarpeterman.com.

55. Danté Stewart (@stewartdantec), "James Baldwin is right: often times the passion with which we love the Lord and the ways we practice our faith 'was a measure of how deeply we feared and distrusted.' And when fear is at the heart of our faith then harm will be the expression of our experience," Twitter, October 7, 2021, 10:03 a.m., https://twitter.com/stewartdantec/status/1446113886042656768?s=20.

56. Danté Stewart, *Shoutin' in the Fire: An American Epistle* (New York: Convergent, 2021), 117.

Chapter 5 Lay Down Your Sword?

1. Cited in Chloe Folmar, "Boebert: Jesus Didn't Have Enough AR-15s to 'Keep His Government from Killing Him,'" *The Hill*, June 17, 2022, https://thehill.com/homenews/house/3528049-boebert-jesus-didnt-have-enough-ar-15s-to-keep-his-government-from-killing-him/.

2. *Official Report of the Nineteenth Annual Conference of Charities and Correction* (1892), 46–59. Reprinted in Richard H. Pratt, "The Advantages of Mingling Indians with Whites," in *Americanizing the American Indians: Writings by the "Friends of the Indian" 1880–1900* (Cambridge, MA: Harvard University Press, 1973), 260–71. Available online at History Matters, http://historymatters.gmu.edu/d/4929/.

3. "On This Day: March 03, 1819," EJI, accessed July 28, 2022, https://calendar.eji.org/racial-injustice/mar/03.

4. Ian Austen, "How Thousands of Indigenous Children Vanished in Canada," *New York Times*, June 7, 2021, https://www.nytimes.com/2021/06/07/world/canada/mass-graves-residential-schools.html.

5. Declan Leary, "The Meaning of the Native Graves," *American Conservative*, July 8, 2021, https://www.theamericanconservative.com/articles/the-meaning-of -the-native-graves/.

6. I recognize that the embrace of violence within Christianity is not unique to the United States. We can trace the relationship back to the first several centuries of Christianity's existence. The marriage of violence and religion is also not unique to Christianity. Numerous world religions have embraced violence in the past and still do today. However, these realities do not excuse us, American Christians, from attending to the mess that idolizing violence makes of our own tradition.

7. This quote is from Mark Driscoll, disgraced former pastor of Mars Hill Church. Greg Boyd, "Revelation and the Violent 'Pride Fighting' Jesus," ReKnew, September 28, 2010, https://reknew.org/2010/09/revelation-and-the-violent-prize -fighting-jesus/.

8. The usual suspects: William Wallace from the movie *Braveheart*, Maximus from *Gladiator*, Neo in *The Matrix*.

9. See Greg Boyd, *The Myth of a Christian Nation: How the Quest for Political Power Is Destroying the Church* (Grand Rapids: Zondervan, 2005); and David Bentley Hart, *The Story of Christianity: A History of 2,000 Years of the Christian Faith* (London: Quercus, 2013).

10. See Philip S. Gorski and Samuel L. Perry, *The Flag and the Cross: White Christian Nationalism and the Threat to American Democracy* (New York: Oxford University Press, 2022), 51.

11. Gorski and Perry, *The Flag and the Cross*, 59.

12. Gorski and Perry, *The Flag and the Cross*, 66.

13. Gorski and Perry, *The Flag and the Cross*, 67.

14. Eric L. McDaniel, Irfan Nooruddin, and Allyson F. Shortle, *The Everyday Crusade: Christian Nationalism in American Politics* (New York: Cambridge University Press, 2022).

15. William M. Arkin, "The Pentagon Unleashes a Holy Warrior," *Los Angeles Times*, October 16, 2003, https://www.latimes.com/archives/la-xpm-2003-oct-16 -oe-arkin16-story.html.

16. Andrew L. Whitehead and Samuel L. Perry, *Taking America Back for God: Christian Nationalism in the United States* (New York: Oxford University Press, 2020), 1.

17. McDaniel, Nooruddin, and Shortle, *Everyday Crusade*.

18. "Remarks by the President upon Arrival," Office of the Press Secretary, The White House, September 16, 2001, https://georgewbush-whitehouse.archives.gov /news/releases/2001/09/20010916-2.html.

19. See Whitehead and Perry, *Taking America Back for God*, 14.

20. McDaniel, Nooruddin, and Shortle, *Everyday Crusade*.

21. This was the same class I had with Prof. Frank Lambert, who opened my eyes to the reality that the founding fathers were not evangelical Christians like we see today.

22. See J. Russell Hawkins, *The Bible Told Them So: How Southern Evangelicals Fought to Preserve White Supremacy* (New York: Oxford University Press, 2021).

23. See Kelly J. Baker, *Gospel according to the Klan: The KKK's Appeal to Protestant America, 1915–1930* (Lawrence: University Press of Kansas, 2017).

24. See Whitehead and Perry, *Taking America Back for God*, 101–5.

25. See Joshua Davis, "Enforcing Christian Nationalism: Examining the Link between Group Identity and Punitive Attitudes in the United States," *Journal for the Scientific Study of Religion* 57, no. 2 (June 2018): 300–317.

26. See Gorski and Perry, *The Flag and the Cross*, 95.

27. See the example pointed out by Samuel Perry (@profsamperry), "It's almost like open Christian nationalists are repeating our survey questions. We find the more whites affirm explicit #ChristianNationalism, the more they say we don't use death penalty enough. And here's a CN stan saying we should expand offenses for which we execute people," Twitter, October 22, 2022, 8:53 a.m., https://twitter.com/profsamperry/status/1583803670072037378.

28. See "Innocence," Death Penalty Information Center, accessed October 12, 2022, https://deathpenaltyinfo.org/policy-issues/innocence. Regarding minority groups being sentenced to death at a rate disproportionately higher than whites, see "Facts about the Death Penalty," Death Penalty Information Center, updated October 6, 2022, https://documents.deathpenaltyinfo.org/pdf/FactSheet.pdf.

29. See "Death Penalty," Equal Justice Initiative, accessed October 12, 2022, https://eji.org/issues/death-penalty/.

30. See Miles T. Armaly, David T. Buckley, and Adam M. Enders, "Christian Nationalism and Political Violence: Victimhood, Racial Identity, Conspiracy, and Support for the Capitol Attacks," *Political Behavior* 44, no. 2 (2022): 937–60; Gorski and Perry, *The Flag and the Cross*; and PRRI Staff, "Competing Visions of America: An Evolving Identity or a Culture Under Attack? Findings from the 2021 American Values Survey," PRRI, November 1, 2021, https://www.prri.org/research/competing-visions-of-america-an-evolving-identity-or-a-culture-under-attack/.

31. Absent any direct knowledge of the firearms, it is prudent to consider them semiautomatic or possibly semiautomatic conversions. Actual machine guns—fully automatic weapons—are quite rare in private ownership in the United States. Weapons capable of automatic fire have been closely regulated since 1984.

32. Adela Suliman and Timothy Bella, "GOP Rep. Boebert: 'I'm Tired of This Separation of Church and State Junk,'" *Washington Post*, June 28, 2022, https://www.washingtonpost.com/politics/2022/06/28/lauren-boebert-church-state-colorado/.

33. Angela Denker, *Red State Christians: Understanding the Voters Who Elected Donald Trump* (Minneapolis: Fortress, 2019), 61. The sign does not explicitly say what kind of "attempt" is in view here.

34. David Moye, "GOP Politician's 'Jesus Guns Babies' Slogan Has Twitter Firing Off Jokes," *HuffPost*, February 17, 2022, https://www.huffpost.com/entry/kandiss-taylor-jesus-guns-babies-campaign-slogan_n_620ebe89e4b0c94bb9a81845.

35. Folmar, "Boebert."

36. Peter Manseau, "Why So Many Guns on Christmas Cards? Because Jesus Was 'Manly and Virile,'" *Washington Post*, December 14, 2021, https://www.washingtonpost.com/outlook/2021/12/14/guns-christmas-thomas-massie-lauren-boebert/.

37. See Kristin Kobes Du Mez, *Jesus and John Wayne: How White Evangelicals Corrupted a Faith and Fractured a Nation* (New York: Liveright, 2020), 296.

38. See Gorski and Perry, *The Flag and the Cross*, 95.

39. See Baylor Religion Survey Wave 6 (2021), https://www.baylor.edu/baylorreligionsurvey/.

40. See Andrew Whitehead, Landon Schnabel, and Samuel Perry, "Gun Control in the Crosshairs: Christian Nationalism and Opposition to Stricter Gun Laws," *Socius* 4 (July 2018): 1–13; Baylor Religion Survey Wave 6 (2021); and the "2019 Chapman University Survey of American Fears," https://www.chapman.edu/wilkinson/research-centers/babbie-center/survey-american-fears.aspx.

41. Paul Gosar (@DrPaulGosar), "Christ is king," Twitter, November 7, 2021, 11:13 a.m., https://twitter.com/DrPaulGosar/status/1457380722197499905. Gosar's tweet about Rep. Ocasio-Cortez no longer exists. See Felicia Sonmez, "Rep. Paul Gosar Tweets Altered Anime Video Showing Him Killing Rep. Ocasio-Cortez

and Attacking President Biden," *Washington Post*, November 8, 2021, https://www .washingtonpost.com/politics/republicans-gosar-trump-ocasio-cortez/2021/11/08 /ead37b36-40ca-11ec-9ea7-3eb2406a2e24_story.html.

42. Danté Stewart, *Shoutin' in the Fire: An American Epistle* (New York: Convergent, 2021), 55.

43. Lisa Sharon Harper, *The Very Good Gospel: How Everything Wrong Can Be Made Right* (Colorado Springs: WaterBrook, 2016), 174.

44. David Cramer and Myles Werntz, *A Field Guide to Christian Nonviolence: Key Thinkers, Activists, and Movements for the Gospel of Peace* (Grand Rapids: Baker Academic, 2022), 7–11.

45. Matthew Peterson, "The Ordinary Goodness of André Trocmé and Le Chambon," *Plough*, February 7, 2022, https://www.plough.com/en/topics/faith/witness /the-ordinary-goodness-of-andre-trocme-and-le-chambon.

46. Cramer and Werntz, *Field Guide*, 56.

47. Cramer and Werntz, *Field Guide*, 35. But see also Cramer and Werntz, chap. 8, on Christian antiviolence regarding sexual and gender-based violence. Here the concept of suffering can be weaponized to shame women experiencing violence and abuse. In this sense, "suffering" can be used to keep the abused in harmful situations as a testament to Christ. I am not speaking of suffering in these terms here.

48. Cramer and Werntz, *Field Guide*, 91.

49. Cramer and Werntz, *Field Guide*, 93–108, here 95.

50. Harper, *The Very Good Gospel*, 175.

51. Stewart, *Shoutin' in the Fire*, 117–18.

Chapter 6 May Your Kingdom Come, on Earth as It Is in Heaven?

1. Bob Jones, "Is Segregation Scriptural?," April 17, 1960, Easter Sunday sermon. Bob Jones was the founder of Bob Jones University. Please see Camille Lewis's transcription and background information at "'Is Segregation Scriptural?' by Bob Jones Sr, 1960," *A Time to Laugh*, March 15, 2013, https://www.drslewis.org/camille /2013/03/15/is-segregation-scriptural-by-bob-jones-sr-1960/.

2. "Race/Ethnicity Report," Association of Religion Data Archives, accessed November 16, 2022, https://www.thearda.com/us-religion/cpb?y=5086543.517162 117&x=-9571469.251585525&b=4&denom=#RACE; "1990 Census of Population and Housing," STATS Indiana, accessed October 13, 2022, https://www.thearda.com/us -religion/community-profiles/build-a-profile-of-your-community. I used 46573 to locate my community and a two-mile radius.

3. "People and Ideas: Jerry Falwell," PBS: Frontline, accessed November 16, 2022, https://www.pbs.org/wgbh/pages/frontline/godinamerica/people/jerry-fal well.html.

4. Quote from Jerry Falwell's now (in)famous sermon responding to Martin Luther King Jr. and the civil rights movement, "Ministers and Marchers," in Randall Balmer, *Bad Faith: Race and the Rise of the Religious Right* (Grand Rapids: Eerdmans, 2021), 73–74.

5. Balmer, *Bad Faith*, 59.

6. See Randall Balmer, *Thy Kingdom Come: How the Religious Right Distorts the Faith and Threatens America* (New York: Basic Books, 2007); and Balmer, *Bad Faith*.

7. Balmer, *Bad Faith*, 41–42.

8. Balmer, *Thy Kingdom Come*, 15.

9. Balmer, *Bad Faith*, 45–48.

10. See Gillian Frank and Neil J. Young, "What Everyone Gets Wrong about Evangelicals and Abortion," *Washington Post*, May 16, 2022, https://www.washington post.com/outlook/2022/05/16/what-everyone-gets-wrong-about-evangelicals-abor tion/.

11. See Frank and Young, "What Everyone Gets Wrong"; and Robert P. Jones, *White Too Long: The Legacy of White Supremacy in American Christianity* (New York: Simon & Schuster, 2020), 73–106.

12. See Samuel L. Perry and Andrew L. Whitehead, "Christian Nationalism and White Racial Boundaries: Examining Whites' Opposition to Interracial Marriage," *Ethnic and Racial Studies* 38, no. 10 (2015): 1671–89; Perry and Whitehead, "Christian Nationalism, Racial Separatism, and Family Formation: Attitudes toward Transracial Adoption as a Test Case," *Race and Social Problems* 7, no. 2 (2015): 12–134; and Perry and Whitehead, "Christian America in Black and White: Racial Identity, Religious-National Group Boundaries, and Explanations for Racial Inequality," *Sociology of Religion* 80, no. 3 (Autumn 2019): 277–98.

13. Joshua T. Davis, "Funding God's Policies, Defending Whiteness: Christian Nationalism and Whites' Attitudes towards Racially-Coded Government Spending," *Ethnic and Racial Studies* 42, no. 12 (2019): 2123–42.

14. Andrew L. Whitehead and Samuel L. Perry, *Taking America Back for God: Christian Nationalism in the United States* (New York: Oxford University Press, 2020); and Samuel L. Perry, Andrew L. Whitehead, and Joshua T. Davis, "God's Country in Black and Blue: How Christian Nationalism Shapes Americans' Views about Police (Mis)Treatment of Blacks," *Sociology of Race and Ethnicity* 5, no. 1 (January 2019): 130–46.

15. Joshua T. Davis and Samuel L. Perry, "White Christian Nationalism and Relative Political Tolerance for Racists," *Social Problems* 68, no. 3 (August 2021): 513–34.

16. Philip S. Gorski and Samuel L. Perry, *The Flag and the Cross: White Christian Nationalism and the Threat to American Democracy* (New York: Oxford University Press, 2022); and Samuel L. Perry, Andrew L. Whitehead, and Joshua B. Grubbs, " 'I Don't Want Everybody to Vote': Christian Nationalism and Restricting Voter Access in the United States," *Sociological Forum* 37, no. 1 (March 2022): 4–26.

17. Samuel L. Perry, Andrew L. Whitehead, and Joshua B. Grubbs, "Prejudice and Pandemic in the Promised Land: How White Christian Nationalism Shapes Americans' Racist and Xenophobic Views of COVID-19," *Ethnic and Racial Studies* 44, no. 5 (2021): 759–72.

18. Ibram X. Kendi, *Stamped from the Beginning: The Definitive History of Racist Ideas in America* (New York: Basic Books, 2016).

19. Mark Charles and Soong-Chan Rah, *Unsettling Truths: The Ongoing, Dehumanizing Legacy of the Doctrine of Discovery* (Downers Grove, IL: InterVarsity, 2019).

20. Jemar Tisby, *The Color of Compromise: The Truth about the American Church's Complicity in Racism* (Grand Rapids: Zondervan, 2019), 36.

21. Jemar Tisby, *How to Fight Racism: Courageous Christianity and the Journey toward Racial Justice* (Grand Rapids: Zondervan, 2021), 9.

22. Charles and Rah, *Unsettling Truths*, 72–73.

23. Jones, *White Too Long*, 73–106.

24. Some reports of this history mention Jesse having an intellectual disability and highlight the suspicious nature of his confession and the discovery of the murder weapon, while others do not. See Patricia Bernstein, "The Lynching of Jesse Washington," *Lynching in Texas*, accessed November 16, 2022, https://lynching intexas.org/bernstein; and Kurt Terry, "Jesse Washington Lynching," *Waco History*, accessed November 16, 2022, https://wacohistory.org/items/show/55.

25. Jesse Washington, "The Waco Horror," *Andscape*, accessed July 28, 2022, https://andscape.com/features/the-waco-horror/.

26. See the EJI map here: https://lynchinginamerica.eji.org/explore.

27. See especially Angela D. Sims, *Lynched: The Power of Memory in a Culture of Terror* (Waco: Baylor University Press, 2016). See Anthea Butler, *White Evangelical Racism: The Politics of Morality in America* (Chapel Hill: University of North Carolina Press, 2021), 30; Jones, *White Too Long*, 28–32; and Tisby, *Color of Compromise*, 107, respectively.

28. See James H. Cone, *The Cross and the Lynching Tree* (Maryknoll, NY: Orbis Books, 2013), chap. 2.

29. See the entirety of J. Russell Hawkins, *The Bible Told Them So: How Southern Evangelicals Fought to Preserve White Supremacy* (New York: Oxford University Press, 2021). See also Butler, *White Evangelical Racism*, 49–50; and Jones, *White Too Long*, 25–71.

30. Curtis W. Freeman, "'Never Had I Been So Blind': W. A. Criswell's 'Change' on Racial Segregation," *Journal of Southern Religion* 10 (2007): 1–12. As Freeman shows in this work, Criswell later shared that his views on segregation had changed, mostly for pragmatic reasons. Hawkins's *The Bible Told Them So* demonstrates this shift and the implications it has for perpetuating the racial hierarchy in American society and the Christian church.

31. Jones, "Is Segregation Scriptural?"

32. Cited in Hawkins, *The Bible Told Them So*, 2.

33. See Richard Rothstein, *The Color of Law: A Forgotten History of How Our Government Segregated America* (New York: Liveright, 2017), 103–5.

34. See Aaron Griffith, *God's Law and Order: The Politics of Punishment in Evangelical America* (Cambridge, MA: Harvard University Press, 2021); and Michelle Alexander, *The New Jim Crow: Mass Incarceration in the Age of Colorblindness* (New York: The New Press, 2010).

35. The statistics in this list are drawn from several sources. See Kriston McIntosh, Emily Moss, Ryan Nunn, and Jay Shambaugh, "Examining the Black-White Wealth Gap," *Up Front*, Feburary 27, 2020, https://www.brookings.edu/blog/up-front/2020/02/27/examining-the-black-white-wealth-gap/; Dedrick Asante-Muhammad et al., "Racial Wealth Snapshot: Native Americans," National Community Reinvestment Coalition, February 14, 2022, https://ncrc.org/racial-wealth-snapshot-american-indians-native-americans/; "Health Coverage by Race and Ethnicity, 2010–2019," Kaiser Family Foundation, July 16, 2021, https://www.kff.org/racial-equity-and-health-policy/issue-brief/health-coverage-by-race-and-ethnicity/; "US Census Housing Vacancy and Homeownership Statistics," United States Census Bureau, September 14, 2020, https://www.census.gov/housing/hvs/data/histtabs.html; Wendy Sawyer, "Visualizing the Racial Disparities in Mass Incarceration," *Prison Policy Initiative*, July 27, 2020, https://www.prisonpolicy.org/blog/2020/07/27/disparities/.

36. It is important to note that PRRI is not measuring Christian nationalism here. However, I share the findings for white evangelicals because, as I shared in chap. 1, a majority of Americans in this religious tradition embrace Christian nationalism to some extent. Furthermore, the diffusion of Christian nationalism throughout American culture is largely due to evangelicals' widespread acceptance of this cultural framework. While Christian nationalism is not synonymous with white evangelicalism, in the absence of a Christian nationalism measure, I turn to this group to illustrate the trends in this paragraph and the next.

37. PRRI Staff, "Summer Unrest over Racial Injustice Moves the Country, but Not Republicans or White Evangelicals," PRRI, August 21, 2020, https://www.prri .org/research/racial-justice-2020-george-floyd/; and Sawyer, "Visualizing the Racial Disparities."

38. Jones, *White Too Long*, 6.

39. Quoted in Cone, *The Cross and the Lynching Tree*, 131.

40. See Butler, *White Evangelical Racism*; Willie James Jennings, *The Christian Imagination: Theology and the Origins of Race* (New Haven: Yale University Press, 2010); Jones, *White Too Long*; Tisby, *How to Fight Racism*; and Tisby, *Color of Compromise*.

41. Cone, *The Cross and the Lynching Tree*, xvii.

42. Jones, *White Too Long*, 70.

43. Cone, *The Cross and the Lynching Tree*, 115.

44. Kat Armas, *Abuelita Faith: What Women on the Margins Teach Us about Wisdom, Persistence, and Strength* (Grand Rapids: Brazos, 2021), 115.

45. Cone, *The Cross and the Lynching Tree*, xviii, 31, 115, 118. See Armas, *Abuelita Faith*, for further examples of the marginalized using the Christian scriptures in novel ways in order to find liberation from their oppressors.

46. Tisby, *How to Fight Racism*, 9, 10. To be clear, Tisby is not arguing that Christianity is the *only* religion or worldview that can show us a way forward. He is not claiming that Christianity is the only religion or worldview that provides the necessary resources for confronting racism, but only that it can. We Christians must remember this as we work alongside others intent on confronting white supremacy and racism.

47. Lisa Sharon Harper, *The Very Good Gospel: How Everything Wrong Can Be Made Right* (Colorado Springs: WaterBrook, 2016).

48. Tisby, *How to Fight Racism*, 29.

49. Hawkins, *The Bible Told Them So*, 166.

50. Cone, *The Cross and the Lynching Tree*, xv.

51. As cited in Damon Mayrl, "The Funk of White Souls: Toward a Du Boisian Theory of the White Church," *Sociology of Religion* (May 29, 2002): 6–7, https://doi .org/10.1093/socrel/srac009.

52. "Christian Nationalism's Influence on American Politics," 1A, NPR, July 11, 2022, https://the1a.org/segments/christian-nationalisms-influence-on-american -politics/.

53. Christina Barland Edmondson and Chad Brennan, *Faithful Antiracism: Moving Past Talk to Systemic Change* (Downers Grove, IL: InterVarsity, 2022).

54. Mayrl, "Funk of White Souls," 7–8, 14; and Victor Ray, "A Theory of Racialized Organizations," *American Sociological Review* 84, no. 1 (February 2019): 26–53, https://doi.org/10.1177/0003122418822335.

55. See https://shalomcc.org/repair/ and https://shalomcc.org/a-reparative-act/.

56. Tobin Miller Shearer's historical work was foundational to Shalom Community Church as they reckoned with the failures of the Mennonite denomination in confronting racial inequality.

57. Author interview, July 19, 2022.

58. Mayrl, "Funk of White Souls," 15–16.

59. See Jones, *White Too Long*, 199–210; and Jones, *UnPromised Land: Finding America's Future by Reckoning with Our Racial Past* (forthcoming), for examples.

60. "Franklin Graham Denies Evangelicalism Has a Race Problem," YouTube, May 16, 2021, https://youtu.be/NO5XT0_Y4xs.

61. As cited in Michael O. Emerson and Christian Smith, *Divided by Faith: Evangelical Religion and the Problem of Race in America* (New York: Oxford University Press, 2000), 47.

62. Robert Jones's chapter "Believing" in *White Too Long* is incredibly powerful in demonstrating just how white Christian theology was designed to oppose Black equality, defend white superiority, and constrict white Christians' moral and religious vision.

63. Danté Stewart (@stewartdantec), "We Have to Dismantle," Twitter, September 1, 2021, 9:14 a.m., https://twitter.com/stewartdantec/status/1433055721956986881?s=20.

Chapter 7 And Who Is My Neighbor?

1. Charles Herbster is an agribusiness executive who sought—but lost—his bid to run for governor in Nebraska in the 2022 primary election. Chris Dunker, "Trump Defends, Endorses Herbster at Rescheduled Nebraska Rally," *Omaha World-Herald*, May 1, 2022, https://omaha.com/news/state-and-regional/govt-and-politics/article _128b9dad-943c-5a26-adf2-c46a883529df.html.

2. Kraig Beyerlein, Jenny Trinitapoli, and Gary Adler, "The Effect of Religious Short-Term Mission Trips on Youth Civic Engagement," *Journal for the Scientific Study of Religion* 50, no. 4 (December 2011): 780–95. But see also LiErin Probasco, "Giving Time, Not Money: Long-Term Impacts of Short-Term Mission Trips," *Missiology: An International Review* 41, no. 2 (April 2013): 202–24; and Lindsey A. Huang, "Short-Term Mission Trips: Developing the Racial and Ethnic Consciousness of White Participants," *Journal of Sociology and Christianity* 9, no. 2 (Fall 2019): 55–73.

3. However, unlawful reentry after deportation proceedings is a criminal offense.

4. Giovanna Albanese, "Piercing the Blue Wall with the Gospel," *Decision*, May 1, 2018, https://decisionmagazine.com/piercing-the-blue-wall-with-the-gospel/.

5. James Dobson, "Dr. Dobson's Visit to the Border: An Open Letter," *The Stream*, July 1, 2019, https://stream.org/dr-dobsons-visit-to-the-border-an-open-letter/.

6. Dobson, "Dr. Dobson's Visit to the Border."

7. See "Facts about Immigration," UnidosUS, accessed August 25, 2022, https://www.unidosus.org/issues/immigration/.

8. PRRI Staff, "A Nation of Immigrants? Diverging Perceptions of Immigrants Increasingly Marking Partisan Divides," PRRI, March 12, 2020, https://www.prri.org /research/a-nation-of-immigrants-diverging-perceptions-of-immigrants-increas ingly-marking-partisan-divides/.

9. D. L. Mayfield, *The Myth of the American Dream: Reflections on Affluence, Autonomy, Safety, and Power* (Downers Grove, IL: InterVarsity, 2020), 98.

10. Dunker, "Trump Defends, Endorses Herbster."

11. PRRI, "Nation of Immigrants?"

12. Eric L. McDaniel, Irfan Nooruddin, and Allyson F. Shortle, *The Everyday Crusade: Christian Nationalism in American Politics* (New York: Cambridge University Press, 2022), 105. This finding underscores the racialized nature of immigration attitudes.

13. Breanne L. Grace and Katie Heins, "Redefining Refugee: White Christian Nationalism in State Politics and Beyond," *Ethnic and Racial Studies* 44, no. 4 (March 2021): 565.

14. See McDaniel, Nooruddin, and Shortle, *Everyday Crusade*, 94.

15. PRRI, "Nation of Immigrants?"

16. See McDaniel, Nooruddin, and Shortle, *Everyday Crusade*, 99–121.

17. Grace and Heins, "Redefining Refugee," 565.

18. Grace and Heins, "Redefining Refugee."

19. See Rosemary Al-Kire, Michael Pasek, and Jo-Ann Tsang, "Protecting America's Borders: Christian Nationalism, Threat, and Attitudes toward Immigrants in the United States," *Group Processes & Intergroup Relations* 25, no. 2 (January 2021): 354–78; Joseph O. Baker, Samuel L. Perry, and Andrew L. Whitehead, "Keep America Christian (and White): Christian Nationalism, Fear of Ethnoracial Outsiders, and Intention to Vote for Donald Trump in the 2020 Presidential Election," *Sociology of Religion* 81, no. 3 (Autumn 2020): 272–93; Ramsey Dahab and Marisa Omori, "Homegrown Foreigners: How Christian Nationalism and Nativist Attitudes Impact Muslim Civil Liberties," *Ethnic and Racial Studies* 42, no. 10 (2019): 1727–46; Penny Edgell, Evan Stewart, Sarah Catherine Billups, and Ryan Larson, "The Stakes of Symbolic Boundaries," *Sociological Quarterly* 61, no. 2 (2020): 309–33; and Darren E. Sherkat and Derek Lehman, "Bad Samaritans: Religion and Anti-immigrant and Anti-Muslim Sentiment in the United States," *Social Science Quarterly* 99, no. 5 (November 2018): 1791–1804.

20. See Samuel L. Perry, Andrew L. Whitehead, and Joshua B. Grubbs, "Prejudice and Pandemic in the Promised Land: How White Christian Nationalism Shapes Americans' Racist and Xenophobic Views of COVID-19," *Ethnic and Racial Studies* 44, no. 5 (2021): 759–72.

21. Dahab and Omori, "Homegrown Foreigners"; and Baker, Perry, and Whitehead, "Keep America Christian."

22. Andrew L. Whitehead and Samuel L. Perry, *Taking America Back for God: Christian Nationalism in the United States* (New York: Oxford University Press, 2020).

23. Cited in McDaniel, Nooruddin, and Shortle, *Everyday Crusade*, 94.

24. Grace and Heins, "Redefining Refugee," 568.

25. McDaniel, Nooruddin, and Shortle, *Everyday Crusade*, 101.

26. In this section, I draw heavily on Obery M. Hendricks Jr., *Christians against Christianity: How Right-Wing Evangelicals Are Destroying Our Nation and Our Faith* (Boston: Beacon, 2021), chap. 5.

27. Hendricks, *Christians against Christianity*, 82.

28. Hendricks, *Christians against Christianity*, 86.

29. Jonathan Wilson-Hartgrove, *Revolution of Values: Reclaiming Public Faith for the Common Good* (Downers Grove, IL: InterVarsity, 2019), 63–79.

30. Lee C. Camp, *Scandalous Witness: A Little Political Manifesto for Christians* (Grand Rapids: Eerdmans, 2020).

31. Kat Armas, *Abuelita Faith: What Women on the Margins Teach Us about Wisdom, Persistence, and Strength* (Grand Rapids: Brazos, 2021), 22.

32. Tisby offers a T-shirt with this phrase on it at https://jemartisby.substack.com/p/drum-rollintroducing-tisbys-merch.

33. "About," Neighbor to Neighbor, accessed October 14, 2022, https://n2nsb.com/about/.

34. Author interview, March 11, 2022.

Chapter 8 Remaking American Christianity

1. James H. Cone, *The Cross and the Lynching Tree* (Maryknoll, NY: Orbis Books, 2013), 160.

2. Kaitlyn Schiess, *The Liturgy of Politics: Spiritual Formation for the Sake of Our Neighbor* (Downers Grove, IL: IVP Academic, 2020).

3. See Lisa Sharon Harper, *The Very Good Gospel: How Everything Wrong Can Be Made Right* (Colorado Springs: WaterBrook, 2016), 175.

4. Schiess, *Liturgy of Politics*, 80.

5. I strongly recommend pastors engage with Schiess, *Liturgy of Politics*, and Drew Strait, "Political Idolatry and White Christian Nationalism: Toward a Pastoral Hermeneutic of Resistance," *Mennonite Quarterly Review* 96 (January 2022): 47–72.

6. Cone, *The Cross and the Lynching Tree*, 36.

7. Cone, *The Cross and the Lynching Tree*, 30–64.

8. Martin Luther King Jr., *The Essential Martin Luther King, Jr.: "I Have a Dream" and Other Great Writings* (Boston: Beacon, 2013), 17.

9. Cone, *The Cross and the Lynching Tree*, 38.

10. Cone, *The Cross and the Lynching Tree*, 41.

11. James Q. Whitman, *Hitler's American Model: The United States and the Making of Nazi Race Law* (Princeton: Princeton University Press, 2017).

12. Reggie L. Williams, *Bonhoeffer's Black Jesus: Harlem Renaissance Theology and an Ethic of Resistance* (Waco: Baylor University Press, 2021), 140.

13. I'm speaking sociologically here—not every single white American Christian enjoys loads of privilege or affluence. You may be saying, "I'm white and Christian, and I sure don't feel affluent. And my parents and grandparents sure weren't affluent." That may be true. But on the whole, white American Christians *as a group* are wealthier and healthier than most any other group. So while you or I may not be personally responsible for the suffering of another group, we still benefit—given our social location—from those historic inequalities. Put another way, being white, American, and Christian may not have made everything easy in our lives, but it sure hasn't made the struggles we (and everyone) face any harder.

14. Danté Stewart, *Shoutin' in the Fire: An American Epistle* (New York: Convergent, 2021), 123.

15. Kat Armas, *Abuelita Faith: What Women on the Margins Teach Us about Wisdom, Persistence, and Strength* (Grand Rapids: Brazos, 2021), 1.

16. Armas, *Abuelita Faith*, 187.

17. Christina Barland Edmondson and Chad Brennan, *Faithful Antiracism: Moving Past Talk to Systemic Change* (Downers Grove, IL: InterVarsity, 2022), 57.

18. Sarah Bessey, *Out of Sorts* (New York: Howard Books, 2015), 205. See also Schiess, *Liturgy of Politics*: "The work that we do now will be redeemed, not extinguished. . . . Our work in the here and now is nurturing our political imaginations for the life to come" (66). "Our hope is its own kind of defiance" (111).

19. Kelly Brown Douglas, *Resurrection Hope: A Future Where Black Lives Matter* (Maryknoll, NY: Orbis Books, 2021), 201.

Andrew L. Whitehead (PhD, Baylor University) is associate professor of sociology at Indiana University–Purdue University Indianapolis, where he codirects the Association of Religion Data Archives in the Center for the Study of Religion and American Culture. He is the coauthor of *Taking America Back for God: Christian Nationalism in the United States,* which won the 2021 Distinguished Book Award from the Society for the Scientific Study of Religion. Whitehead has written for the *Washington Post, NBC News, Time,* and Religion News Service and speaks frequently about Christian nationalism.